THE ROOTS OF
PSYCHOTHERAPY

BRUNNER/MAZEL CLASSICS IN PSYCHOANALYSIS
AND PSYCHOTHERAPY NO. 9

THE ROOTS OF

PSYCHOTHERAPY

By

CARL A. WHITAKER, M.D.
and
THOMAS P. MALONE, Ph.D., M.D.

WITH A NEW INTRODUCTION
BY THE AUTHORS

BRUNNER/MAZEL, *Publishers* • New York

Library of Congress Cataloging in Publication Data

Whitaker, Carl A.
   The roots of psychotherapy.

   (Brunner/Mazel classics in psychoanalysis; no. 9)
   Reprint of the 1953 ed. published by Blakiston, New York.
   Bibliography: p. 234
   1. Psychotherapy.   I. Malone, Thomas Patrick, 1919–   joint author.
II. Title.   III. Series.

RC480.W48 1980   616.89'14   80-24437
ISBN 0-87630-265-7, cloth
     0-87630-498-6, paper
Copyright © 1953 by The Blakiston Company
Copyright © 1981 by Carl A. Whitaker and Thomas P. Malone

Published by BRUNNER/MAZEL, INC.
19 Union Square, New York, NY 10003

MANUFACTURED IN THE UNITED STATES OF AMERICA

10 9 8 7 6 5 4 3 2

Dedicated to
Muriel, my wife,
and
Nancy, Elaine, Bruce, Anita and Lynn Whitaker
and to
Deirdre, Patrick, Sheila and David Malone

Preface

This monograph proposes a scientific formulation of the art of psychotherapy. The recent recognition of this treatment process as a separate discipline makes imperative the understanding of its nature and the comprehension of those features common to all forms of psychotherapy, regardless of differences in technique or in school orientation. We are interested in providing a conceptual framework which will serve as a point of departure for the common effort to develop both research and the pragmatic aspects of psychotherapy. Much of the writing involves making explicit what is implicit in many previous formulations.

Psychiatry and, more significantly, medicine in general seek a clearer idea of the roots from which any form of psychotherapy derives its validity.

The book is divided into three sections: (1) *Foundation* deals with the relationship of psychotherapy to general biology, especially to growth and adaptation, and with the common features as well as the differences in the major approaches to psychotherapy; (2) *Process* presents a formulation of the essential phases and the dynamics of any psychotherapeutic relationship; and (3) *Techniques* presents some techniques which the authors have found useful in their own work as psychotherapists.

We are not interested in developing a "new school" of psychotherapy. This book will be significant in so far as it clarifies the common features of all psychotherapy. It differs, we feel, from other publications on this subject in its attempt to integrate psychotherapy within the field of general medical therapeutics.

In addition, its emphasis is upon the wellness of patients, making psychotherapy more than a by-product of the theory of psychopathology. Lastly, the book is unique in its endeavor to set forth the doctor-therapist as the essential dynamic in psychotherapy, including some evaluation of the importance of his feeling-responses to the patient. Effort is made to stress the reciprocal quality of the relationship between the two persons who are called "doctor" and "patient."

The book is intended for anyone, no matter what his training, who has the experience of treating patients or who has been a patient himself. We believe anyone who has had experience either as a patient or a therapist should have little difficulty comprehending the essential meaning of the book. This includes, therefore, the psychiatrist, the clinical psychologist, the social worker, and most important, the practicing physician, no matter what his specialty. Many others, of course, approach the problem of helping patients with different orientations, e.g., religious, vocational, industrial, educational, recreational, and rehabilitative. For these we hope the book offers some explicit verbalization of what many of them know empirically. Finally, students of human behavior and of society, be they medical, academic, or pragmatic, should find this useful in their preparation for the all-important task of helping others.

Although the book's practical significance is relatively limited, the final section does attempt to give practicing therapists some real, concrete notion of what can be done to increase the effectiveness of their psychotherapy and of some of the pitfalls which jeopardize their effort. The practicing physician may, in addition, be reassured by our belief in the potential effectiveness of a brief form of intensive psychotherapy suitable to a busy practice.

Though we have written this monograph, the ideas presented, along with much of the actual clinical investigation through which the ideas were refined, have come from the members of the department of psychiatry in which the authors have worked for the past six years. This also is their work, even though we have written it. In this sense we are deeply indebted for our personal and research association to Dr. John Warkentin, Miss Nan Johnson, Dr.

Ellen Finley, Dr. William Kiser, and Dr. Richard Felder. We are also indebted to the administrative and teaching faculty of the Medical School at Emory University for their help in providing us with an opportunity and an atmosphere within which this work was possible. We are indebted to our secretary, Mrs. Ralph Bodfish, who suffered with the responsibility for stenographic preparation and considerable editorial help. Finally, we are indebted in no small measure to numerous colleagues here and throughout the country: Dr. John Lilly, Dr. George Devereux, Dr. Malcolm Hayward, Dr. Edward Taylor, and Dr. Harlow Ades, Dr. Hugh Wood, and Dr. Paul Beeson, who have stimulated us in many instances through vigorous negative criticism to better clarify and integrate the theory of psychotherapy presented in this manuscript.

Our efforts to teach psychotherapy to medical students have done much to force a tighter formulation. Their questions and incisive comments induced much new thinking. Lastly, we owe a debt of gratitude to those many patients with whom we have collaborated in the effort to mature the patient and the therapist.

CARL A. WHITAKER and THOMAS P. MALONE

February, 1953

Contents

Preface vii
Introduction xiii
Introduction to the 1981 Reprint xvii

FOUNDATION

Chapter

1. SCIENCE AS A CREATIVE METHOD 1
2. RESEARCH IN PSYCHOTHERAPY 8
3. THE BIOLOGICAL BASIS OF PSYCHOTHERAPY 16
4. ADAPTATION 26
5. CATALYZED REPAIR 34
6. THE COMMUNITY AND PSYCHOTHERAPY 40
7. IMPLICIT AND EXPLICIT PSYCHOTHERAPY 46
8. DYNAMIC PSYCHIATRY AND PSYCHOTHERAPY 59

PROCESS

9. THE PATIENT AS A PERSON 67
10. THE PROCESS OF PSYCHOTHERAPY 80
11. ANXIETY AND PSYCHOTHERAPY 125
12. THE THERAPIST AS A PERSON 141
13. PATIENT-VECTORS IN THE THERAPIST 165
14. RESTATEMENT OF THE PROBLEM OF PSYCHOTHERAPY . 186

TECHNIQUES

15. SOME TECHNIQUES IN BRIEF PSYCHOTHERAPY 194
Glossary 231
Bibliography 234

Introduction

Psychotherapy in recent years has become more and more a separate discipline dealing with a recognizable process. Professional people in medicine and in the social sciences have developed some consensus about the general nature of this process. Underlying this consensus has been the conviction that there is an emotional exchange (process) in interpersonal relationships, which, when it occurs successfully, speeds up the growth experience of one or both participants in that relationship. This appears to be true regardless of the specific content of the relationship, the techniques utilized in it, whether it be professional or occurring in the everyday human relationships, or whether it be consciously or intuitively understood. Moreover, the type of emotional pathology involved appears to make little difference. Interested in this process of catalyzing emotional growth, we faced at the outset a disturbing lack of any conceptual framework within which to formulate our thinking.

Despite the difficulty in communicating something to a large degree implicit, the effort may offer at least a means of comparing the thinking of various investigators. It should be possible to integrate all learnings about the process of psychotherapy into some tentative theory. Such a theory might provide a pattern around which one could develop more adequate research designs for the investigation of what the psychotherapist experiences but only partly understands. Such a theory might also enable us to teach psychotherapy more adequately and allow the student to develop his own unique capacities within some common groundings. The essentials of psychiatric treatment might be accomplished in a shorter period of time with less cost to the patient if these essentials were agreed on by psychotherapists. Underlying all of this lies the professional necessity to get behind the differences of technique and arrive at some understanding of the essential process common to all forms of psychotherapy.

Psychotherapy in the broad sense includes any acceleration in the growth of a human being as a person. Such growth has many directions. This book is not concerned with all of these, but limits itself to understanding growth in the sense of integration. Increased integration may be expressed as greater maturity or as more adequacy. Maturity and adequacy refer to different dimensions of growth. Increases in maturity occur through emotional experiences which alter some of the intrapersonal structures. These alterations result from an increasing ease in the exchange of energies within an individual. The person's dynamics become more flexible. He thereby frees energy previously bound in conflict and now available for interpersonal use.

Such an individual, however, may still apply these available, but labile energies quite inadequately in his interpersonal and reality-bound experiences. Growth in this latter area can better be thought of as an increase in his adequacy. In developing maturity the therapist makes more energy available. In developing adequacy he improves control and understanding so that the patient better utilizes what energies are available.

Growth in maturity occurs through emotional experiences. Growth in adequacy ordinarily occurs through an educative social experience. Obviously an individual, who has developed greater power and strength but who cannot adequately use such capacity, may present as serious a social problem as an individual who has poorly developed strength, but who utilizes what power he has with adequacy. Each has failed to develop his potential either as a separate individual or as a member of society. Full growth includes abundant energy adequately used in interpersonal relationships.

All non-physical forms of psychiatric treatment deal in some way with both immaturity deficit (intrapersonal) and inadequacy deficit (interpersonal). Some psychiatrists are far more interested in the development of the individual's adequacy in his social adjustment. Many techniques have been developed to increase the adequacy of individuals. By contrast, techniques for the development of maturity have, until recently, been somewhat neglected.

This book deals with those processes in psychotherapy which catalyze the emergence of the individual's potential energy, i.e., his maturity. If the processes which are known to be important in the development of patients' adequacy (adjustment) are neglected, this is not out of any conviction of their unimportance or ineffectiveness to the environment, but rather out of the need to expand this other aspect, the understanding of which seems significant to the authors at this point in the development of psychiatry.

The emphasis on maturity as against adequacy reflects the authors' increasing concern for the better integration of psychotherapy within the field of medicine. Medicine is essentially biologically oriented. Maturity is a biological concept representing growth within the organism. Adequacy is a social-science concept representing relations between organisms.

It may well be that the practicing physician is, to some degree, a bridge between these two areas and carries a certain amount of responsibility, not only for the health of the individual organism, but also for the social adjustment of the patient. The physician must accept responsibility for those measures which augment the psychological health of his patient in the same sense that he is responsible for those measures which assure the patient's physical well-being. This holds true even though his responsibility for the patient's social adjustment is not clear-cut.

The point at which the responsibility of the physician ends, in the final analysis, must be decided by the individual physician. His decision reflects the extent to which his living is interwoven with the community in which he practices. Certainly the patient's well-being, biological and psychological, as well as the manner in which he uses himself as a member of a community, are all-important. Generally the physician is more concerned with biological well-being and, except where medicine becomes also a social science as in psychiatry, his concern for the behavior of his patients in the community is personal rather than professional. Any concept of physician responsibility must orient him toward aiding the continued growth and well-being of the total individual.

The medical approach implies that psychotherapy can best be understood only by including the principles of general biology. On this basis an effort to integrate the principles of psychotherapy with a theory of biological growth and adaptation has been made. Such welding of theory is highly specious at many points. It follows also that the authors have neglected, to some extent, some aspects of psychotherapy which more properly belong in the area of the social sciences. This indicates not any feeling that the social sciences are unimportant in psychotherapy, but rather our conviction that, at this point in the development of therapeutic theory, grounding such a theory in biology may serve to integrate psychotherapy in the field of medicine more securely than if it were dealt with as a social process.

The definition of a descriptive pattern for the dynamic interpersonal relationship is liable to misunderstanding either by its artificial quality or by the semantic difficulty included. Any human experience can be only partially relived by words. Thus, also, problems in the evolving pattern of emotional recovery and the technical adjuncts to recovery are all but impossible to communicate unless the reader has touched them in his own work or his "outside living." Added to this has been the conviction that psychiatric language is too restricted for use here.

Any conceptual framework for a process so implicit as psychotherapy must be tentative and must be presented largely in an effort to find a means of communicating with other workers in the field, even with those who are not professionally indoctrinated. If our work proves to be a stimulus for the further refinement of a conceptual basis for psychotherapy, this will provide ample justification for the effort.

Introduction to the 1981 Reprint

(*Publisher's Note:* For the Introduction to this Reprint, the authors have chosen to exchange letters, reflecting on their work together and sharing their individual insights on the growth of and changes in psychotherapy since this book was first published.)

Dear Tom,

Republishing *The Roots* leaves us with an opportunity to talk about how the book evolved. The evolution of psychotherapy since 1953 seems partly an expansion of our formulation. The book was a step in the formulation of one system of psychotherapy. Psychiatry had mainly dealt with diagnosis, prognosis and support for psychoanalytic research and its therapeutic offspring. Since 1950, the evolution of intensive psychotherapy, psychotherapy of groups and the psychotherapy of couples and families has escalated and with great variety.

The Roots evolved from the creative power of our own co-therapy teaming. That eight-person group of ours was so close that we prevented burnout in the therapist, tended to neutralize pilot error, and evolved a systems-to-system format which espoused a circular causation theory which we termed reverberating anxiety. Our co-therapy team provided an inter-personal framework and support system for those intrapsychic changes that took place in the individual patient. It opened also the possibility of a *me-they* group experience used to reen-act the triangular dynamics of parenting. We saw this process as a symbolic but not symbiotic relationship. That teaming provided the patient with more freedom to regress and also more freedom to effectively end the therapy. There was less Oedipal fixation on the therapeutic team and therefore less guilt in the patient at inducing the empty-nest syndrome. Teaming in psychotherapy also prevented much of the cross-generational confusion that's so painful in one-to-one therapy.

The evolution of psychotherapy as a process followed the public acceptance of psychodynamics as a science. People did change. The playroom was an effective system for understand-ing children and, furthermore, many of those children bene-fited. Group therapy did relieve symptoms. Play therapy often resulted in dramatically increasing creativity. Deliberate strat-egies to induce change were emerging.

I also see the evolution of psychotherapy in these 27 years as massively supported by the cultural evolvement from the social groups pseudomutual therapy game characteristic of those "good old days." The emerging of group therapy sys-tems, of sensitivity groups, and of family therapy have been actively supported by establishment changes which resulted in empty state hospitals, the birth of crisis intervention clinics, of walk-in clinics, of the women's liberation movement, and freedom for massive personal exposure. This might also be called a covert population control system and thus include abortions, homosexuality, birth control, and the not-so-happy emergence of child abuse, rape, and the discovery that psycho-therapy isn't a magic bullet that cures all psychosocial dis-tortions.

The Roots was our attempt to postulate a common under-structure to the interactional process of psychotherapy. In that effort to picture therapy as a system, we specifically withheld the electrifying agony and ecstacy of the daily struggle. However, psychotherapy as a professional change induction experience, like all parenting, is punctuated by an endless series of episodes—now boring, now painful, now delicious.

Hereby we add a few lemon squeezings, some garlic and a dollop of honey. Flavor isn't always nourishing, but it does spice the dish. The penetrating stories of pre-socialized children are often too penetrating to be recalled. Just so the quotes of schizophrenics cut through our adult white lie communication pattern. Those humanity samplers have a disease of abnormal integrity and we "professional" mothers often get beaten as if they were still in the notorious stage of the "terrible twos."

Hidden within *The Roots* is another dynamic, the force of the teamwork in the co-therapy process. Just as parenting includes an endlessly increasing investment by each spouse in the other and in the we-ness, so does teaming increase concept forming and warms the writing.

Jane was a schizophrenic for 15 years, finally got off drugs, and, having been offered the chance to be my consultant on a couple of "psychotic" family interviews, decided that she would live without going psychotic again. Part of the decision was the statement that I would not treat her at any time because I didn't believe she was crazy. I thought her craziness was an act that she had perfected over time. Although it seemed very real to her, it was not real to me. "Since you know craziness, I'd hire you as a consultant, but we have a problem. I don't trust you, and since I am so involved and so intrigued with craziness, I don't trust myself." She said, "Well, I don't trust you either, and I don't trust myself, but I trust us."

One chronic psychotic had been working in a bank for five years, but came in for therapy because tranquilizers made her feel even further away from people. After some months of treatment, the therapist said, "I suddenly became aware that you owe me $400 and I want us to stay straight. I don't want to be your banker." She said, "All right, I'll pay you." Two weeks went by and he confronted her again. She blew up, "Listen, you should be paying me. You get more from me than I do from you." Therapist: "You're paying me for my time; this is not a friendship. Yet you expect me to love you more than you love yourself and more than I love myself. Neither is true. Not only that, I love myself first, my wife second, my children third, my colleagues fourth, my reputation fifth and you come in sixth." Several years later, the patient said, "You know, that was the most important confrontation we ever had."

The schizophrenic was a sculptress, had had ten hospitalizations, much electric shock and was into her second year of ongoing individual therapy. She suddenly became massively depressed, carefully planned suicide and told the therapist about it. His response was immediate, explosive and direct, "If you kill yourself, I will jump up and down on your grave and curse you." And he would have, too.

Another patient, weighing 300 pounds, threatening suicide, refused to bring her sister, the only family member, into her therapy. She was told, "If you don't bring your sister in and you do kill yourself, I shall tell her that it's her fault you're dead." Sister arrived next interview.

Middle of the third interview, the therapist said to the patient, "I think you're lying." Patient, "I'm not." "I didn't say you were, I said I think you are." "Well, you think wrong." "Sorry about that. My thinking is my own and I insist on maintaining it. You don't have to agree with it, but you can't change my thinking, although you're welcome to try. However, I may change it any time."

It was 1944. I was seeing a patient just back from the South Pacific. In the middle of the first interview, I suddenly became terrified that he was going to kill me. I excused myself, went across the hall, interrupted Dr. John Warkentin's interview: "I need you." He came to my office. I explained, "John, I was sitting here with this guy taking an ordinary history and all of a sudden I'm terrified he's going to kill me." John looked at the patient, "I don't blame you. Sometimes I want to kill the bastard myself," then got up and walked out. This intervention had a magic way of changing the dynamics. I wasn't terrified, the patient wasn't dangerous, and we went on with our interview.

John Warkentin and I were working with a schizophrenic and one day I arrived an half hour late. John said to the schizophrenic, "You sit right there and don't say a word 'cause he's always late and we're going to have the most awful fight you ever saw and if you stick your nose in, we'll probably both clobber you." We fought for an half hour. The schizophrenic sat over in the corner glowing; he had never seen his parents fight lovingly and honestly with each other.

One night at 11:00 I got a call from the police department. They said, "There's a young lady down here. We called her mother and her mother said to call you. When she came in, we asked what she wanted. She said she wanted to report a murder and when we asked her who had been murdered, she said she was the victim. We don't quite know what to do with her. She'll talk with you." The schiz got on the phone, "Mr. Whitaker, this is Sue." I said, "Sue, I hear you reported a murder to the police. I think that's fine of you. Would you please be sure to report any other murders you know about?" She laughed gaily, said, "Thank you," and hung up.

The group therapy had been going on for several months and of the ten members, five or six were always talking. Three didn't ever say anything. Finally, the talkers became very indignant at the silent ones. One replied, "Just because we don't talk doesn't mean nothing is happening. The chassis in a car doesn't turn like the wheels, but it goes just as far."

My own situation has led me more and more into working with families. I sometimes feel very different from those old days when I spent all my time with individuals. I don't even believe in individuals anymore; I think they're only fragments of a family and I do no treatment except with families. I'm also more and more convinced that the dyad that we call marriage is merely the remnant of an extruded third. One marriage component that makes for great pain is the fact that these two individuals are also scapegoats sent out by two unique families. Thus, the groom and the bride may well spend a lifetime deciding which family to reproduce.

One other exciting component in the evolution of psychotherapy is our increasing courage to bypass the microdynamics of the individual. The research in individual dynamics delayed putting the interpersonal world of couples, families and groups into a therapeutic frame to facilitate change. Furthermore, while we clearly don't understand the dynamics of the family's living, it's still true, as Barbara Betz said, "The dynamics of psychotherapy are in the person of the therapist." The utilization of the cybernetic model with negative and positive feedback and the endless rediscovery of the double bind, of paradox and counterparadox make the training for psychotherapy more and more the development of a free transfer across the corpus collusum, from the right brain to the left brain and from the left brain to the right brain.

Our writing about a pragmatic system for understanding the therapeutic process still seems relevant and useful. Much of my current thinking about the pragmatic components in family therapy is quite closely tied to this original frame. The reciprocating anxiety concept is very much a part of the interactional thinking that I see now in all systems of psychotherapy.

Tom, as I think about the 15 years of our separation, they're filled with many moments of deep reverence and tenderness for the 17 years of teaming and cross-fertilization that produced the book and many other by-products which still echo in my therapy. The learning of our professional family years doesn't fade. It's a rich heritage with its own patina.

CARL A. WHITAKER, M.D.

July 28, 1980

Dear Carl,

Sitting and talking with you last month was an exciting and affirming experience. Your move into family therapy in these recent years seemed a distant cry from my involvement with experiential psychotherapy, particularly as it relates to the dynamics of the intimate dyad. All of the implications of this are toward a more relevant general theory of personality, as well as some effort to develop a more useful concept of psychopathology than the traditional one. My excitement and affirmation came with the realization as we talked that through the years, separate as we were, we essentially had come to an identical space in our concept of the psychotherapeutic experience. Most importantly, after these many years we were both still youthfully excited with the promise of psychotherapy to grow humans into more of their potential humanity.

Of the basic concepts presented in *The Roots of Psychotherapy* some remain clearly relevant and, if anything, still inadequately and insufficiently explored. The most fundamental of these is the simple notion that the dynamics of psychotherapy reside in the person of the therapist. This concept has of course been paid enormous lip service by many of the psychotherapies developed since we wrote *The Roots*. I feel, however, that its implications have been only superficially developed. I would anticipate that in the years to come, if psychotherapy as an art ever succeeds in separating itself from its imprisoning medical model of the educated caretaker treating the benighted pathology of the dependent patient, then we will see an explosive advance in psychotherapy. The move from medical content has been deceptive in my mind. As long as technique remains paramount, the medical model will continue to obscure the underlying dynamics of how a person participates in the psychological growth of another person or persons. Medicine is inherently interventive and not participatory. As you noted in our conversation, training in medicine, clinical psychology, and social work appears to be basically anti-psychotherapeutic. Where will future psychotherapists come from? These disciplines produce an abundance of psychopharmacologists and psychoeducationalists or counselors, but few psychotherapists.

The Roots of Psychotherapy was a rather brazen statement about psychotherapy. In retrospect, we would have been wise to more clearly define what we meant by psychotherapy. In the years since I have come to see it as having a very precise and limited meaning. Psychotherapy specifically refers to those *experiences* occurring between or among two or more persons which increase the *capacity* of any one of the participants to experience more of either his/her inner life or his/her living relationship to everyone and everything surrounding him/her. The important words are *experience* and *capacity* for experience. Obviously such experiences can occur in a variety of relationships, one of which is the professional contractual relationship to the trained psychotherapist. Psychotherapy in this sense has to be distinguished from counseling. Counseling is patient-activated, the relationship is relatively incidental, the process is very goal-oriented, the experience is basically educative and cognitively energized, the experience is mostly conscious in intent, technique is of paramount importance, the process is sequential and linear, and the experience is mostly verbal. In contrast, psychotherapy is therapist-activated, the relationship is most significant, it is non-goal-oriented (if anything the goal is to get rid of goals), the process is affectively energized, the mode is unconscious rather than conscious, technique is subliminal, the process is nonsequential and repetitively rhythmic, and the basic content is nonverbal. I am, of course, aware that in doing psychotherapy I very frequently do counseling. I am also aware that such counseling has enormous value to the patient. But it is not psychotherapy. It is not an *experience* and increases neither my nor the patient's *capacity* to experience.

Based on these differences, were I to presently write *The Roots* I would shift somewhat from left lobe to right lobe. I am increasingly aware that the dynamics of psychotherapy are more spatial than temporal, more colored than black and white or gray, more circular and rhythmic than linear, more musical than verbal, more holistic than analytical, more unconscious and metaphorical than logical and rational, more relational than individual, more aesthetic than scientific, and more of an art than a craft. We said all of these things, but we said them too timidly.

In our conversation you remarked that you say what you say these days with little concern for whether the patient accepts or denies it. I recognize that experience. I, too, have come to have less investment in the patient's response. I am very clear that as I have come to this kind of non-investment, what I share with patients has had significantly more impact. We spoke years ago of the importance of a co-therapist, a person who could allow you to be less self-conscious, less technical, and more personal. It is as if I have come to that without the presence of a co-therapist.

As you can surmise from what I have written so far, I am less impressed with regression and transference than I was when we wrote *The Roots*. Currently, I would consider replacement therapy to be probably impossible. There is no way I can replace deficient parenting. I can only be with patients as the person I am. Psychosexual development, fixation and regression, concepts basic to replacement therapy, can be limiting concepts, however rationally attractive they may be. We were not sufficiently courageous in our involvement with the unconscious. The unconscious is ageless, and its expressions are little modified by the vagaries of psychosexual development. Its nondevelopmental characteristics are undeniable. The unconscious of the child is only minimally different from the unconscious of the adult. We were, in *The Roots*, too impressed with the developmental input. In this regard we paid too little attention to the archetypes of Jung and the message of Groddeck. We did have a germinal idea in our concept of the therapeutic "psychosis," but I feel we backed off from it.

It has enormous implications both for psychotherapy and an understanding of psychoses in general.

I have had no regret about our biological orientation in the early chapters. Were I to write the book again, I think I would expand these. It intrigues me that the psychological sciences have analogically used the physical sciences over the years. Presently they seem more like the rigid physical sciences of the past century, while in contrast physics and biology became far more free and fanciful, and thus creative, in the past two decades. I am more than ever convinced that psychotherapy lacks an adequate philosophical and epistemological basis. Traditional philosophies are essentially dualistic, separating mind from body. To date, monism lacks an adequate philosophical skeleton. If and when this develops I am encouraged that we will see unbelievable advances in human growth enhancement, both psychologically and chemically, plus biologically-environmentally-ecologically. In our biological chapter in *The Roots* I feel now that we were constrained and perhaps too analogic. The current non-mechanistic and increasingly phenomenological biochemistry, and physics with their imaginative explorations of interfaces, coupled with system theory methodologies, would lend themselves gorgeously to the illumination of basic psychotherapeutic dynamics.

Our failure to confront the traditionally defined categories of psychopathology is another regrettable, although understandable, blindness in *The Roots*. Regrettable because concepts of psychopathology have not significantly changed for the past half century. They remain imprisoned in the early psychoanalytical developmental boxes. It seems reasonable to have expected that the enormous proliferation of psychotherapeutic innovations would have greatly illuminated our understanding of psychopathology. They have not, at least not in print. I remarked that our slighting of psychopathology was at that time understandable. We did need to shift the emphasis to the dynamics of the therapist. In the ensuing years we have certainly learned a great deal about the dilemma of patients, and it needs to be shared and looked at.

The most important concept involved is that of experience. The clear implication of experiential psychotherapy is simply that all psychopathology can *psychologically* be understood as a variety of *non-experiences,* or lessened experiences, or attenuated experiences, or manufactured experiences. If you are willing to look at all psychopathology without reference to its assumed etiology, immediately all "psychopathology" has the common dimension of non-experience. Experientially, depressions depreciate experience, anxiety overcomes experience, phobias abhor experience, hysteria ignores experience, obsessions deny experience, compulsions override experience, psychopathy precludes experience, and psychosis manufactures experience. The common underlying dynamic is the fear or inability to experience, a learned aversion or inability to experience. Developmental factors simply determine the specific ways in which this is accomplished. This different perspective significantly alters the way in which we look at hysteria, or depression, and all of psychopathology. Most importantly, it illuminates what is happening in psychotherapy. The task of therapy becomes one of uncovering, reactivating or reassociating, i.e., integrating the experiential dimensions of the *ordinary* experience.

An oddity of *The Roots* has been that it apparently became the basis for the development of a "school of psychotherapy." There are thousands of experiential psychotherapists throughout the world. This happened despite our explicit admonition in *The Roots* that we had little interest in developing a school of psychotherapy. We were interested in illuminating the basic dynamics of all psychotherapies. In a delightfully paradoxical way, it appears as if these thousands of "experiential psychotherapists" agreed with our position. They use a myriad of psychotherapeutic systems and techniques. They use their experience of their persons in psychotherapy and apparently are convinced that technique and system approach is significantly subordinate to their use of their personal experience to cata-lyze the patient's growth. Thus they confidently and with as-surance refer to themselves as "experiential psychotherapists."

The oddity occurs when these "experiential psychothera-pists" convene. In the vacuum of system and technique no one appears to know exactly what experiential psychotherapy is. Yet they know it is! I have written in recent years that the ex-periential psychotherapist is one who finds techniques and theoretical systems that are most congruent with his/her per-son, and so allow him/her the fullest and most feeling expres-sion of their personality and character in relating to patients. The key concept is congruence. The congruence between the therapist's technique-system and his/her person allows the maximal personal participation in the relationship to the pa-tient. This differs for different therapists.

More recently I have begun to explore the possibility of filling this vacuum. It is still very clear to me that experiential psychotherapy has little to do with technique or systematics of psychotherapy. However, I have decided that a description of the *essential experiences* in psychotherapy might be helpful, particularly if I am able to refrain from suggesting how the therapist might bring these about. This might correct a serious deficiency in *The Roots*, the absence of clinical material. Con-crete clinical examples would do much to fill this vacuum. Concepts are difficult to effectively confront because they are so easy to challenge. Data are inexhaustible. Concrete clinical material might offer a more meaningful dialectic.

There are some central concepts outlined in *The Roots* that continue to be fundamental in our thinking about psycho-therapy. These concepts have been neglected, and deserve to be more explicitly developed. It would take at least two vol-umes to explicate these. I wish we had both the time and in-clination. Suffice it here to simply identify some of the more important dormant concepts. The first is that of the ambiguity of anxiety. We described in *The Roots*, as in subsequent writ-ings, the dual quality of anxiety. Much anxiety freezes and immobilizes humans, and has to be reduced to allow growth to take place. In contrast, many frozen and immobilized humans remain so because of the absence of experienced anxiety. In these persons their growth depends on their capacity to sustain their anxiety, and in some instances, growth depends on the capacity of the therapist to develop anxiety in the patient. The qualities that distinguish negative anxiety from positive anxiety should be explored and elaborated. I was visted recently by a representative of a drug company who asked me if I had any research suggestions. I shared with him the importance of anxiety in growth, and wondered if they had any plans to research a drug which would induce anxiety that could be constructively used by the patient. He appeared certain that I was putting him on.

Associated with this is the concept of relational disequilibrium as a positive dynamic in change and growth. In contrast to this would be the notion that equilibrium and stability in relationships, whether psychotherapeutic or marital, can often be the kiss of experiential death. A dynamic balance between equilibrium and disequilibrium seems so much more characteristic of creative life.

Despite the emphasis on growth in the humanistic psychologies, the specifics of growth dynamics inherent in all psychopathologies have been grossly neglected. We pay clinical pejorative attention to the fear of the phobic person, but seldom describe the growth thrust of the desire in that phobic fear. We condescendingly listen to the dissociative pseudo feelings of the hysteric, but seldom deal with his/her thrust to manufacture more feelings. We are both frightened and entertained by the fabricated realities of the psychotic, but seldom attend with respect his/her dedicated effort to challenge cultural realities that are more insane than his psychotic dreamings. Gregory Bateson has written that most alcoholics drink because of their nagging awareness of the inanities of the "real world." He may be right. Granted that being a drunk is hardly a constructive way to deal with these inanities, this should not shelter us from dealing with the appropriateness of his awareness.

There are many other central concepts, e.g., the person of the therapist, the reciprocity of the therapeutic relationship, the dynamics of ending, and others. One that deserves much more attention is the nature of the unconscious to unconscious communication. For example, I would be very interested in the unconscious component of verbal communication. We are aware of the nonverbal aspects of verbal communication, i.e., the posture, the vocal tone, the nuances of the verbal sequences, the slips of the tongue, etc. Words, however, are primary carriers of the unconscious, and we remain relatively naive about the unconscious substrate of linguistics. I assume that every human being fully understands unconsciously the evolved meanings of all words, meanings that transcend the current cultural usage. And I assume these meanings to be more significant in psychotherapy than the culturally bound conversation. If you as a therapist tell a patient his wife seems to be a "nice" person, I assume he knows that is an insult.

I will end as I began. It was a delightful and recreative experience to spend the time with both you and Muriel. It seemed full circled. The fact that we did not go on to describe the trunk, or the branches, or the leaves, or the ecology seems less important than the wonderful feeling that we both agreed that *The Roots* are still viable.

THOMAS P. MALONE, Ph.D., M.D.

August 24, 1980

The Quest*

A thousand years ago two philosophers met on a slope of Lebanon, and one said to the other, "Where goest thou?"

And the other answered, "I am seeking after the fountain of youth which I know wells out among these hills. I have found writings which tell of that fountain flowering toward the sun. And you, what are you seeking?"

The first man answered, "I am seeking after the mystery of death."

Then each of the two philosophers conceived that the other was lacking in his great science, and they began to wrangle, and to accuse each other of spiritual blindness.

Now while the two philosophers were loud upon the wind, a stranger, a man who was deemed a simpleton in his own village, passed by, and when he heard the two in hot dispute, he stood awhile and listened to their argument.

Then he came near to them and said, "My good men, it seems that you both really belong to the same school of philosophy, and that you are speaking of the same thing, only you speak in different words. One of you seeks the fountain of youth, and the other seeks the mystery of death. Yet indeed they are but one, and as one they dwell in you both."

Then the stranger turned away saying, "Farewell, sages." And as he departed he laughed a patient laughter.

The two philosophers looked at each other in silence for a moment, and then they laughed also. And one of them said, "Well now, shall we not walk and seek together?"

* From KAHLIL GIBRAN, "The Wanderer,"
Courtesy Alfred A. Knopf, Inc.

1

Science as a Creative Method

The pleasure is the pleasure of powers that create a truth that cannot be arrived at by the reason alone, a truth that the poet recognizes by sensation. The morality of the poet's radiant and productive atmosphere is the right sensation.

Wallace Stevens

Since research is a common denominator of all science, the application of this method to psychotherapy requires a preliminary clarification. This is a difficult task since the philosophy of science is at present undergoing tremendous changes.

The scientist investigating the inorganic world takes precautions against distorting his observations because of defects in his capacity to observe. As an example, with defects in visual perception, of which he is unaware, his data include a constant error in perspective. To guard against this, he has implemented his observations with various types of sense extensions, e.g., the microscope, which minimize the variability of the human observer. Even so, particularly in the physical sciences, there has been considerable discontent about the error of a personal definition of physical phenomena. To correct this, the physicists define physical phenomena in terms of the ways in which these phenomena are observed and measured. This is called operationalism, i.e., data defined in terms of the operation by which they are observed or measured.

One of the central issues of current controversy between philosophers of science is the place of the scientist as a person in his investigations. This methodological controversy is a crucial one in that its outcome will clarify not only the importance of the observer in research, and of the scientist in science, but will also alter the definition of science per se, which will have to be viewed as a creative method as well as a method of experimentation.

Role of the Unconscious (Intuition)

It is a strange paradox that our understanding of the unconscious bears fruit in just about every area of human creativity except in science itself. Science has revealed and explored the power of the unconscious. However, it continues to be used mainly in the field of the creative arts. In fact, the last half century marked the inception of a new era in all the creative arts (modern art). This new movement, whatever its limitations may be, has a breadth and fullness which, even though it may not match the perfection and brilliance of the classical forms of art, does nevertheless express the true character of human experiences. This realism was achieved by the artists' recognition of the central role of the "unconscious" in their work. By contrast, science avoids the use of the unconscious as a means of broadening and deepening its own method of obtaining knowledge. Yet in many ways, creative scientific method is much more intimately associated with the method of art than with laboratory techniques. Much of science still relies on traditional procedures and refuses to alter the method that has been so productive in the past. However, in order to remain valid, the method must change through use, and must constantly re-design its own tools of understanding. The authors feel convinced that in all science, and more particularly in those disciplines which deal with life processes, the unconscious will assume greater significance in the new methods. Historically, major advances in our knowledge have grown out of unconscious experiences. The history of science records, essentially, a pyramiding of intuitions. Many of the foremost scientists have also made outstanding contributions to the arts.

The phrase "the inscrutable face of nature" sums up for many investigators the difficulties encountered in research. In fact, Whitehead has affirmed that "Nature is closed to the mind." One sometimes feels that there is something playful and protean about nature. She reveals her truths in paradoxical ways. She seems chaotic and inscrutable until someone has a flash of insight and sees a new interrelationship among natural phenomena. Sometimes these "revelations" offend our logic and we find them difficult to tolerate and much more so, to digest. The history of science time and again records the same sequence: A sudden, blinding light of understanding followed by decades of retrenchment and of unwillingness to believe. This has been true in astronomy, physics, biology, and in psychiatry. We seem unable to integrate on a conscious level the breadth of our understanding. We have always been a bit childish in our personification of nature. Like primitives, we make her alive, playful, inscrutable, seductive, and droll. Like primitives, the scientist often sees in nature qualities which reflect his own personality. We do know that the unconscious is, in fact, playful, chaotic, and droll. It reveals itself in sudden fleeting insights, the integration of which with conscious comprehension is a difficult task indeed. The problem of comprehension may lie within the scientist rather than within nature itself. It may not be the inscrutability of nature, but that of the deeper layers of the unconscious which forms an obstacle to insight. It may not be nature which is reluctant to reveal its truths, but the scientist's unconscious which reluctantly reveals itself. Nature does not suddenly open her doors, nor does she keep them closed. The scientist as a person suddenly knows consciously—because he is emotionally ready for this knowledge. Scientific conservatism does not impel us to challenge or deny these intuitive advances. The scientist reluctantly accepts the validity of his own experience. The frontiers of nature are not set by nature, but by the extent of the scientist's acceptance of his intuitive understanding of nature. Major advances in science and the rapidity with which they are made are determined by the scientist's ability to tolerate this unconscious faculty and to use it in his scientific endeavors.

"The Creative Unconscious"

One of the transitions in our own work was the growing belief that the unconscious is more than a reservoir of pathology. It is also a healthy segment of our persons to be used productively and creatively.* Unconscious processes determine not only hysterical gaits, but also the coordination necessary in normal gait. They integrate and coordinate essential functions of life and therefore contain an inherent knowledge of these life functions. The unconscious is more than the total residue of our life long repressions. It also coordinates our most fundamental life experiences which may at times be pathogenic, but most often constructively formative. In many ways the rightness and appropriateness of certain basic life processes depend upon their remaining unconscious.** The complexity of simple locomotion, involving, as it does, the integration of many specific muscles, would overwhelm our conscious capacity were it burdened with the task of negotiating a simple step. One may think in this context of the little poem describing the plight of the centipede paralyzed by the malicious request that he explain the manner in which he coordinates his legs. Yet locomotion involves only processes which seem crude and elementary indeed when compared to kidney function, endocrine function, and cellular metabolism. Looked at from this point of view, it becomes strikingly clear that only an infinitesimal part of our life function is integrated on a conscious level.

Much scientific stumbling stems from the fallacy that nothing is valid except the rational. Deeper insight into essential life processes might stem from our freer use of those levels of our nervous system within which these functions are primarily integrated. Operationally, this amounts to a greater use of, and confidence in, the unconscious in scientific investigation. This, in turn, amounts to a plea for including the unconscious in our epistemological theories. At this point the authors are only interested in the straightforward recognition of the importance of this faculty in the

---

* See Hans Sachs, "The Creative Unconscious."

** See Heinz Hartmann, "On Rational and Irrational Action," (in Geza Roheim, Ed., "Psychoanalysis and the Social Sciences," II, New York, 1950).

method of science. It has always played a central role even when we have not realized it. The unconscious is a productive colleague of the conscious in efforts to know nature. Even to know how droll the unconscious can be is an advantage. Knowing this, one is a little more apt to be objective and careful about one's subjective intuitions. This might provide not only greater objectivity in the classical sense, but also more productivity in the modern sense.

In any branch of human biology, control of the observer requires careful attention. In psychiatry, since the investigator observes the subject in its total complexity, control of the observer becomes more crucial. The distortion introduced has demanded some modification of our methods of investigation. Those who insist that man cannot study man objectively in his total functioning beg the question. Others naively have assumed that the techniques and methods suited to inorganic phenomena were just as appropriate to the study of man, the most complex biological system. This lack of appropriate method underlies a current dilemma in the biological sciences, and more particularly, in the psychological sciences.

In the physical sciences, most of the revolutionary discoveries were not produced by mechanical and logical inference from empirical observations and experimentation. They came as creative insights. What is it that enables one scientist with a mass of facts before him suddenly to see relationships which make them meaningful, while another scientist with the same factual knowledge "creates" no new ideas? There must be some crucial difference in the way the two relate their observations to their total experience. The creative scientist in some way relates experience of his data (his observations) to his experience of himself (his introspection) in a manner not achieved by the non-creative scientist.

Descriptions of our own bodily functions, as in physiology, are modelled after our picture of the external world, e.g., circulation as a hydraulic pump system, the nervous system as an electrical communication system, and the musculo-skeletal system in terms of physical leverage. We understand least those physiological functions which have no ready counterpart in the physical world, e.g., the endocrine system. The contrary of this may not be so obvious.

How much of our understanding of the external world is simply a projection of our implicit understanding of our own body functions? The concept of energy seems hardly different from our experience of "will." "Relativity" was implicitly assumed by every human being in even his simplest perceptions long before the "creative scientist" could translate his implicit understanding into generalizations from a mass of data. Such correlations are innumerable. Indeed, if you assume that man has some implicit understanding of his physiology, then he has, in his own experience, a basis for understanding heat, light, electronics, mechanics, etc. In this sense, the observer and what is observed have a real unity. Many of the fundamental concepts in physics and physiology have their equivalents in the subjective, though unconscious, experience of every individual. Anything known is known essentially by the experience of it directly in the observation and indirectly in the scientist.* This may be of negligible significance in the physical sciences, a matter of some concern in basic biological sciences, but in the psychological sciences it assumes paramount importance.

Objective observations are of fundamental importance, but particularly in psychological science such observations mean little without honest cognizance of the personal component in the observation. Such emphasis on inner experience does not mean a reversion to the introspective efforts of nineteenth century scientists. Today we have better access to the determinants of the observer's experience. Moreover, we can communicate these experiences more accurately. For this understanding we are indebted primarily to the development of modern psychiatry. The validity of the internal experience as a datum of science stands better assured because of these advances. Despite this control, the very instrument (scientists' inner experience) which can be most useful and illuminating can lead to great distortions and confusion. Nonetheless, the positive value of this objective-subjective approach outweighs the dangers inherent in it. If conscientious application of the procedures of the physical sciences to the more complex biological phenomena continues to be as sterile as it has in the past, these new methods must be developed. Whatever methods

---

* A. Whitehead, "Science and the Modern World."

we finally arrive at, the importance of the scientist's experience as the final source of creative achievement is indisputable. Since the subjective experience of the observer is of such critical importance, the honest recognition and acceptance of it will antecede further advance in method.

2

Research in Psychotherapy

Always the beautiful answer who asks a more beautiful question.

E. E. Cummings

Methods of Research in Biological Science

An unfortunate gap in the development of science, particularly that of psychotherapy, is the failure of scientists to record their methods of investigation. Science has developed a highly specific experimental method which applies only after certain initial hypotheses have been set up and certain inferences have been drawn from them. Although hypotheses provide the moving force in science, the manner in which scientists arrive at these remains unclear. Few hypotheses emerge out of sheer induction. Nonetheless, induction may validate these hypotheses. Their origin in the biological sciences remains even more obscure since mathematico-deductive methods have little applicability here, at least up to the present. A knowledge of the steps by which the biologists have developed new theories would be helpful.

It is difficult to use traditional methods where the sources of one's data are living human beings seen in a clinical situation.

Many areas in medicine have had to content themselves with rather gross statistical approximations, based on masses of clinical material. Yet in almost every instance, the differences obscured by the statistical approach may be as important as the similarities on which the statistics were based. Even so, the generalizations from material studied in this manner have a static quality very unlike their living source. The other possibility in clinical medicine has been the searching out of so-called "natural experiments." These consist of changes in the organism, naturally or therapeutically induced, which imply the modification of a specific factor, and the observation of the resultant effect of this modification on other functions. In such cases the controls are, of course, pitifully inadequate. This problem becomes magnified many times in the field of human behavior, where nature's experiments are seen day after day in clinical situations. The variables are so numerous and so interlocking that it is almost impossible to generalize safely. Other factors, such as the humanness of the observer and the unique meaning to each observer of his data, represent important additional pitfalls. Even if we assume observation to have been accurate, the problem of communicating to another person is awesome.

Methods of Research in Psychotherapy

At the present time, the difficulties of research in clinical psychotherapy appear as insurmountable as many problems in clinical medicine did a few decades ago. However, some very real compensations exist. No scientist is more pervasively exposed to, or more intimately in contact with, his material than the practicing psychotherapist. The scientist has no instrument more accurate or delicate than the therapist's personal capacity to react to his material selectively and subtly. No scientific instrument is as refined or discerning as the human nervous system. Our failure to define rigorously the methods for precise use of this instrument of observation is lamentable.

It would be helpful to know the early history of the science of psychiatry, written from the point of view of the growth of understanding by the early masters. Precisely what methods did they use which enabled them to abstract from their clinical experiences the data upon which the science was founded? What personal capacities had they which other individuals with the same clinical exposure lacked? What was the importance of the group in the pioneer days of the science of psychoanalysis? How did they communicate and share their clinical experience? In what manner did they stimulate understanding in each other, and how did they serve as controls for each other? If we knew these things, we might know better how to utilize our own clinical data to feed into the common body of shared experience, which is the core of the science of psychiatry.

The Group Approach to Research Problems

One lesson we can learn from the history of science generally is the importance of group research. Some of this research involves a group of people physically working together in the same research building. There are, however, many more instances in which the members of the group work physically in separate areas but maintain a constant exchange on a subjective level, because of their intense emotional involvement with each other in terms of their specific research areas. Some of these groups are integrated by positive affect, others are integrated by differences which frequently go beyond intellectual disagreements. Many times, after attending scientific meetings, one leaves with a feeling of belonging and increased emotional involvement, not because other individuals agree, but more often because those disagreeing expressed a great deal of feeling in their disagreement. From this point of view, even though an individual may prefer to do his research alone, he is part of an ill-defined group or groups made up of other individuals working in the same area and affectively related to him in either a positive or negative sense. In medicine particularly, one rarely sees at the present time, any research not produced by a group of individuals working together. The inability of any single person to comprehend the complexities of the human organism sharply limits individual research. In addition, the group approach also appears to provide a more adequate stimulus for, and a more rigorous control of, the subjectivity of the individual scientist. In a sense, group research is based on an increasing recognition of the importance of including the observer along with the observed. This approach is especially significant, but for that very reason especially difficult in psychiatry. The personal intimacy of the small original group of analysts may have been a significant factor in their productivity. Such intimacy, however, may have been purchased at the price of intensive psychological demands made upon the individuals and upon the group as a whole.

The differences among Freud, Jung, and Adler, and their final separation may reflect, in part, the cost of this continued intimacy in a research group where the "data" dealt with were the personal reactions of these men to their patients. Had these men had the cultural and professional support on which psychotherapists rely today, their continued association might have been possible. Their mutual support might have increased the contributions of each in preventing some rifts still unhealed—might have advanced the integration of the total science.

Finally, such a group with a particular research problem presents a matrix to which even therapists who are not members of the group refer data from their contemporary experiences with patients. The authors frequently clarified their conceptual framework by presenting it to groups of medical students and taking up with them, at length, the relationship of this to their own experiences in therapy with out-patients in the teaching clinic. Their contributions to our research effort has the validity of insights that one gets from patients themselves. A very similar example of this type of research learning is furnished by contributions of members of our staff doing child psychiatry. Their experiences in this different area form a challenging medium for a better conceptualization applicable to the over-all field. In a somewhat different framework, we have spent considerable time as a group discussing the role of science in the therapeutic process. The experience of each individual is unique. His perceptions of a particular facet of therapy are frequently quite divergent from those of another group member, and the effort to hammer the different observations into a common framework is stimulating even though arduous.

The establishment of a research team composed of actively practicing psychotherapists promises some refinement of our methods of investigation. The team must function as a group on a fairly deep psychological level. It involves the development of an emotional honesty, a personal security in expressing deep reactions to patients, and the development of methods of communicating which go deeper than any technical terminology. These are achieved through a process closely related to group therapy. In such a group, when a research problem is presented, each person brings his total experience to bear and to a much greater extent than would be possible if each individual contributed separately. Group insights emerge only after communicability about central issues is achieved.

After five years as members of a research group, the authors are just beginning to develop the kind of security necessary for productive research. We develop some of the subjective intimacy through which such a group functions through a continuing process of what approaches group therapy. In research we utilize a method of joint fantasy. A problem area is presented, e.g., a spontaneous, free-associative fantasy integrated by the affect of each of the participants for the group. Out of this fantasy, unbound by any conceptual or pragmatic limitations, there gradually emerge some tentative hypotheses which are then more rationally conceptualized and empirically tested against available data. These hypotheses are later put to work in a therapy situation with patients. Our next step is to narrow down the area of investigation within approachable limits, and establish those generalizations which our experiences as psychotherapists gave some common basis for accepting. In scheduled research conferences, these generalizations are gradually refined and qualified. Inferences from them are re-evaluated continually in the light of our total available experience as psychotherapists. To implement this research method, we have used various recording methods. At the same time, we vary the type of patient and, within limits, the character of the therapy, in order to obtain data on areas of specific interest at any given time. Any such implementation and refinement, however, is secondary to the fundamental importance of the personal participation of each investigator and his ability to transmit his own observations and emotional reactions in a clinical situation to a critical but productive group matrix.

Problems of Communication

An intuition proffers little unless it can be communicated. Insights with an unconscious component are very difficult to communicate. Much of the struggle in science consists of an effort to achieve a common basis of communication. The discipline of semantics has endeavored to answer precisely this need.

The inadequacies of the written word in the communication of understanding in the natural sciences are apparent. The physical scientists have evolved a less subjective and less variable sign language involving essentially de-personalized and acultural symbols, i.e., mathematics. The problem in the biological sciences differs somewhat. To date, we have not found a language suitable to convey the complexity of biological data or one comprehensive enough to express its integration. Dissatisfaction with the use of personal signs in scientific communication provoked the recent effort to provide an impersonal, symbolic language suitable to the biological sciences which would be, in many ways, a counterpart of classical mathematics in the physical sciences. Symbolic logic has attempted to answer this need. One is still left, however, with a sense of deep dissatisfaction. Semantics has not significantly clarified the problem.

Science repeats its experiments, presumably in order to affirm or negate the original findings. Such repetition assures communication together with verification. Repetition of the experiment is not simply a technical procedure, but it exposes a second scientist to an experience similar to the one which the first scientist utilized as a source of knowledge. Repetition of the experiment serves more than further validation. In inducing a similar experience for another, the first scientist succeeds in communicating much more than he could have on a verbal or sign level.

To write this text, the authors had to communicate separate experiences in their treatment of psychiatric patients. This treatment process is not an impersonal objective experience; it is deeply personal. As we will describe later, some adequacy in communication emerged only when we shared not only words but experiences. This led to the conviction that what is of fundamental importance in the field of psychotherapy is essentially non-verbal. The communication of it must utilize those forms of communicating which functioned in the initial experience. We know very little of the precise kinds of communication utilized. Many are non-verbal but, despite this, unbelievably accurate. When the spoken voice is involved, qualities such as intensity, modulation, timbre, pitch, tempo, and pauses seem to be the important ones. More important even than sound are the primitive perceptive systems which involve postural changes, changes in muscle tone, proprioceptive and somesthetic perceptions. These necessitate shared experience, and words are valuable only to the extent that they stimulate in others a total experience similar to the experience which the teller is attempting to describe. When this happens, we communicate.

Our problem with you, the reader, is even more difficult, because our words do not adequately stimulate in you those fundamental *perceptive* systems which mediate accurate communication. We hope, at most, that you respond to what we write as you respond to a patient, i.e., to the underlying philosophy. Concern with specific and highly abstracted parts of the whole will blunt communication of the basic concepts presented.

Psychiatry and Psychotherapy: Art of Psychotherapy

In many ways the art of psychotherapy stands in striking contrast to the science of psychiatry. There is some justification for this. Every society develops psychotherapeutic techniques, and its basic values have become part of every culture. The science of psychiatry, in contrast, has been more recently developed, more explicitly denoted, more exactly recorded, and more easily communicated. Only recently has the art of psychotherapy emerged as a neophyte science. The abstruse quality of psychotherapy as an art accounts for some of this delay in its formulation as a science. Any effort to look at the process of psychotherapy implies some abuse of the sacredness of the therapeutic relationship. The psychotherapist faces many of the same problems as the medical clinician in his role as a medical scientist. In addition, the communication of the psychotherapist's observations and insights presents other difficulties. He must violate his own subjective integrity and utilize the momentary character of his conscious insights to make the data, which are subjectively unearthed, objectively available to someone else. Nonetheless, to the degree that he does this, he is a scientist who makes known some aspects of human nature. The art of psychotherapy often conflicts with, and limits the development of, psychotherapy as a science. The formulation of an art into a body of knowledge may lead to its enfeeblement as a creative process. Nevertheless, of the people dealing with the science of human behavior, the therapist most immediately and pervasively deals with the raw data of human experience. Potentially then, he has the most to offer to the science of psychiatry.

3

The Biological Basis of Psychotherapy

Man is born child, his power is the power of growth.

Tagore

Inasmuch as psychotherapy deals with the whole organism, it comes within the province of general biology. The science of biology has matured through the incorporation of the principles and data of more basic sciences, e.g., chemistry. In a similar way, the principles and data of biology should foster the growth of the science of psychotherapy. Psychotherapy, as a specific form of medical treatment, provides biological repair, especially by effecting changes in the growth or adaptation of the organism, and we will therefore be especially interested in biological generalizations concerning growth and adaptation. The purpose of this chapter is to present a biological frame of reference for psychotherapy. What follows, then, is necessarily brief, and comprises a condensation of those biological principles developed by others which seem to be most representative of current thinking as well as useful to us in understanding the process of psychotherapy.

16

This approach implies a recognition of the close interrelationship between all the fields of science. This, in turn, implies the belief that generalizations valid in one area of science are apt to be valid in all areas unless proof to the contrary is adduced.

The lay person has no difficulty accepting the unity of the sciences since, despite his confusions, he is reassured by the feeling of his own unity. Not only do we, as individuals, find unity within ourselves, but we find a unity with others in our shared experience. Our subjective judgment (insight) about life has a certain validity.

It helps us in our thinking, at any rate, to assume that whatever is known about anything organic holds true, no matter what phase or aspect of life one approaches, whether it be physiological, biochemical, ecological, or psychological. Knowledge itself has this same kind of unity. This is particularly so when the subject of the knowledge is the knower himself, as is true in psychotherapy. The above orientation gives us some basis on which to discuss the complex relationships with which we deal in this chapter. If knowledge simply reflects the knower, then the reflection has as much unity and integrity as the knower. Professional concern with different aspects of the source stem from the training of the investigator. Nevertheless, biology, physiology, or psychology are simply aspects of the same basic phenomena. It may be that one way of looking at the human organism is more gross and more fundamental than another. Thus, biological truth may be more clear-cut than psychological truth. We feel that the relationship between the basic biological sciences and the more recent psychological sciences presents a problem not only of the relationship of whole to part, but also, and more significantly, of function to structure. Since we cannot, as yet, see many of the more subtle functional relationships, we rely on the theory of the biological scientists for our orientation concerning human functions, including psychotherapy, utilizing their findings as a critical measure of the validity of our own concepts. A science of psychotherapy must be developed within the framework of the biological sciences. In summary, physiological principles are validated by comparison with the more basic biological and biochemical truths, and psychological principles, in turn, may be critically altered by what is fundamental in all of these more objective sciences.

Unity Within the Biological World

Within the unity of all life, any living system has all the properties of the single cell, even though it may also have other properties by virtue of its multicellular arrangement. This amounts to more than an academic classification; this continuum of complexity has a dynamic reality, which extends from the most primitive structure to the most subtle function. All forms of life relate to all other forms of life, either ecologically or phylogenetically.

The single organism has the same unity. Divisions or disciplines are more heuristic than real. Any change in a part of the organism, regardless of whether the change comes in the province of the physiological, genetic, chemical, or psychological, results in changes which affect every other aspect of the total organism. The dynamic continuity between these different levels of integration means that any change in a lower level will result in corresponding changes in higher levels, and vice versa. Thus, physiological changes have very clear psychological effects, and presumably, the reverse is also true: the interpersonal changes the psychological; the psychological changes the physiological; and the physiological changes the anatomical. The effect of structural changes on function is, of course, obvious. The effect of function on structure, although logical and apparent from a common sense view, is not so obvious.

In the human organism, one finds much the same continuity of functional levels. In keeping with recent developments in biological theory, thought and ideation are viewed as highly integrated feeling, feeling as highly integrated emotion, emotion as highly integrated physiological change, and physiological change as simply a highly integrated electro-chemical change. The basic dynamics of each level are pertinent to any other level, and all reflect the same plan of organic function.

The lowest level of integration with which the psychiatrist deals entails physiological functions as these relate to growth and total function, e.g., the motility and secretory activity of the gastrointestinal tract as these are experientially integrated into the personality structure, as in the ulcer patient. More significantly, as in the newborn, he studies the growth of personality as it evolves out of the matrix of mother-child symbiosis, taking its basic forms from the physiological systems which are centrally implicated at various stages of growth. This early personality and character growth can be more accurately called physiopsychogenesis rather than merely psychogenesis. From the matrix of these early undifferentiated "physio-psychic" energy systems, the adult personality emerges through successive differentiation and integration under the impact of an ever-expanding and complex experience. In the adult, one can speak of dependency as a purely psychological phenomenon, but its intimate relation to basic physiological processes is impressed on us in times of stress or disease.

The underlying process, whether applied to such a vagary as "the total personality," or to something as specific as gastrointestinal function, involves successive differentiation, accompanied by a more refined and delicately balanced integration with other systems within the organism. Very early the "total organism" develops some over-all integration which, though changing, is identifiable. We term this "personality." This, in turn, is further differentiated and integrated under the impact of expanding social and cultural experiences—so that the whole process becomes more physio-psycho-sociogenesis, with the underlying life principle of growth as expressed through emergent integration providing the continuity.

Other scientists, e.g., the embryologists, anatomists, geneticists, biologists, may concern themselves with the determinants of the physiological systems with which the psychiatrist begins. From this point of view, although the level of differentiation and integration with which the psychiatrist deals primarily in the newborn may seem primitive to him, the newborn itself represents a level of complexity which the psychiatrist appreciates only when he turns his attention to the amount of growth which anteceded the birth cry. The concept of growth applies in the area of evolution, also, and the same principles of emergent differentiation and integration underly the development of species.

Change Within Biological Systems

The actual biological capacity of the individual cell for change and for adaptation to stressful situations is itself almost fantastic. The evolution of the fertilized cell, with constant and unique adaptations to changes surrounding the developing organism, beautifully illustrates this. The potential of the individual cell for ordered mitosis during the first days after conception highlights its growth potential. The whole panorama of evolutionary change can, in a sense, be viewed as empirical evidence of the ever-present urgent life principle pushing toward increasing growth and more refined adaptations. Organic life is change. The study of biological systems is the study of constant flux.

The application of this same principle to the individual organism concerns us here. How much does the quality of change, of flux, characterize the human organism? How much of this change involves increasing efforts for better adjustment, either physiologically or psychologically? How much of the total capacity of the human individual organism do we ordinarily use in the accomplishment of these tasks? What are our potentials for change? In regard to the first question, the answer seems fairly simple subjectively. Our lives entail constant change with the need to adapt to ever-changing and unique stress situations. In each adaptation one seems to alter somewhat one's orientation toward personal experience. The actual constitutents of body structure differ from day to day, and from week to week; the human body contains little of the constituent substance present within it a year earlier. The fat deposits in the body are constantly replaced by ingested fat, so that at the end of seven or eight days, as much as 15 to 20% of our body weight is metabolized and replaced with new tissue. Within the organism itself, constant interchanges of chemical substances occur in the tissue matrices by the processes of trans-amination, the conversion of fats to carbohydrates, etc. The flux characteristic of the human organism then becomes increasingly apparent even in the actual substance of organic structure, to say nothing of catabolic-anabolic changes characteristic of organisms as a whole during the total life span. How much of this change is adaptive? The same cycle of creation and destruction holds true of the blood cell, the protein structure of the body tissue, and even of bone. This capacity of the body to restructure itself, to transpose fats and proteins and carbohydrates as the need arises, illustrates well the biological potential of the human organism.

In describing what seems to be the fundamental quality of change or flux which characterizes all biological phenomena, one must discuss, also, psychological growth in the human being as a particular type of growth. There are more specific principles which pertain to growth and adaptation in this area. The unity of all life phenomena, nonetheless, should provide some generalizations which would hold true and help integrate our thinking about psychotherapy.

Four general areas stand out as significant to our purpose: (1) those principles which apply generally to the process of growth and orderly change, both in the individual organism and in the species; (2) those generalizations which are implicitly assumed concerning the functioning of an organism during any given period of time; (3) those principles which govern exchange of energy; and (4) those principles governing the interrelationships among organic systems at any specific time. We refer to these areas in order as growth, adaptation, energetics, and field theory. We will consider each area separately, discussing adaptation separately in the following chapter.

GROWTH. Life denotes constant flux and change. This change seems to have a certain orderliness. Orderly change with direction we can call growth. Growth in this sense means life, and refers, as such, to the fundamental process in organic systems. The beginnings of growth in any biological form have qualities so peculiar to their beginnings that the description of this phase of growth has been formulated as the principle of incubation. Every organic system has a period of incubation, a period within which the organic system organizes in a definitive enough fashion to continue the process of growth through a maturation phase. No matter what their final form, biological systems are more similar if compared in the incubation period than when compared later during the phase of maturation. The most primitive growth forms obtain in incubation. Subsequently, growth as maturation characterizes any organism until it reaches the stage at which the organism has ceased maturing and has begun maintaining itself. This seems to be an arbitrary distinction, and all growth after incubation may be termed maturation so that, in a sense, an organism matures to death. The growth curve, however, usually reaches a characteristic plateau, at which point maturation has all but stopped. Even here, change does occur which the plateau may not truly reflect. Nonetheless, incubation and maturation do involve more fundamentally the process of de-differentiation, while growth in the plateau entails more fundamentally the process of integration. The dual function of differentiation and integration is operative, however, at any phase of growth and even in the incubation period.

During the incubation period, many structures regress and may even disappear in order to permit the further differentiation and integration of the total system. These temporary distortions or reversals of the growth pattern we call regression. The principle applies not only in incubatory stages of growth, but also in the period of maturation, particularly psychological maturation. The process of growth then implicates incubation, maturation, and regression. Distortions in the growth curve may occur because of overdevelopment or inhibition of growth, in addition to regression. Growth in this sense follows the principles of inertia, based on the need to maintain the present level of growth, and also, a tendency to persevere in a growth process once it is started and, in a sense, to grow beyond the point where growth is adaptive.

ENERGETICS. Accompanying growth and change there are always quanta of energy in any organic system unavailable at any given time and particular circumstance for expression in growth and change. This is the principle of *entropy* (bound energy). The unavailability of that energy is a function primarily of the field in which the system reacts. The amount of unavailable energy varies, depending on the extent to which the organism has developed access to its own potentials, and the tolerance of the system within which the organism functions. Bound energy is nonetheless potential energy. Its expression and availability depend upon an increase in the efficiency of the organism through growth.

The principles of thermodynamics best express the energy exchange among biological systems at any given time. The energy of any one system is ordinarily available to any other system, and within the single organism different forms of energy are transmutable. Any form of energy can be converted to another form of energy and most of this energy, whatever its form, is available for work, e.g., growth.

Persisting throughout change or growth, the organism maintains its identity throughout the whole cycle of life. This provides a constant by which it can be identified at any stage in the life cycle, and reflects specifically the operation of the genetic principle in biology, and more generally, the principle of continuity. Continuity of the organism persists despite changes in its integral parts. An English shepherd dog never becomes a dachshund. This reflects the genetic principle. At the same time, a particular English shepherd never becomes another English shepherd. This reflects the principle of continuity. In historical perspective, of course, growth becomes evolution. The growth seen as evolution, though seen more clearly empirically, continues to confound us conceptually so that the actual processes involved remain ill-defined. Growth in any sense is directional, and has recognizable form which leaves its imprint on the growth sequence itself. Which determines the other is a moot question. In a sense, this directional quality appears to resemble the earlier vitalistic principle of _entelechy_, which, when defined as "a vital influence which guides living organisms toward the right direction," seems particularly pertinent to psychological growth, and is implicitly assumed by many physicians in their clinical function.

There are innumerable examples of conversion of energy in normal behavior. Thus, anger in an interpersonal relationship may be converted into compulsive work, random motor behavior, misdirected feeling, rigidity or, in many instances, deep hate may be rather suddenly converted into deep love. Any psychodynamic is simply a way in which these "conversions" occur. In the example of an angry person who represses his anger and converts it into rigidity, work, or displaces it onto another person, there is always the possibility that the direct expression of his anger will deepen his relationship with the person with whom he is angry, and such expression is most often growthful. Psychotherapy necessitates the freeing of affect in order to provide some basis for a growthful interchange between the patient and the doctor. Not only are biological energies interchangeable, but the manner of exchange reflects differences in the potential of two systems. The relationship of the mother to the infant presents this interchange most revealingly. The mother gives protection, love, and support to the dependent child since she has greater potential for such giving. As the child develops, the difference between the potential of the mother for support and emotional giving and that of the child decreases, and frequently examples are seen of the five- or six-year old supporting the mother emotionally during periods of stress. On a more subtle level, the same differences in potential are seen in psychotherapeutic relationships, whether they be social or professional in nature.

FIELD PRINCIPLES. When viewed in panorama, the relationship among all biological systems within a relatively large area reveals a fundamental principle of modern ecology. Not only are the parts of an organism so interrelated that the whole is more than the sum of its parts, but the relationships among different organisms in the bionomical field are such that the whole is more than the sum of the organisms involved. This principle has led to the recognition of the importance of treating the whole family when one member of the family undertakes psychiatric treatment. We have all seen dramatic changes occur in children, both physically and psychologically, when they were moved from one environment to another. The most striking example of the sensitive interdependence among members of a family is that seen in the case of a patient who undergoes psychiatric treatment successfully. The new-found capacities in one member of the family upsets the total economy of the family so that the other members are precipitated into a different type of pathology or therapy, or both.

This gestalt principle itself has meaning only when seen as an expression of homeostasis. The maintenance of the gestalt character of the organism and of the field within which it lives seems to be the central concern of most of the adaptative dynamics. There is a tendency toward completion or closure achieved through adaptation. Any healing of the skin surface involves closure, and fundamentally this differs little from the effort at closure seen in the individual, interrupted in some task, who develops some anxiety until he completes the task. On a more gross level, the same need for closure arises in any disturbed interpersonal relationship. Each individual struggles with some anxiety to achieve some definite ending to the particular phase of his relationship. The husband who leaves home in the morning after an exchange of inhibited anger with his wife will suffer during the day with generalized anxiety which may be resolved in a few minutes after his return home. During the day, he is acutely aware of the unfinished quality of his feeling.

The principles of biology outlined above are so broad that disagreement in terms of particular instances would be quite easy. Nevertheless, they indicate some of the principles which investigators assume when they deal with organic systems. The dynamics of psychological growth are simply specific expressions of these broader principles. They comprise the wide framework within which the authors set their research efforts.

4

Adaptation

Allah gives light in darkness, Allah gives rest in pain.
Cheeks that are white with weeping, Allah paints red again.
Seigfried Mahlmann

Classically, adaptation consists of the process of change within the organism in response to stress forces from the outside which better enables the organism to function in any given set of circumstances. Such reciprocity of internal and external change results in stress in either area modifying the whole organism to reduce the stress vector. At any period of growth when we look at the organism in its current functioning, we deal with a type of adaptation. Thus, even when we are dealing with the flatness of a schizophrenic or the paralysis of the hysterical patient, we are dealing with a patient who adapts and not merely regresses. The adaptation of any psychiatric patient has some of the qualities of the physiological adaptations, e.g., the syncope resulting from blood loss. The total organism responds in either case so as to maintain the whole by defending itself from further stress. Thus, syncope results in certain circulatory changes (vasoconstriction, negation of postural hypotension), which assure more adequate blood supply to vital organs.

Some of the major biological adaptations, however, occur in response to not external but internal stress. Recently, internal stresses have assumed increasing significance in medical science, e.g., collagen diseases, endocrine diseases, etc. Just so, psychiatry now sees much psychopathology as a way of responding to stresses within rather than external to the person. The theory of adaptation takes on a new perspective when seen as a problem of adjustment within the individual and not of the individual to external insult.

Adaptation functions via the irritability of the biological system. When viewed in conjunction with irritability, the process of adaptation expresses the principle of homeostasis. According to this principle, in a stress situation, whether the stress be internal or external, the total organism reacts in such a way as to restore equilibrium, including a maximum reduction of irritation achieved with a minimum response on the part of the organism. This principle normally applies in any organic system, and needs no psychological illustration since it underlies most of dynamic psychiatry. Every symptom has its economy and its meaningfulness to the individual. Moreover, the organism responds with the most integrative response adequate to adapt to any disequilibrating stimulus. Disequilibrium, in very general terms, arises out of conflict or antagonism among competing systems, e.g., an individual provoked to anger by another individual may simply suppress his anger and remove himself from the situation, provided that in so doing he does not frustrate any of his deeper personal needs. In another case, for example a child, responding to the father's provocation, may be unable to handle the stress economically except by a very primitive regression. He curls up on the floor, weeps, wets, and sucks his thumb. Presumably in this latter instance, the child responds on the most economical level available to him in this given circumstance. The character, intensity, and direction of the adaptative response algebraically sums up the antagonistic vectors. The child has the impulse to attack, but at the same time, needs the continued love and protection from the father. His upset derives from the antagonism between these two needs. His response, in this particular instance, reflects the unique intensity of both these needs and their resolution in a single adaptative response. Another child, in the same situation with different intensity of need, might well respond by a physical attack on the father. The principles are analogous to those involved in the buffer systems of the blood and the selective excretion of electrolytes in the maintenance of constant pH of body fluid.

We can distinguish between simple adaptation, which involves transient changes in the organism aimed at reducing the immediate stress in the environment, and those adaptations which involve more lasting alterations within the organism. These latter relate directly to the immediate stress situation, but also, produce in the organism increased capacity to adapt better to subsequent stress of a similar nature.

In line with the concept that the psychological processes are part and parcel of these biological principles, and in line with an orientation towards the function of the therapist, pathology develops a new dimension. It isn't enough to say that pathology results from stress either from within or without the organism. One must go beyond this to envision any pathology as a disruption of the growth process of the organism. Seen thus as an operational rather than a descriptive concept, certain differences emerge and demand further evaluation. Specifically, adaptation of the organism to stress becomes part of the general principle of growth. The same general principles which apply to growth as a process apply also thereby to adaptation. Hence, adaptation functions not only in the specific systems under stress but in the organism as a whole. The whole organism endeavors to reassert its growth potential with the greatest possible economy and maintenance of the most adequate homeostatic balance, not only of the particular systems under stress, but with regard to the over-all performance of the organism. Simple adaptation has a certain passive quality and tends to automatically counteract the precipitating stress. More careful consideration shows the incompleteness of this concept. The organism not only orients itself towards reduction of the stress involved and maintenance of its over-all functions, but it may go further. There are many examples in the biological realm of the organism's struggle to go beyond adaptation to stress and to bring about a state in which the organism will be less overwhelmed by similar stress at a subsequent time. In the development of immunity, the body not only undertakes the struggle against stress, but also the long range effort to develop highly specific methods of preventing further inroads. The effort of an adolescent girl to dissociate herself from the pain of her father's death almost inevitably initiates, also, an effort to dissociate the affect she has cathected on other father figures, resulting in an increased capacity for tolerating the loss of the loved object. In a sense, she has developed immunity to father figures.

These might well be called autotherapeutic functions of the organism. Labeling them as such involves two additional concepts: (1) The organism orients itself toward its continuance, not merely at this instant in time, but in an over-all sense. (2) In this therapeutic effort, the organism extends its own functional capacity, and makes dynamic that which has been potential. Thus any therapeutic adaptation decreases the entropy (bound energy) so that what was potential becomes kinetic and available for use in the life function of the organism.

The Problem of Repair

The outstanding characteristic of natural repair is the fact of it. The capacity of the body to repair itself, whether grossly or in an exquisitely specific manner, underlies all medical therapeutics. Repair distinguishes organic systems from inorganic. This process is inherently a part of any organism and pervades all of the activity of the organism. The continuance of life itself depends on the adequacy of these repair mechanisms as they daily involve the ever-changing adjustment of the organism to stress, either from without or from within. Thus, a person expects a wound to heal, inflammation to subside, pain to cease, infections to clear up within a reasonable period of time, and these expectations are ordinarily justified. Just so, a person expects anxiety to subside, grief and depression to pass away, and even compulsions and psychotic episodes to subside. In each instance, the individual somehow or other expects to take care of his psychological and social pathology without outside help, and fundamentally this expectation is justified. The processes of repair involved in all of these instances resemble each other.

Repair, viewed superficially, involves only a small part of the organism as a whole. Thus, the healing of a superficial wound involves primarily local mechanisms in the area of the wound, but also involves responses in other parts of the organism to facilitate or compensate for the local reaction. In contrast, fever as a disease phenomenon involves the total organism. In diseases there is a recognizable difference in the importance of the local mechanism in contrast to the total physiological response. In a patient with pneumonia, the greatly increased supply of blood to the lungs serves to engulf the invading bacteria, and finally, the organism develops humoral antibodies. Subsequently, the diseased lung tissue repairs itself. All these responses occur spontaneously and in an ordered sequence; some are more in the nature of *defense*, for example, prostration, fever, leukocytosis and congestion. Some others are specifically *reparative*, for example, the replacement of diseased lung tissue. The final group of responses involve both immediate defense and *lasting adaptation*, for example, the humoral antibodies. All of these processes occur in the patient with pneumonia, and looked at holistically, make up the reparative process.

The defense, repair, and therapeutic functions are as closely interwoven and interdependent in psychiatric diseases. During the second World War, a new clinical entity emerged, commonly known as Acute (Three-Day) Schizophrenia. The soldier who, in the midst of front line fighting, developed an acute psychosis, utilized the hallucinations and delusions as a method of defending himself against the reality stress. Simultaneously, by his dissociation from the reality situation around him and retreat into his psychosis, he brought to bear reparative processes which would decrease the stress. This regression brought about a retreat from reality demands, and an access to the psychological reparative processes of the organism in much the same way that fever and leukocytosis increased the reparative capacity of the individual with pneumonia. It is difficult to describe in a few words how this psychotic episode results in a greater capacity for tolerating subsequent reality stress, but we believe this is a fact and one which we will take up at length in the chapter on *The Process of Psychotherapy.* Thus, the psychosis, as does pneumonia, entails specific reparative and therapeutic processes.

Anatomical, physiological, and psychological factors limit any repair process. The body can grow a fingernail if the bed is intact, or a peripheral nerve if the myelin sheath is intact. In contrast, the body does not regrow an amputated finger or replace degenerated nerve cells. The limits, then, depend upon the tissue involved and the nature of the trauma. Bacteria, for example those with a capsule, are inadequately phagocytosed because of their morphology. Again, antibody response may provide immunity against a limited number of invading organisms, but the invasion may be so overwhelming that the antibody response either temporarily or quantitatively cannot overcome the invader. The site of the bite of a rabid dog may determine the adequacy of the immunity response. Thus multiple and deep lacerations in an area with a large number of sensory nerve endings, e.g., the face, may overwhelm the nervous system, and the antibody response may be totally inadequate. The above represent physiological limitations, of which there are countless examples.

In our present state of psychiatric knowledge, the psychological limitations are not clear. For many years, psychiatrists assumed that intelligence and very early experiences were so ingrained and unalterable that they conditioned the degree to which an individual could change his personality. It is likely that there are many such limiting factors in personality, but the most fruitful approach to psychotherapy, with our present knowledge, is to assume no unalterable psychological traits.

A further biological restriction has to do with the total economy of the organism: the automatic reparative process itself may be modified grossly if its demands are such that they endanger the economy of the whole. The best examples of this arise in the psychological area. Many individuals in stress situations may react inadequately, but are seen to develop greater tolerance for the same stresses subsequently. Successful adaptation to a stress increases the individual's tolerance for that same stress. Even an inadequate reaction to a stress situation which does not succeed initially may lead to a greater capacity at a later time. This increase in tolerance (immunity?) is not mechanical or simply summative. The availability of this increased tolerance ordinarily takes a long time. As in bacteriology, after a period of incubation the effects of the stress experience become integrated into the total personality of the individual. Beyond the mechanical notion that successful adaptation to stress increases the tolerance for that particular stress, adaptation to a specific stress increases the general capacity of the organism to adapt to any stress, whatever its nature. We will discuss the implication of this in relation to psychotherapy in a later chapter.

Generally speaking, the repair response depends on the interaction of four factors:

1. The intensity of the stress, whether the stress be trauma or infection, physical or chemical, internal or external. Thus, the extent of burns on the body surface, the virulence of an infecting organism, the number of infecting organisms, an overwhelming rage response, the depth of guilt associated with behavior, all represent different intensities of stress.

2. The resistance of the organism, by which is meant the capacity of the total organism to respond defensively and reparatively to any stress. Resistance may vary either constitutionally or situationally, and seems to be the most variable and most fundamental factor in determining the ability of the organism to survive exposure to stress.

3. The level of maturation, e.g., liability to many infectious agents, varies with age. In none of these instances does resistance totally disappear, but more or less serious reductions take place in the maximum possible efficiency of the total repair process.

4. The cost of the repair effort to the organism as a whole. The repair mechanism may be even so exaggerated that it becomes of negative value. Many of the hypersensitivity diseases represent just such a mechanism. The antibody formation, as part of the general repair process, may actually become converted into a process far more detrimental to the total organism than the original in-

fection as, for example, in rheumatic fever and glomerulonephritis. The same general principle applies in the metabolic compensations which occur in the diabetic patient. He produces increasing quantities of carbohydrates from fats only to come under greater and greater stress by virtue of the ketone bodies produced as a by-product in this chemical reaction. Thus, the repair process, local in nature, may, although complete in itself, markedly reduce the capacity of the total organism for adaptation. The repair of a broken femur in poor alignment may produce a degree of crippling which grossly incapacitates the organ for its normal functioning. In fact, it has been suggested that the reparative process following chronic irritation may be in certain instances the etiological factor in the production of neoplastic growth which finally destroys the organism itself. Many of the schizophrenic reactions represent an exaggeration of a repair dynamic to the detriment of the organism as a whole.

5

Catalyzed Repair

The physician must have two special objects in view in regard to disease, namely, to do good, or at any rate to do no harm.

Hippocrates

Therapists must recognize the principles which apply in the catalyzed natural repair processes. These are fundamentally based on natural self-repair mechanisms, differing to the extent that the catalyst interferes with or alters the process of natural repair. Most treatment in modern medicine represents a considered interference with the natural history of disease either chemically or surgically. More recently, greater emphasis is being placed on the natural defenses of the body with increasing concern for timing and the manner in which the physician contributes to the natural repair, i.e., interferes. The physician aims for a better balance between self-repair and pharmacological or surgical interference. Medicine has increased its understanding of the bodily responses, and therefore has greater assurance about the advisability of interfering with or of relying on the natural self repair. Certainly the less one knows about a particular disease process the more the natural repair mechanisms should be relied upon. Medicine has been forced historically to rely on natural repair since little was known of many diseases and certainly even now little is known of the process of repair in many diseases. Psychiatry, at the present time, occupies much the same position as medicine did three or four decades ago. Recently, gains have been made in understanding some of the grosser aspects of mental disease, but as yet we have no understanding of the natural processes of personality repair. This being true, any interference must be evaluated empirically with the greatest reliance being placed on catalyzing the natural process of self-repair.

Critics of psychiatry rightly condemn the tendency to usurp natural repair processes in psychological illness where the ultimate effect or limitations of such interference remains unknown, e.g., electroshock therapy. Psychiatry has, of course, harmed patients by disrupting mechanisms of repair which, if helped to run their natural course, might have brought the patient out of his illness with greater adaptative integrity. In World War I, cases of battle shock were intensively but irrationally treated with the result that many remained lifetime cripples. In World War II, such cases were simply sedated and sent back to combat where the patient's natural repair mechanisms could work, with the result that few became chronic casualties. The failures in World War I were due to over-treatment which prevented natural repair; in contrast natural repair was catalyzed by the approach used in the second war. Psychiatry will be able to interfere with greater assurance and certainly greater justification as more of the repair dynamics are better understood. Until then, therapeutic procedures must rely on natural repair mechanisms. At best, the present day psychotherapist acts as a general catalyst to natural repair processes. In the exercise of this role, the lack of knowledge of the repair dynamics in psychiatric disease is a serious limitation. But the failure of the therapist to understand his function as a catalyst to these processes presents a more immediate limitation.

Understanding of the pathophysiological defense mechanisms of the body has lagged behind investigation of the action of various medications and therapeutic procedures in medicine. In direct contrast, an understanding of psychotherapy has lagged behind the investigation of psychopathology in psychiatry. Since the therapist himself becomes the primary catalyst (medication), psychiatry needs a more adequate understanding of the relationship of the therapist's personality to the repair process in the patient. In a sense, further development in psychopathology depends on this better understanding of therapy.

Some general problems arise whenever one interferes with a natural repair process. Such interference may disrupt the repair process. The organism may become dependent on the catalyst, and as the arthritic patient may relapse after cortisone is withdrawn, the psychiatric patient may regress after the therapist withdraws. In some instances the catalyzed process may leave the person less capable than he might have been if he had been left to adapt to the stress without aid. Many examples from medicine illustrate this principle. Ill-considered use of antibiotics comes to mind as a striking example. The treatment may attenuate the natural defenses of the body and leave the individual less capable of resisting other infectious stresses. This untoward outcome, unfortunately, occurs quite often in psychiatry also. Early institutionalization of an acute psychotic reaction may prolong the disease. Supportive measures as used with neurotics, and often out of desperation or ignorance, may preclude exposure to sufficient stress to foster recovery and further growth.

The physician, and the psychotherapist, has the right to interfere with natural repair mechanisms only when his understanding of, or clinical experience with, them has convinced him of their inadequacy in a given patient. This means cautious calculation of the risk of creating enduring dependence on the therapeutic agent as against the risk of collapse or serious sequelae if the natural history of the disease is not arrested. The psychotherapist can often delay a psychotic break in a neurotic patient by putting him in a protective environment. Living through such a psychotic experience, on the other hand, might enable the patient to mature so that he no longer needed a sheltered environment. In psychiatry, adequate therapeutics seem to require maximal utilization of the natural repair process of the body in the broadest sense. In psychiatric illness, efforts at repair are frequently confused with disease itself.

Where the disease process is poorly understood, ideal therapeutics involves interference only to the extent that the organism cannot handle the disease by its own mechanisms. Thus lobotomy in the early stages of a schizophrenic reaction has no justification since, although the disease is poorly understood, clinically most of the patients recover without any treatment. When a therapeutic procedure is used, all the known natural repair mechanisms should be maximally used. This may be beset with dangers, since many therapeutic dosages are very near toxic doses. In much the same way, adequate psychotherapy with many neurotic patients may bring them near to clinical psychosis.

Many of the body's natural defenses develop only under conditions of continued stress. On the basis of this principle, as stated above, many psychiatric casualties were salvaged during the last war. Soldiers with battle neuroses were kept near the front lines after their breakdown. This policy greatly reduced the number of postwar casualties. Its effectiveness should not surprise us, since many of the common sense rules of thumb in child raising are based on the parents' willingness to demand greater capacity from the child and to allow the child exposure to stress situations, e.g., pugnacious, belligerent play companions, without over-protecting the child. The physiology of bone formation and bone repair also confirms this principle since osteoblastic activity is almost directly proportional to the stress placed on the bone structure. Furthermore, any part of the body which temporarily becomes unnecessary to the body's function will atrophy, e.g., arm in a sling or leg in a cast. Psychological faculties are bound by the same general principle, and the treatment of psychological disorders depends on the acceptance of this. Recently, outpatient treatment of psychotics who remain exposed to the stresses of normal living has shown promise of becoming a major advance in the treatment of some disorders. Such an approach correlates with a greater appreciation of the self-limiting character of many serious psychiatric diseases.

Subclinical disease itself is frequently a therapeutic method. It may occur naturally, as in tuberculosis and poliomyelitis, or it may be instigated by the physician as in the use of immunization procedures. Subclinical psychiatric diseases also occur, and many have the same beneficial effect. Many patients who recover from an acute schizophrenic reaction emerge with what in the literature has been called "massive resynthesis and insight." There develops a significant improvement in the integration of that person with a greater capacity to tolerate stress. This same principle underlies much of the theory of frustration tolerance. In fact, therapy often involves a "therapeutic psychosis" which, in many ways, effectively "immunizes" the patient against subsequent stress. As in medicine, this "immunization" through increased tolerance is relative and may be inadequate protection against severe stress. Unlike antigen-antibody reactions, successful tolerance of psychiatric stress seems to mobilize capacities which are more general, and provides protection against a broad range of stresses.

A physician who interferes with the natural defenses of the body must not only recognize the immediate implications of his interference; he must also take account of the long range effects. More specifically, the physician must recognize that he has therapeutic responsibility for the organism as a whole. Treatment of the presenting problem, for example, the relief of a headache by an analgesic, may be detrimental to the whole organism. Similarly, supporting measures which serve to tide the psychiatric patient over his immediate problem, e.g., by environmental manipulation, may significantly reduce his capacity to handle future stress. Overprotection of the growing child certainly prevents adequate integration. The mother, by protecting the child initially, facilitates his growth; but by continuing such protection, she fosters weakness and insecurity, leaving the child susceptible to minimal stress. At times, an actual increase in the stress may be necessary for the individual's growth. An aggressive demand by the parent on the child may augment the child's growth considerably. Such an approach follows a basic principle underlying surgical repair.

A few illustrations of the interrelationships between the natural process of repair and the function of therapy have been presented. Seen within the framework of the governing principles of biology, psychotherapy takes on new meanings. The principles which pertain to growth have immediate and practical significance. Acceptance of the tremendous potential for growth in less complex biological organisms as true also in the human being will further the development of effective psychotherapeutic procedures. New directions for experimentation will also emerge. Viewing psychological energies as merely a specific form of organic energy, governed by all of the laws which apply to energy (dynamics), will make more meaningful a study of the flow of energy in the relationship between the therapist and the patient. An acceptance of the governing functions of homeostasis and adaptation will likewise make for more security in altering disease process with techniques the exact effects of which can not be predicted. Most specifically, the principles of general self-repair and of therapeutic, catalyzed repair apply directly to the area of psychotherapy. The principles of therapeutics which have been developed by medicine, generally, should obtain in psychotherapy as well. Medical therapeutics can teach psychiatry a greater reliance on the process of natural repair and the dangers inherent in disturbing normal physiological reponses to stress. Thus, environmental manipulation, supportive procedures, and symptomatic treatment, generally, may result in a state in which any new stress can be responded to only on the basis of continued therapeutic support. Such procedures may facilitate simple adaptation, but remove the opportunity for developing greater stress tolerance through the natural repair function. The patient becomes dependent on the therapist so that, although the therapeutic process may help the individual in his response to the immediate stress, the end result may be greater disability than would have occurred had he been left to his own devices. Medicine has learned many lessons, some of them at great cost, relative to interfering with natural defenses and repair dynamics. Psychiatry, particularly psychotherapy, would do well to profit by the history of such success and failure.

6

The Community and Psychotherapy

For to him that is joined to all the living there
is hope. For a living dog is better than a dead lion.
Ecclesiastes 9:4

Who, during centuries past, has functioned as therapist to the
overwhelming number of individuals with psychosomatic, psy-
choneurotic, and psychotic disorders? The culture, at any phase of
its development, provides mechanisms for handling its own needs
and the illnesses of the individuals within the culture. For example, the highly developed religious and political systems of the
Middle Ages had a certain supportive and therapeutic value for
most of medieval society. Indeed, each individual in medieval culture had therapeutic responsibilities imposed on him, and he constantly responded to the needs of other members of the community. Nevertheless, there were at all times, certain groups in
whom these potentialities were developed to a higher degree. The
most conspicuous of these was the primitive medicine man. In the
Hellenic period, these functions were taken over primarily by the
priest class. Thus, we see King Oedipus visiting an oracular shrine
in order to abreact on a deep unconscious level, but within the

religious setting, his anxieties about his father's death and his own marriage. We also see the Hellenic philosopher-teacher function as a therapist to large groups of students, managing profound anxiety problems with an ease which would bring credit even to some of our prominent present-day psychiatrists. In another area, and in a different cultural setting, the government handled the hostility problems of the populace by staging spectacles with human life and death as trophies. These cases exemplify how variegated were the agents upon whom therapeutic responsibility was placed.

In our own western culture, there occurred a gradual cultural delegation of part of this responsibility. It devolved first upon the priest class, then upon the surgeon and the physician, and finally, upon the psychiatrist and the psychotherapist.

Psychiatry has accepted this responsibility, and during the past half century has made significant steps toward transposing the responsibility into a science. The science has developed historically through many divergent and seemingly contradictory paths which only recently seem to be converging toward some common understanding, i.e., toward a true science. The problem, at present, appears to be the application of this common knowledge. This has necessitated a re-evaluation of our responsibilities as physicians to the community, and a re-examination of the nature and limitations of the responsibility which the culture has delegated to psychiatry.

Such divergent approaches as those of Mesmer, Bernheim, Kraepelin, Janet, Jung, and others, all of which were based on different theoretical assumptions about the process of treatment and the nature of psychiatric disease, seemed to achieve results which, when honestly evaluated, were fairly comparable. On the whole, in the early days of psychiatry, the effectiveness of therapy seems to have been more deeply influenced by how able the therapist was as a person, rather than by the soundness of his theory. Today, one can find equally adept practitioners of the art of psychotherapy among religious converters, client-centered counsellors, or orthodox analysts. The Meyerian, who uses the personal history, the social worker with her process-interviews, and the clinical psychologist using his own techniques, all practice various forms of psychotherapy. Other psychotherapeutic groups include industrial counsellors and group psychotherapists. Yet in our own culture, the practicing physician, no matter what his avowed function may be, does, in fact, handle the largest percentage of emotional illness. Often he does so without any formal psychiatric orientation or knowledge of psychotherapy. Whoever meets this responsibility, and in whatever manner, the responsibility, along with the final judgment of the adequacy of the therapists, resides ultimately with the culture.

Disregarding the personal differences which predispose each of us as psychotherapists, the manner in which one sees psychiatry and psychotherapy, particularly their limitations, seems to be fundamentally a matter of the person's cultural background, and more immediately, a matter of his professional training. Psychiatrists, historically and at the present time, are rigidly bound by the level of the culture within which they live in much the same manner as the artist in any age is limited in his expression by his culture and the impact of his professional training. The therapist constantly struggles with these cultural limitations.

The authors hope to formulate some principles which reflect a different synthesis of the art of psychotherapy as it has developed currently in modern medicine, and more important, in our culture as a whole. Such a synthesis is difficult at the present stage of our knowledge of psychotherapy. Thus, one of the authors, by virtue of his training in practical medicine, limits his perspective by his need to validate his thinking by clinical case studies. The other author, by virtue of his training, limits his perspective by his need to integrate his thinking about the art of psychotherapy within the framework of the systematic sciences. Aware of these limitations, one can only hope to push the knowledge of psychotherapy a little further. The burden of developing it will fall on those psychiatrists who grow up in the more advanced, integrated professional training of the present day, which reflects the increasing synthesis of psychotherapy within our system of cultural values.

Psychotherapists, in a very specific way, are simply individuals who perform in crucial situations the therapeutic function of the culture itself. With the widespread interest in psychopathology and its etiology in the past few decades, there has been a tendency to overemphasize the repressive and inhibitory aspects of the culture. There is a more positive side to both the culture and its prime representative, the parent. Cultures develop very comprehensive patterns with therapeutic potential for satisfying the deep needs of the individuals within them.

The insecure individual does not have available these cultural therapeutic patterns for constant use in his life experience. The unavailability of his parent provides the prototype of his relationship to his culture. The positive feelings in the parent may be present but appear unavailable to the insecure child. The psychotherapist has the job of increasing the availability of the culture to the patient. He facilitates the transition in the patient from a sense of personal, parental, and cultural isolation to an ability to participate in, and increasingly to avail himself of, the culture for his constant use. Since this is true, the relationship of psychotherapy to the cultural pattern assumes critical significance.

In the past decades, we have been prone to set up psychiatry as an operational philosophy isolated from accepted cultural values. Nonetheless, patients who leave psychotherapy must enter a community of cultural values and function adequately in a real sense. Therefore, psychotherapy must be based on some of the given values around which the culture is patterned. There must be a unity in purpose between psychotherapy and the culture. In a punitively patriarchal and neurotic culture, which over-values masculinity, adequate psychotherapy does not function at its optimum if indeed it functions at all. Psychotherapy here might achieve certain changes in the patient which would place him, as he re-enters the culture, in a position of fundamental conflict to it. Our concept, then, of the relationship of psychotherapy to the culture is not simply one of relativism. The given values in both need not be identical, but both sets of values should be interdependent and based on a recognition of the more fundamental qualities of man as a biological and social animal. Such values include the opportunity for the expression and gratification of his deep biological needs, as well as the need for independent, integral functioning along with the opportunity for dependence on other individuals as he requires this to achieve both physical and emotional maturity. These imply acceptance of a sense of interpersonal and group responsibility. Such a value system, therefore, would need to present a nice balance between the individual in his independent uniqueness and the individual as a member of a group. The value placed on individuality as against conformity would be central both to the optimum culture and the most adequate psychotherapy. One could multiply these instances *ad infinitum.* Psychotherapy arises as an integral part of the culture. To operate most effectively, it must have in common with the culture, a similar set of human values. However, for both to be most effective in terms of human gratification, these sets of values must, in turn, be based on a recognition of the more fundamental biological qualities of man.

The implications of such an orientation to psychotherapy, relative to the responsibility of psychiatry to the community, are many. The only adequate approach to psychiatric illness, true also in other fields of medicine, necessitates a prophylactic and preventive orientation. The emphasis on insight and intelligent control has led, in recent years, to the assumption on the part of psychiatrists of the responsibility for educating the community. The effect of this extensive educational program has yet to be measured. Judging by the number of state hospital admissions and the rejection rate for emotional disturbances among men examined by the Army, this program has not made any appreciable dent in the problem of emotional illness. Prophylaxis involves radical changes in some of our most fundamental cultural values and patterns. These involve, primarily, the early socialization of the child. We know that the overt aspects of such socialization are much less important than the covert. These latter are based on unconscious needs, and are primarily affective rather than ideational.

Psychiatrists need to retrench and redefine their community responsibility with a more honest recognition of their limitations. Many of us psychiatrists have difficulty raising our own children and still we presume to tell other individuals how to raise theirs. A more limited sense of responsibility may provide a functional framework within which more profound changes in our culture can be achieved. Psychiatry can do this only if its therapeutic endeavors produce enough social therapists with adequacy and maturity to function with leadership in the culture. Their capacity to alter the cultural values within a small segment, for example a neighborhood, is limitless. The teaching responsibility to prepare the general practitioner as a psychotherapist broadens the base of our contribution to the community. In developing future medical practitioners as psychotherapists, we geometrically multiply the number of social therapists who, as active members of the community, can function on an experimental and feeling level to originate new patterns of cultural socialization and, in doing so, provide some real basis for preventive psychiatry. At any rate, psychiatry may be far more successful in this limited task than it would ever be by setting itself up as a judge of the total culture with all of its religious, economic, political, and social complexities.

7

Implicit and Explicit Psychotherapy

It is wisdom to trust a heart . . .
to trust the soul's invincible surmise.
Santayana

The modern effort to formulate a theory of psychotherapy has been stimulated by overt pressure from the community and pressure from physicians for a practical application of psychiatry in the general practice of medicine. In thus criticising psychiatry, both the community and the medical profession have accepted some responsibility for the emotional health of the individual. Psychiatry must provide an orientation and procedure for meeting this responsibility in the same way that pharmacologists developed methods of therapy specific enough so that the general practitioner could adequately treat his patients. The physician's function as a psychotherapist is as essential a part of patient care as is his use of antibiotics. He cannot rely simply upon his development of a bedside manner, nor can he deny the responsibility by saying, "I am not a psychotherapist." The modern physician must assume the responsibility for adequate use of antibiotics. In a similar manner, he must assume certain responsibilities in the area of psycho-

46

therapy. He should be equipped to refer to psychotherapists those patients with profound needs and grave disease processes, although the responsibility for treating minor emotional disturbances and the emotional upset associated with physical illness remains with him. He must be able to go beyond this and apply preventive psychotherapy in much the same sense that he is now responsible for giving tetanus antitoxin to prevent the development of serious disease.

In adding the burden of psychotherapy to the responsibility of the physician, the authors recognize that he must be protected in some way from the excessive demands of patients, insofar as these overwhelm his personal living. Psychiatry can help with this problem in two ways; it can (1) reinforce the physician as a person so that he can utilize his maturity as a tool in the practice of medicine, and (2) develop methods of practicing psychotherapy which can be taught on a level specific enough for use in general practice. The physician who learns how to do psychotherapy and how to function in an emotional relationship with his patient develops some protection from the excessive stress brought about by the sense of unlimited responsibility for all of his patients. He can accept the limited, but deeper responsibility for helping the patient become more self-sufficient. Unfortunately, it is only recently that psychiatry has been prepared to offer training in psychotherapy. Many practicing physicians have been forced to develop therapeutic patterns in isolation from the modern teaching of therapy. Adequate though these therapeutic patterns may be, they are often limited in their applicability. Some agreement among psychotherapists on what constitutes adequate therapy would help to expand the physician's therapeutic effectiveness. To go further, three terms need definition: physician, psychotherapy, and psychiatry. As individuals, physicians come closer to being psychotherapists than do any other group, not excluding even psychiatrists. Historically, one of the duties of the physician has been to catalyze the integrative adaptations of his patients. He also deals with problems of simple and segmental adaptations, that is, with the reduction of some immediate stress. In such instances, he often makes no attempt to increase the capacity of the individual to handle further stresses. Again, frequently the focus of his efforts is only some segment of the total person, e.g., the various organ systems. The physician as a psychotherapist should resemble more the old general practitioner than the modern internist. At present, the increasingly specialized physician is more and more concerned with certain aspects of the individual's total functioning. He thereby has given up to an ever greater extent his function as a psychotherapist. Nevertheless, psychotherapy remains an essential responsibility of the physician.

Why do the majority of practicing physicians eventually develop a competence in psychotherapeutic medicine? Why is it that, despite the differences in their therapeutic approach, most physicians do succeed with many emotionally disturbed patients? Psychotherapists are agreed that certain specific methods of treatment are more effective than others. Yet it is nonetheless evident that an individual using the most adequate method of therapy may achieve very poor results, while certain individuals using apparently inadequate methods do remarkably effective work as psychotherapists. Both the method and person using the method are crucial in psychotherapy. The term psychotherapy has been used for many years in a rather nonspecific and generic manner. Only recently have psychotherapists been able to teach the art of psychotherapy.

Psychotherapy occurs in many different relationships and under many different guises. Such psychotherapy is _implicit. Explicit_ psychotherapy, or the science of psychotherapy, has but recently emerged. It has been accompanied by labor pains similar to those which characterized the birth of other medical therapeutics. The relationship of these implicit forms of therapy to the present day explicit science is still unclear. The art of medicine as practiced by the country physician resembles the esoteric work of the psychiatrist. It is difficult to make explicit what has helped the patient emotionally in either instance. The experientially developed capacity of the professional psychiatrist was presumed to be related to both his knowledge of psychodynamics and psychopathology, and his appreciation of the relationship of the individual to the culture. The intuitive, clinically developed capacity of the general practitioner was assumed to come from his long and intimate contact with patients. Ideally, treatment by the professional psychiatrist is *explicit* psychotherapy, in contrast to the implicit methods of the physician. In either instance, however, psychotherapy may occur and is *an interpersonal operation in which the total organismic adaptation of one individual is catalyzed by another individual in such a way that the patient's level of adaptative capacity is increased.*

def. of psycho- therapy

In this sense, the psychotherapeutic process is a sub-type of what earlier was defined as a catalyzed therapeutic adaptation. Increase in adaptative capacity consists specifically of an increase in integrative adaptations. The emphasis on integration means simply that the area of growth relevant in this context is psychological. Such a definition excludes from the province of psychotherapy all of those operations, social or interpersonal, which trigger adaptation and do not lead to an increase in the individual's total adaptative capacity, as well as those therapies which are partial and increase only the adaptative capacity of some segmental aspect of the total person. Environmental manipulations which relieve economic or social stress, directive counselling, simple supportive or repressive measures, efforts to increase the capacity of the person to function better in some limited area of his total function, are viewed as nonpsychotherapeutic because they do not seek to produce an increase in the individual's capacity to adapt himself to all kinds of stress and on a higher integrative level.

The specific operations through which psychotherapy, so defined, comes about vary. Thus, the quality of the counsellor's relationship to the patient may result in some *implicit* psychotherapeutic gain. Many other forms of relationship may also be therapeutic in this sense. Some may even have as their stated aim an increase in the integrative adaptative capacity of the person and still fail to be truly psychotherapeutic. The techniques utilized, or the "therapist" involved, limit the depth of experience possible. Psychotherapy in the limited sense defined above may, however, result from the implicit quality of these relationships.

Regardless of the type or explicit intent of the relationship, whenever one individual engaged in an interpersonal relationship with another functions in such a way as to increase the integrative adaptative capacity of the latter, psychotherapy has taken place. Quantitatively restated, psychotherapy occurs whenever there results an increased actualization of the individual's adaptative potential, with a corresponding decrease in the difference between what that person actually is and what he has the potential of being. Previously bound (entropic) energy is thus made available to the organism.

It must seem very presumptuous to define as an objective the formulation of the basic process of psychotherapy. Why should it not be left as an implicit part of the culture, and why should not the psychotherapist go on functioning in an implicit manner since the basis for his functioning has to do with his own deep needs and his effort at satisfying them? It is true that psychotherapy is an art, and as such, must always be the expression of the total individual. Therefore, the value of any formulation must perforce be limited. Nevertheless, there are very definite analogies in the field of medicine. The art of aligning the two parts of a broken femur has been practiced for generations. Physicians over the years became more adept, and the teaching of medical students made each generation more effective than the past. However, it is not enough in our time for the physician to exercise his manual capacities. He must attempt to align the bones in such a way that x-ray pictures show the alignment to be anatomically as well as clinically adequate. Thus, he must not only be implicitly adequate, but he must be scientifically accurate. The same is true of psychotherapy. The modern practitioner must live up not only to his own capacity as an individual, but also to the growth of psychotherapy as a science and a discipline. Further justification for the effort to formulate an art of psychotherapy lies in the fact that explicit denotation may serve, as it does with the x-ray picture, to enable the therapist better to evaluate his experience and, therefore, to develop his capacity more rapidly and critically. By thus endeavoring to formulate the art, psychiatry also demands more of itself and of those who account themselves professional psychotherapists. It is possible to push the capacity of every mature psychotherapist to new levels of achievement. His potential is much greater than he assumes it to be, just as the patient's potential is greater than he, himself, envisions.

It may seem that in thus defining the significance of the explicit factors in psychotherapy the more intangible factors which so far are labeled as intuitive become explicit. As a matter of fact, the opposite is true. There is no doubt that one of the problems of the modern physician is immediately in this area, that having become increasingly adept at the science of medicine, he is apt to deny the evidence of clinical judgment. This is also one of the problems in psychotherapy. The psychotherapist has become increasingly uneasy in his clinical judgment without the security of an adequate scientific formulation. Lacking a definition of the process of psychotherapy, he has been forced to retreat to the safety of the sciences of psychopathology; and if the process can be explicated, the therapist may be freed so that he can more comfortably rely on his intuitive capacities. No matter what is said about psychotherapy on an explicit level, no matter how well it will be formulated in the years to come, there will always be a major place which can be filled only by the willingness of the mature therapist to respond as a whole person on a subjective level to the patient. It might even be said that in this capacity to be subjectively involved and to function on a personal level lies the art—and no amount of description will ever make the operation scientific.

Psychiatry and medicine, at the present time, seem to be developing along similar lines. In medicine, the classical anatomist was concerned with the structure of the body, and the classical pathologist was interested mostly in disturbed structure and, at best, concerned with ways in which the observed pathology developed. By contrast, the modern internist is chiefly a student of pathological physiology. He is interested not only in how pathology developed, but also in the *function* of the pathology itself. The same development also occurred in psychiatry. The classical psychiatrists were interested primarily in the structure and content of the disease, whose dynamic genesis was then studied by the classical psychoanalyst. The psychotherapist goes one step further. He studies not only the psychogenesis of emotional illness but, even more, the dynamics of present pathology and the function and therapeutic import of symptoms. In this respect he is primarily an empiricist and, like the internist, relies to a great extent on that intuitive reaction which medicine ordinarily calls "clinical judgment."

"Help" for psychiatric patients is such a nonspecific term! It may resemble suppressing the cough of the tuberculous patient, i.e., it may be temporary and possibly more dangerous than no help at all. Medical scientists are most interested in such questions as: "How many patients do you cure?" and "What do you mean by curing a psychiatric patient?" The solution of this problem, i.e., the attempt to prove to the statistically-minded scientist that psychotherapy is worthwhile, has been extremely frustrating. To date, the most comprehensive effort to find a possible answer is the establishment of an institute whose purpose would be to assay a large percentage of the variables involved in cure by a pre-therapeutic and post-therapeutic evaluation of patients. Nevertheless, this long range type of program must wait, and psychiatry must think more clearly about the present results of psychotherapy.

The most obvious definition of cure is the resolution of the symptoms for which the patient consulted the physician. This definition, however, is as inadequate in psychotherapy as would be a similar definition of the "cure" of cardiac pain. In psychiatry, the situation is further complicated by the fact that even the resolution of the pathology itself may not necessarily constitute an adequate cure, since it may involve the individual in even more profound pathological problems. The situation becomes more complicated when one stops to consider that the term "cure" is used differently depending upon the method of therapy. The psychiatrist using administrative methods considers cure to be a situation in which the individual disturbs the group or community less, or even more simply, merely to involve the patient's carrying out his directions. Those who manipulate the environment consider that they have brought about a cure when the relationship between the individual and the situation has been altered towards a more adequate functional relationship. The educational therapist utilizes the term "cure" to describe a more adequate understanding of his immaturities on the part of the individual; so, too, the therapist who does "ego therapy" may feel that cure involves merely a person's better adjustment to reality. In a repressive therapy or a conditioned-reflex type of therapy, a cure may merely mean the cessation of objectionable behavior, and thereby the elimination of that particular irritation in the social structure. To those to whom therapy is fundamentally experiential, the cure involves a reorientation of the individual's emotional energies in such a way that they are more *personally* satisfying in addition to being more socially acceptable.

Thus, the term cure has many facets, and any effort to find common denominators must deal with this problem, the solution of which necessitated, at the outset, a redefinition of the term psychotherapy itself. The reorganization of the energy factors existing between the individual and his culture, and the realignment of the energy factors of one or another aspect of his personality may be useful and, socially speaking, desirable. The term "cure," however, when used by the psychotherapist, should be defined more carefully and reserved for a more specific result of his interpersonal contact with a patient. Any cure in the realm of psychotherapy must be relative to a whole person. This must not merely increase the present functioning of the individual as a whole. In addition, as noted, to increasing his capacity currently, therapy actuates his potential capacity. Psychotherapy does not cure in the sense of assuring maturity in the patient; it simply inaugurates growth. It is the process of helping the individual learn how to remove the blocks to utilizing his inherent growth impulse. The growth and attainment of maturity occurs through experience in the community matrix.

In contrast, many dynamic psychiatrists generally consider the aim of therapy to be the extension of ego control over unconscious impulses. To the extent that unconscious material is made conscious, the patient is thought to be well. This is the fundamental basis of so-called insight therapy. This approach grossly underrates the adaptative and growth capacities of the unconscious and its usefulness biologically. The more unconscious the responses or the greater the participation of the unconscious in his total functioning, the more likely is the individual to function personally and socially on an adequate and gratifying level. Biologically, life is fundamentally an unconscious process, and in the degree to which internal stimuli must be handled on a conscious level consciousness is under stress and, therefore, less able to perform its limited but appropriate function of reality testing. In a very real sense, the individual becomes "self-conscious." Intelligence itself is something to be used by the deeper core levels of the personality, i.e., those levels that have to do with the gratification of the more fundamental and unconscious needs of the individual.

In this sense, one of the primary aims of psychotherapy would be to restore to unconsciousness functions which seem to work best when the person is unaware of them. An example in physiology might clarify the issue. In many ways, cardiac action is less adequate to the extent that it is conscious. Frequent, continued and prolonged treatment, if it makes the patient more acutely aware of his heart action, may leave him with greater disability and sometimes precipitate final physical failure. Cardiac patients frequently have trouble ridding themselves of heart consciousness. This example could be multiplied in the areas of physiology, for example, breathing, digestion, muscle coordination, vision, excretion, etc. Here, as with cardiac action, increased awareness and attempts to control and direct our physiology consciously lead to poor functioning and often physiological breakdown. Much the same principle obtains in the area of psychological functioning. This is expressed culturally in the description of the mature person as someone who is "natural." Even our professional evaluation of the adequate person as someone capable of expressing his feelings, of gratifying his deeper needs, and of never sacrificing his fundamental personal gratifications for conformity to external social pressures, reflects this same orientation.

One can easily reduce this principle to absurdity. For instance, the unrealistic person who obtains his gratifications in defiance of any nonpersonal considerations might, by this principle, be considered mature. There are some crucial qualifications to equating "natural" with "mature." The defect in such a belligerently "natural" person is the compulsive rather than natural character of his behavior. Part of being natural involves an implicit recognition of one's social responsibilities. Another example of pseudonaturalness would be the schizophrenic patient. His unconscious expresses itself with little restraint. Despite this, he certainly is not mature or even natural. The answer to this is rather paradoxical. The schizophrenic individual has more of his unconscious made conscious, and sums up in his sickness precisely the principle illustrated. In this respect, he resembles the pseudoanalyzed patient who is aware of all of the symbolic implications of his simplest natural behavior. Finally, it is paradoxical that while in psychiatry one leads the neurotic to express the kind of unconscious material which the psychotic individual has readily available, nevertheless, psychiatry often hesitates to treat the psychotic patient. The problem in treating the psychotic is considered to be one of increasing the reality component of the patient, in contrast to the effort to force the neurotic individual to express his fantastic component.

Patients in psychotherapy reflect a deep need to restore to the unconscious those capacities freed during therapy. The neurotic needs to "re-repress" the symbolic material which was so readily available during the process of therapy itself. Re-repression seems to be inherent in the ending process. Thus, after a very deep fantasy relationship, the patient in the final interview may react to any fantastic orientation with a starkness which is chilling. In essence, the patient completely denies any fantastic involvement in the relationship. He may subsequently greet the therapist impersonally, leaving him with the feeling that, if nothing else, the patient is certainly ungrateful. This may not be far different from the need of the analyzed patient to deny the analysis. For instance, one patient visited a chiropractor after two years of analysis, got one treatment, and came back to the analyst saying, "Look here, you have spent two years with me and haven't helped me at all. I went down to the chiropractor for one treatment and I feel much better." The analyst has traditionally assumed that this was an effort on the part of the patient to handle his guilt about the transference relationship. It may partially be his need to re-establish the integrity of the unconscious through re-repression. This re-repression is, in some very fundamental respects, far different from repression as we ordinarily use the concept. Repression involves fear, guilt, shame, or anxiety. It represents one of the most pervasive unconscious dynamics for the resolution of conscious conflicts. Re-repression has more positive aspects. The relegation of a function to the unconscious, in this instance, does not stem from fear or guilt, but more from the biological fact that some functions operate with maximum integrative effect when they operate unconsciously.

The importance of the individual patient as a source of data for the study of dynamics and psychopathology has been recognized. Yet the patient's dynamic formulations of the therapeutic relationship have been relatively neglected. This is true even of the therapist's intuitive and personal understanding of therapy, which arises out of the use of his own unconscious in therapy. Actually, his slips of the tongue and his therapeutic errata provide an excellent source of learning about the process of psychotherapy as well as psychodynamics and psychopathology. Only recently has psychiatry accepted the usefulness of studying failures in psychotherapy. The denial of the patient as a person implies a doubt that he has any real concept of what he wants when he comes to the professional therapist, that he has any real understanding of what he is getting and that, furthermore, he has any perception of when he has gotten all that is available. It is as though psychiatry believed in the unconscious when it fitted into the need for intellectual understanding of the personality and then denied the same unconscious as a force for the patient's understanding of the therapeutic process as such. The principle of the fitness of the unconscious, with its emphasis on the fundamental importance of the patient in determining the process and the objectives of psychotherapy, has other corollaries. One is a recognition of the inherent growth capacity in even the sickest patients. This capacity is as relentless in the psychological sphere as in the area of organic growth. Every expression of the psychiatric patient, even his most complex psychopathology, seems to reflect directly his effort toward growth. A reassuring aspect of psychiatric disease is that no matter how complete and endless the rejection may be, patients continue in their effort to obtain satisfaction for their growth needs. The psychotherapist functions most critically in the area of catalyzing these self-growth mechanisms. Once the process is begun in the patient, the importance of the psychotherapist decreases. Having overcome a certain inertia, the patient obtains from reality and from the culture whatever his continued maturation needs.

Viewing this orientation in its total perspective, two practical points of departure in psychotherapy emerge. One has to do with the process of therapy, and the other with its objectives. Both are implied in the principle that the initiative for psychotherapy must begin in the patient, be broadened in the process of psychotherapy, and become a capacity which the patient takes from therapy and applies in real situations. This final development occurs only if the patient has taken the major initiative for ending the therapeutic relationship and separating himself from the therapist. Much of modern psychotherapy, whether it be of a supportive nature or based on the development of insight, has very serious drawbacks because of the failure to recognize the importance of keeping the initiative with the patient. Many patients who have achieved some adequacy in therapy are in a very real sense crippled because of failure to take from therapy the initiative which is necessary for mature realistic gratification. This stems usually from failure to resolve their dependency on the therapist. Often the therapist fails to provide the kind of relationship which the patient can resolve. The hallmark of adequate therapy is a clear-cut ending, that is, an ending for which the patient is responsible and from which he takes initiative to use in his real life experience. It is precisely this characteristic which distinguishes the results of adequate depth therapy from so-called transference cures. The technical aspects of therapy involve a pervasive application of the concept that initiative in crucial areas must rest with the patient. The decision to begin psychotherapy, the decision to return to the therapist, are matters which only he can decide. A reluctance, even unwillingness of the therapist to participate in real-life decisions of the patient reflects the same orientation. Whether he should accept this job, marry this individual, or leave his family are all decisions which for purposes of his own growth he had better make. If the therapist attempts to make them for him, he creates a dependent relationship and impairs the growth process of the patient. Judgments on the part of the therapist about the patient's adequacy to handle these real situations are most often, if not always, presumptive. The patient is quite able delicately and subtly to evaluate his own tolerance for stress. If the therapist can always accept the patient's capacity in this area, he will more effectively catalyze growth, while at the same time keep from crippling the initiative and retarding the maturing of the patient as a whole.

Summary

This chapter began with a notation of the urgent need for a transmissible theory of psychotherapy. Physicians need help with their psychotherapeutic responsibilities. This is further augmented by the public's increasing demand for more adequate, less expensive, and simpler forms of psychiatric treatment. Medical schools have assumed some responsibility for developing these capacities in students, but practicing physicians today need some clear-cut concepts of therapy.

A promising beginning lies in psychiatry's awareness of the fact that physicians continually practice psychotherapy under many different guises and with various techniques. The conviction was presented here that, despite the variety of techniques used in psychotherapy, there must be an underlying process common to all types of therapy. The immediate problem of psychiatry lies in making more explicit this underlying process which, to date, has been implicit. Pragmatically, the most important variable in all forms of therapy appears to be the adequacy of the therapist as a person, be he internist or psychiatrist.

More specifically, a working definition of psychotherapy was presented, along with some concept of cure, and a statement of the objectives of therapy. These will be developed in later chapters. Since there are many differences concerning these concepts among psychiatrists themselves, these are presented in the next chapter.

8

Dynamic Psychiatry and Psychotherapy

> . . . It then became increasingly clear, however, that the aim in view, the bringing into consciousness of the unconscious, was not fully attainable by this method either (interpretation and analysis of resistances). He (the patient) is obliged to *repeat* as a *current* experience what is repressed, instead of, as the physician would prefer to see him do, recollecting it as a fragment of the past.
>
> *Freud,* "Beyond the Pleasure Principle."

The systematic science of psychopathology and psychodynamics, developed through clinical and experimental investigative efforts, is the core of the science of psychiatry. Although it provides the basis for psychotherapy, nevertheless, it differs from the latter. Much of psychiatry deals with the therapeutic operation which, in its essential features, more closely relates to psychiatry than to any other medical science. Yet some of psychiatry only indirectly involves psychotherapy. For example, so-called administrative psychiatry seeks primarily to facilitate simple adaptations in patients by the administrative manipulation of interpersonal, organizational, and/or cultural stresses. Social psychiatry and mental hygiene are concerned with the problem of psychiatric prophylaxis.

The operation of psychotherapy, though based on the science of psychiatry, has a slightly different orientation. It focuses not on pathology *per se,* but on the therapeutically relevant dynamics of current pathology. The psychotherapist is essentially an empiricist, interested in the relationship of pathology to growth. He attempts to understand the psychodynamics of a specific individual's psychopathology, but primarily as a means of facilitating the therapeutic growth of the person. His interest in the genesis of the pathology is subordinated to his influencing the therapeutic potential in the pathology at the present time.

Psychoanalysis and Psychotherapy

The relationship of analysis to psychotherapy is a different problem. Of the holistic therapies, psychoanalysis stands as the most comprehensive and, in the judgment of many, the most effective. Although very radical changes in the total person may be achieved with various types of brief psychotherapy, these can be understood only in terms of the fundamental contributions which psychoanalysis has made to the science of human behavior. The most significant concepts and the most precise theory of psychodynamics available stem from this source. An honest evaluation of the achievement of analysis as a form of psychotherapy finds its contributions, in this respect, less profound than its contributions to the understanding of psychological growth and psychopathology. It is a lengthy and expensive procedure. If equivalent results are possible with a briefer procedure, then there is some urgency to develop these briefer techniques. Beyond techniques, we are even more in need of isolating precisely the fundamental factors in psychotherapy, whatever its form.

One wonders if some psychoanalysts have not abandoned their early therapeutic orientation to some extent, under the pressure of the emotional demands of patients. The therapist who continued to do psychotherapy on a deep, unconscious, living level, despite the lack of cultural support, so obvious in the early days of psychoanalysis, required considerable stamina to survive. Much of psychoanalysis today appears to be simply a very competent, comprehensive form of ego or educative therapy. These forms of educative psychoanalysis sometimes come close to being repressive in character. On an ego level in a deep-transference relationship, a learning process can occur in which certain ego judgments are made about what can be gratified and what costs (repressively) one has to pay for these gratifications. Many nonprofessional people criticize analysis for blocking, in some patients, areas of personal and cultural creativity. We are not so sure that this is the case, although some analyzed individuals do emerge with a certain flatness in their living capacities, girded up by an almost religious adoration of the analytic philosophy of life. Admittedly, the benefits various patients obtain from analysis differ strikingly. Even though analysis utilizes a definitive technique, the success with any particular patient depends on the unique therapeutic capacity of his analyst.

Many assume that psychoanalysis as a form of therapy involves what we have defined as therapy proper, but undertakes, in addition, rather extensive "re-education" (analysis) which cannot be said to be therapy defined as catalyzed growth. The recent upsurge of many forms of so-called modified psychoanalysis stems from the need to better isolate the therapeutic component of analysis, e.g., corrective emotional experience. A questionable assumption of orthodox analysis seems to be the generalization that libido, fixated and repressed as an energy system, and cathected to an infantile ideational representation, continues to function unconsciously just as is. When this representation is recovered through the devious route of free association, interpretation presumably frees these energies for other, more real uses, first, by making them conscious and, secondly, by "working them through" in the transference relationship. This formulation seems incomplete. In this connection, it is interesting to note that the emphasis has been shifting from making these repressed systems conscious (insight), to their "working through" in the transference relationship, primarily by dealing with resistances. When you examine more closely this "working through," particularly as expressed immediately in the resistances, it becomes clear that the paramount factor in the efficacy of therapy is not the "working through" of the infantile transference. The relationship has other than historical determinants. Actually, the therapist also has other qualities which are perceived by the patient, in addition to those which the latter projects onto him. The transference projection constitutes only part of the relationship of patient to therapist. By virtue of these differences, an interpersonal relationship between therapist and patient exists which competes with the transference relationship. This involves the interaction between the noninfantile aspect of the patient (the part of the patient which brings him to therapy and which expresses his positive growth potential) and the nonprojective or personal part of the therapist. This particular aspect of the relationship underlies the therapeutic process, as distinct from the analytical process. It accounts for much of the success of brief psychotherapy, and may even be the measure of success in a good deal of any depth psychotherapy.

Whatever may be the most effective dynamic of psychotherapy, whether brief or extensive, understanding will be based on psychoanalysis as a theory of personality. Nonetheless, we do question the view that analytic techniques are, by virtue of their efficacy as methods of investigation, also the most efficacious therapeutic techniques. Many experimental procedures, though extremely fruitful, may not be pertinent to clinical situations. To some extent, the most systematic psychoanalytic theory would, paradoxically, contraindicate psychoanalysis as the most generally appropriate form of psychotherapy.

Psychotherapy and Time

Is psychotherapy necessarily a procedure which requires prolonged treatment? At this time, we feel safe in categorically answering, No. A comparison of depth to the superficial, of brief to intensive, and of genetic to nongenetic psychotherapy, will clarify the basis for our conviction. Depth, as a description of therapy, does not seem very pertinent. Any therapy which deals with the whole person is deep. Any procedure which does not deal with the whole person may be educational or supportive, but it certainly is not psychotherapy. Brevity or lengthiness, we are convinced, is an accidental quality of psychotherapy, and has nothing to do with the essential process. It certainly does not, at any rate, preclude depth in therapy.

Therapy aims at a reorganization and different integration of areas of the personality in a total sense. This has two dimensions:

(1) the genetic, has to do with past experience as it determines present experience; (2) the nongenetic, or what we prefer to call the dimension of experience, has to do with the present experience as it determines the relationship of other current experiences to each other and to past experiences, and summatively integrates current experiences and their projection into the future. In the case of the genetic dimension, one looks at current experience from the point of view of its past determinants. In the case of the nongenetic, one looks at current experiences as emergent determinants in themselves.

Therapeutic movement, then, can theoretically result from a "working through" or re-experiencing of past experiences that have determined present pathology. This therapeutic approach deals at length with the longitudinal dimension and takes up intensively the genetic causal interrelationship. Such a therapeutic procedure is properly called analytical therapy. The quality of consciousness, particularly ego function through insight, assumes considerable importance in this process. This results from the fact that one integrates retrospectively, in order to extend the control of conscious ego over the unconscious. In contrast, therapeutic change can also result from certain current experiences which, because of their pervasiveness, change the relationship of other current experiences to each other and somehow mitigate the pathological effect of past experience on the organization of one's current living. This therapy could properly be called experiential. It is essentially a nonhistorical, atemporal one and uses, primarily, the current interpersonal experience in all of its facets, and depth as the means of altering personality.

Assuming that this distinction can be made, therapy in the first instance has to do with how deep the analytical process penetrates in terms of reworking various genetic experiences. In the second case, the depth of psychotherapy has to do with how pervasive and integrative the experiential process is in terms of the two individuals involved at the time. Presumably, the same depth may result from either approach. Superficiality in analytical therapy is considered by some as "working through" the less significant genetic experiences. Superficiality in brief therapy would have to do with a limited personal involvement on the part of both individuals in the current therapeutic experience. Depth therapy through either approach involves mainly unconscious experiences. In the case of analysis, these are presented, worked through, and analyzed away. As such, the conscious-ego segment of the patient becomes more immediately involved. In experiential therapy, unconscious dynamics are again most significant. Comparison of depth in analytical therapy and experiential therapy can be justified only if the experiential in some way reverberates to the genetic and, conversely, if the genetic working through has resonance in the current experience. That some relationship exists between the genetic and the experiential may be assumed on the basis of our present knowledge of brain function which, though timeless, has at the same time adequate genetic representations. Furthermore, the fact that memory—and certainly every memory involved in current experience—can be changed by an alteration in the total experiential *gestalt*, substantiates the relationship between the genetic and the experiential. The unconscious itself seems to be atemporal in its function, and certainly its reflections in experience as, for example, in dreams, are nontemporal.

We could go on buttressing the conviction that the relationship of past experience to present living may be altered simply on the basis of one's current experience. This holds true even if this current experience be looked upon as "working through." If the current experience pervasively involves sufficiently deep areas of the personality, without any consideration for time, the whole relationship of past experience to current function can be altered radically. Generally, the genetic approach to biological phenomena causes the fragmentation of a unitary process by imposing on it a time measure. Process studies may, therefore, have little relationship to the process *in vivo*. No therapist is interested in anything as much as the individual's current capacity for gratification and life function. The scientist may be interested in other matters, but to the therapist, these others are of secondary interest.

Psychiatry needs a denominator which is common not only to the schools of therapy, but to the functions of individuals in the therapeutic process. The authors are trying to describe those aspects of the therapeutic process which are implicit in all successful therapy. It can probably be said with equal validity that psychoanalysis, to the degree to which it is successful, is implicitly experiential, and that experiential therapy reinforces the concepts of psychoanalysis. In the search for a common denominator in the therapeutic process as such, one must disregard a great part of the explicit formulation of what all therapists (including the authors) think happens in the therapeutic process. The common denominator is the interpersonal relationship, an interpersonal relationship fundamentally subjective in character. The relationship of the unconscious of the therapist to the unconscious of the patient underlies any therapy. This provides the ultimate in depth, the ultimate in experience, and, as such, must be both quantitatively and qualitatively the common denominator of therapy. One of the reasons for the effectiveness of therapy, even though it may be brief in character, may be the emphasis it places on the potential biological growth capacity in the patient. A genetic approach by necessity focuses attention primarily on pathology, i.e., on what is wrong with the organism. The possibilities opened up by stimulating and expanding the capacities of the organism deserve more emphasis. The readiness of the individual to grow in keeping with his potential may explain why one can achieve so much in therapy in such a short period of time. The rigidity and the complexity of the determinants of psychopathology may serve to explain why analytical therapy is so time consuming.

Summary

From this point of view, psychotherapy becomes not so much a social as a biological process. Being biological, it has a certain unity which centers around the integrative effect of certain current experiences in the growth of the total person. We have spoken of this orientation in psychotherapy as being experiential, involving, as we have pointed out, emphasis on the ahistorical, the atemporal, and the unconscious processes. This contrasts with the historical, analytical therapy, with its emphasis on insight and consciousness. The three central comparisons involve experience as against insight, unconscious as against conscious, integration and synthesis as against analysis. The willingness to involve one's self totally with the patient, and the recognition of the patient's fitness to judge more adequately than the therapist the process of therapy and its objectives, is based on an acceptance of the principle of homeostasis, as it operates psychologically. The patient can quite adequately maintain and protect himself within the therapeutic relationship. The recognition of his ability to do so is of critical importance in the effectiveness with which the therapy is achieved.

The concept of the synthetic grows out of this orientation. Unfortunately, the word has many connotations related to the artificial. Perhaps it would be better to speak of an emphasis on synthesis and integration as against analysis and insight. The therapist's or patient's understanding of the genetic panorama of his current inadequacies assumes less significance than the development of the patient's capacity to function as a person integrated within himself and with the surrounding culture. This synthesis can be achieved by experience and seldom simply by understanding. It may or may not be pertinent for a patient to understand that his inability to be aggressive toward a parental figure is due to certain infantile fears and guilt. In contrast, the experience of being aggressive toward a parental figure, even if he does not understand what occurs, will be helpful if the patient finds that after such expressed aggression he does not suffer and is not rejected. This is the precise difference between synthesis and analysis, between experience and insight.

9

The Patient as a Person

The general public has accepted for years the quip that to the psychiatrist every person is a patient. Although we deny this publicly, the accusation comes very near to the truth. It has many implications. Among ourselves, we recognize that a person sees in others only what he has seen in himself. It may be then that the psychiatrist sees others as patients since he so frequently faces his own patient facet. This appraisal may provide us with a more honest basis for our orientation in psychotherapy. As we will see further on, the therapist sees himself as a person only after he has been a patient. From this we recognize that all persons have similar potentialities and that, therefore, all persons are *potentially* patients. We must, however, differentiate between these potential patients and the actual patient who comes into the office for treatment.

*From Kahlil Gibran, "The Wanderer," Courtesy, Alfred A. Knopf, Inc.

The Genesis of a Patient

Psychotherapy can be utilized in two fundamental ways: It can provide help for the patient in need of psychiatric treatment for very specific symptoms, and it can help the socially adequate and fairly mature individual to become more creative than formerly and, in general, to develop more of his capacity to function as a well-integrated adult. Accordingly, psychotherapy may help the "sick" individual, or it may actualize the potential capacities of the average "normal" person. Potential patients fall, roughly speaking, into three groups: those who come with pathology grossly apparent to the outside word (society), those whose pathology becomes obvious only in the interviews, and those whose pathology is discernible only to the patients themselves. The mere fact that the individual has gross pathology, however, does not mean that he becomes automatically a patient. Many people continue to operate on a compensated level and repeatedly deny all offers of help. In this group, even those who obviously should be patients are not. As a matter of fact, one of the growth experiences of the young therapist evolves from his effort to convert a sick person into a *patient*. In his enthusiasm as a professional person, the young therapist will often respond in a professional manner to a bit of pathology revealed in a social setting. He thereby shows little recognition of the importance of the patient's initiative in bringing his problem to a therapist, or the importance of isolating his "therapeutic role" from the realities of ordinary social living. Thus, the young therapist may respond to the depression of a friend while at a cocktail party. Such an approach often succeeds in freezing the depressed friend and making him more anxious. The next day, the therapist may realize he has lost a friend, or be startled by the distant reaction of his erstwhile friend and "patient." Furthermore, even a patient who comes to the office with gross pathology may reject his offer of help in the same way. Both these individuals could be patients and could benefit from therapy, *but they do not accept their patient status*. What does this mean?

Previously, we discussed the implication that psychopathology represents, in one sense, a request for therapy. This request may be consistently and aggressively denied consciously and may be detectable only on a symbolic level. A patient, then, is simply defined as a person who asks for help from the psychotherapist. An individual may be able to ask for help from one therapist and not from another. Even when the patient asks for help, there remains the problem of the therapist's "hearing" him. Some therapists can hear a request for help even when expressed in the obtuse symbolic language of the schizophrenic, whereas others seem to have difficulty unless the patient demands help more directly. One schizophrenic patient, who had rather rigid paranoid feelings, kept demanding in the initial interviews, "I want to get out of here. Please let me out of here. I've got to get out of here so that I can lead a normal life." Superficially, she was talking about leaving the interview room. On a symbolic level, she was speaking of getting out of her schizophrenic isolation and, in this sense, symbolically begging for help. Even with this request, she still was not a patient. She was not a patient until the therapists not only theoretically knew, but more important, subjectively felt, that she was asking for their help. With the concurrence of her need felt in both herself and the therapists, she became a patient.

Patient status, in general, involves acceptance on the part of both parties of a felt need. Patient status has, therefore, two ingredients. First, the concept "patient" as used here becomes a biological concept. It implies the existence of a discrepancy between the individual's current effectiveness in his living and his biological potential. This deletes from the concept of "patient" the cultural relativity which has caused psychiatrists so much concern in the past. One culture may satisfy certain needs more fully than others or accept one type of personal deficiency more readily than another. However, the objective basis of the individual being a patient is precisely the difference between what he is and what he could be. The second ingredient of patient status is a subjective acceptance of his need, and its presentation, whether consciously or unconsciously, to another person in order to obtain help with it. Finally, the therapist must accept that need as something with which he can struggle. Only when these objective and subjective ingredients occur together can it be said that this person has become a patient.

Patient status, then, is defined by the therapeutic process itself. It does not antecede it, nor does it exist apart from therapy. It is not equivalent to pathology. An individual may have gross pathology and not be a patient, or have minimal pathology and be a patient. In the case of the deteriorated schizophrenic previously discussed, she became a patient when the therapist developed the capacity to recognize her need so that it became meaningful to him personally, and consequently provoked some emotional response in him. As this developed, she demanded, with increasing urgency, the rights of her patient status.

The above dynamics appear most openly in collaborative therapy. The authors frequently qualify their acceptance of a patient with the understanding that his parent or spouse obtain therapy simultaneously. This poses a difficult task since these individuals see themselves as normal in comparison with the "real" patient and have no conviction of their own need. The problem has additional facets since, just as frequently, the therapist to these latter individuals has little advance conviction of their need. The initial struggle in this therapy, thus, seeks to achieve a bilateral, felt acceptance of their need on the part of both patient and therapist. The relative's acceptance of his patient status usually follows the therapist's recognition of his emotional involvement in it. We have belabored this point to give force to our conviction that the process of psychotherapy is bilateral, even to the extent of insisting that the therapist's reaction may constitute the determining factor in bringing about patient status in an individual. From here on, we are going to discuss, primarily, the patient's dynamics despite the artificiality of such an abstraction.

Barriers to Patient Status

The patient's decision to see a therapist is no easy one. What brings the patient to the therapist? The pressures which force him to take this step must be fairly urgent ones. He has essential barriers to overcome. The first, and probably most important of these, evidences his unwillingness to upset his own neurotic equilibrium. This compromise, even though it limits his gratifications in life, also satisfies him in certain ways. For example, it provides him with some kind of protection and enables him to live on a fairly safe, though sterile, level. He senses that therapy may cause him to reverse the defensive compromises of a lifetime. The fact that he lacks much appreciation of the possibility of achieving a more adequate level of living makes it all the more difficult for him to seek treatment. Sometimes the patient comes to the therapist because he wishes, not so much to grow, as to repair those self-therapeutizing patterns through which he has obtained certain "subsistence level" gratifications, and which, for various reasons, are now breaking down. For example, one overt homosexual wanted to make sure that he would not fall in love. Yet, despite all this, the patient's coming to the therapist, in the face of years of compromise living, implies a deep recognition of the tremendous power of the long-suppressed growth impulse in himself as an individual. To see the almost unprovoked stirrings of the need to grow in the deteriorated schizophrenic forces one to respect the dominant role of this urge in the hierarchy of living impulses.

The person who comes to a therapist defies, in a sense, many of his own cultural values. This constitutes a serious deterrent. For example, in seeking therapy, he tacitly blames his culture for its failure to provide him with adequate "growth nutrition," i.e., with therapy. Thus, the very act of coming to the therapist points up many of the deficiencies of the community within which he lives. More particularly, he implicates those members of the community who live in close association with him. One wonders, therefore, just how much of the hostility which our culture expresses against psychiatry, and against psychotherapy, reflects some latent recognition of the fact that the need of its members to seek therapy constitutes a reflection upon the community in which they live. Be that as it may, the patient comes only because something powerful in him overcomes both a lifetime of compromise living and the cultural pressures enforcing submission to the parents and parent substitutes. The patient must also overcome the anxiety mobilized by the recognition that his auto-therapeutic functions have failed. Indeed, he has to reject the culture and its therapeutic function in order to isolate himself from the culture by coming to the professional therapist. Lastly, he must reject an earlier therapeutic relationship to some individual (social therapist) within the culture, e.g., the referring physician. Even the individual who has not been referred has usually struggled for satisfaction of his emotional needs with some other individual or group in his community at some time in the past.

The Social Therapist

Patients seldom, if ever, come to a professional therapist without having first experienced some growth in a previous therapeutic relationship. Social therapists often help patients therapeutically, though their relationship may not be a professional one. Everyone in the community functions at one time or another as a therapist to the needs of others. We call this process "social therapy." They usually are not conscious of the process of therapy and, as therapists, have marked limitations. Nevertheless, in their relationship with a specific person, they frequently provide a modicum of gratification. This measure often gives the patient a first glimpse of the possibility of growth through therapy. In this sense, we are convinced that most, if not all, patients are referred from social to professional therapists. What happened to the patient prior to his first interview with the professional therapist represents what we will call, in a later chapter, the "pre-interview phase of therapy." This implies that an increase in the number and adequacy of social therapists in any community might be a partial answer to the problems of preventive psychiatry.

Many difficulties beset the transfer of the patient from a social to a professional therapist. An almost inevitable hostility develops toward the social therapist, resulting from his failure to be completely effective. Part of this hostility toward the social therapist represents transference of infantile feelings of rejection. Whatever its source, these feelings are transferred onto the professional therapist to whom the patient responds, early in their relationship, much as the patient had responded to his social therapist.

We frequently hear such remarks as, "You sound just like my husband," or "I don't see why my doctor sent me to you." This last illustration contains the core of another difficulty. Patients develop deep transference to their social therapists, e.g., referring internist which, later on, hinders the development of a deep relationship to the professional therapist.

The therapist must "work through" his own response to this hostility and his competition with the social therapist before the relationship can go beyond the point of the previous rejection. This "working through" on the part of the therapist brings to the patient, at the outset, some indication of the limitations and immaturities of the therapist. Acceptance of these by the patient expands the initial professional relationship into a more personal one. In a sense, it implies a recognition by the patient that the therapist has a fantasy life of his own, which will inevitably play a part in the development of his own fantasy life.

Culture: The Last Barrier

As mentioned above, the patient's fantasy of therapy includes the fear that therapy is possible only in defiance of the culture. In order to conform to his culture, the patient has had to develop a façade of maturity. He has denied repeatedly those deeper needs which he felt were antagonistic to cultural demands. Now, confronted with an opportunity to express his childlike needs, the patient must first break through his pseudo-adult pattern. In doing so, he fears that the therapist will respond to his needs as his culture has done, i.e., by denying these infantile needs. Were this to happen, he might then be unable to re-establish his protective façade. Furthermore, he intuits that the therapist will offer him such satisfactions that he will become a helpless child and might be held forever dependent. Patients frequently say, "I'm afraid that if I really let myself become a little baby, I'll never grow up (again), and you wouldn't take care of me." This wish opposes the hostile, aggressive demand that the culture (or therapist) take care of him. The ambivalence of dependence and assertion of adequacy characterizes the initial period of psychotherapy.

The patient turns to the therapist as a possible escape from the struggle within himself. His concept of the therapist reflects a cultural stereotype which includes some of the following characteristics: the therapist has all the magic which the child ascribes to the parent, i.e., in his presence the patient will suddenly and miraculously be cured. In this sense, the physician becomes the witch doctor of our culture. In his fantasy, the patient depends on this omnipotent parent to share his burden and to carry the onus of his disease. The therapist also engenders hate, as someone who deprives the patient of part of his individuality. The unique needs of each individual patient mold his interpretation of the cultural stereotype. Its specific characteristics are determined by the constellation of that individual's "intra-psychic family." When the intra-psychic family of the patient comes to include in this manner also the doctor-therapist, the process of therapy, as an intra-psychic phenomenon, begins. Conversely, and in much the same manner, the patient is, in turn, an introject, and so becomes part of the intra-psychic dynamics of the therapist. This means that the process is a bilateral one. The patient's stereotype of the therapist fuses with the members of his own intra-psychic family. In this sense, the doctor may be anybody—God, teacher, the devil, the nurse, or society. The individual patient's projections are numberless.

These cultural barriers to the patient's obtaining psychotherapy find their most direct expression in the patient's family. The family has a deep sense of guilt since the patient's sickness attests to their failure to mature him adequately. They have further difficulty in bringing him to the therapist, since often the emotional homeostasis (economy) of the family centers around the patient. They sense that if the patient changes, they too must change. For example, the "martyred" wife of the alcoholic patient not only fulfills a mother role, but satisfies her own neurotic needs by keeping her husband dependent. Therefore, if the alcoholic husband comes for therapy, this disrupts her compensatory neurotic patterns by breaking up the dovetailing of two previously complementary neuroses. Often the resentment, guilt, and neurotic dependence of the family expresses itself as a fatalism about the patient being able to recover. They say to the patient, "We want to give you whatever is necessary for you to get well," but beneath this is the fatalism and resentment engendered by their own failure to have given him what would have kept him well. When the patient comes to the therapist, much of the family's ambivalence falls upon the therapist, and the patient now has to adjust to the added problem of their feelings about the therapist.

In spite of the projections of the patient and the cultural barriers, the therapist must maintain himself as a person in his own right, so as to be able to alter the make-up of the patient's intrapsychic family. Antagonism between the patient and the culture (particularly the family) presents the therapist with many administrative and personal problems. A psychiatrist often accumulates hostility toward the family of the patient. He senses how the family rejects the patient, and he resents this. This resentment in turn increases the family's antagonism toward him. Ordinarily, neither the family nor the therapist can openly express their resentment since each feels bound by the culture. Should the therapist express his personal feelings to the family, he frees himself for a more adequate relationship to the patient but endangers his professional status with them.

This may only become a problem after therapy has begun and the patient begins to get well. For example, the father of an adolescent schizophrenic, recovering at last as a result of intensive therapy, decides suddenly that the treatment has failed and withdraws the patient from therapy. The patient's recovery apparently provokes guilt and anxiety in the parent, which he resolves by this withdrawal. Not only does the patient's therapy upset the family by removing the patient from *them* and thereby changing the family's dynamics, but often in removing the pre-psychotic from the family, one deprives the latter of its most functional therapist member. A portion of the family's aggression toward the professional therapist originates in these same dynamics.

Confronted with such uncertainties, the patient brings to therapy all the mechanisms at his command in order to protect himself from further rejection. These protective mechanisms, when manifested in therapy, are thought of as resistances.

Resistances also have a very specific therapeutic function. They do not simply provide the patient with protection from anxiety but, on a deeper level, they also protect him from this new parent whose feelings and capacities he presumes but must discover for himself. Resistances thus occupy a central place in the beginning phase of therapy, and require a bilateral relationship for their resolution. If one looks at resistance from this point of view, one notes at once that the therapist, too, frequently brings to the initial interview a good number of his own resistances, and uses them in the same manner. In both persons, resistances function to provide protection against rejection by the other person. A new rejection would be more painful than the mere recall or re-enactment of past rejections, because of the additive effects of the repetition compulsion.

Of course, many of the patient's resistances are derived from his recognition of the therapist's inadequacies. The patient constantly searches for the real potential in the therapist. Once he discovers it, he may force the therapist to function at his fullest capacity. We have all seen patients whose resistances disappeared rapidly. This rapid movement derives from the more or less complete personal involvement of the therapist and from his readiness to give to the patient that which is more than implicit in his professional role. We would even suggest that the ideal therapist would encounter no resistance whatsoever.

The ways in which personal involvement of the therapist occurs at the onset of therapy will be more fully discussed later, in the chapter on the *Therapist as a Person* (Chapter 12). At the outset of treatment, the patient means little to the therapist, except as a representative of all previous patients, and in a reality sense, a professional responsibility. He may also perceive the patient as a symbol of the culture. Finally, of course, the therapist has unconscious motivations which facilitate the transition to personal involvement with the patient.

The growth impulse provides the positive motivational factor which enables the patient to struggle in order to get beyond the above barriers. This is identical with those biological forces operative in the structure and function of the body itself which impel the growth of the total organism. Certain internal tension systems may bind the patient's energy in such a manner that very little free energy remains available, yet the power used in the therapeutic process, to a large extent, derives from the patient himself. The implications of this for the conduct of the therapeutic relationship are many and pervasive, but not different in general character from similar implications which are obvious to the biologist or the physiologist on the basis of his understanding of the body's function, and especially, of its reparative function. We have already, in some detail, taken up the implications of this finding for the therapeutic process, although we did not discuss its pertinence to the understanding of the problem of psychopathology. The self-reparative capacities of the patient can be brought to bear in the therapy by utilizing the free energy components of the patient's personality to the limit. Indeed, in order to free further quanta of energy, the patient must find even greater access to his own unconscious energies. This means that he does more in therapy than just learn how to use his already available energy more constructively. Since the neurotic binding of this energy has been brought about by the pressures of the culture, this bound energy must be liberated on a level more primitive than a cultural one. The therapist can, and does, use forces available within the individual in order to release this bound energy. The therapist may then become concerned because of some doubt of the patient's capacity to reorient himself in terms of reality, and his undervaluation of the capacity of the culture to reintegrate the patient into its framework. In general, psychiatry tends to *underestimate* the constructive capacity of the human being. This reflects a general medical bias, since many physicians also *underestimate* the physiological potential of the human body, even though they have scientific proof of the capacity of tissue to continue to function despite seemingly insuperable difficulties.

Conclusion

We have followed the patient from his initial impulse to seek therapy, which he derived from his social therapist, into the process of therapy with a professional therapist. Once in that process, the patient can only be seen within the bilateral relationship. This makes it difficult to discuss him as a separate person. His limited separateness as an individual in the central therapeutic process may be compared to the limited autonomy of the nursing infant as a person. The infant can be understood fully only within the framework of his relationship to the mother. We will discuss this process in detail in a later chapter. Here we will simply "pick up" the patient as he leaves the process of therapy. Assuming an adequate therapy, certain minimal changes have taken place.

This, at once, raises a controversial question which has been bandied about in psychiatry for many years: What is a cured patient? Let's ignore the superficial conception of treatment as consisting of the alleviation of symptoms. We agree with those who say that successful therapy may not always require a complete redirection of the dynamics of the person's energy. This concept can perhaps be best expressed negatively. Patients do not enter therapy with a large infantile segment in their makeup and emerge from it as adults. Neither has the child finished his growth when, as an adolescent, he leaves home. Restructuring of the personality does not always occur in therapy, and perhaps not even growth itself, but rather, therapy means an overcoming of the inertia in the all-but-static growth process. The patient does not leave the therapist "mature." He leaves "different," in that he has gained access to those processes within himself and within society through which he can become mature. Further, he leaves with the understanding that he must struggle time and time again in his lifelong effort to achieve more and more maturity. The experience of relating himself to another human being on a primitive level has taught him to go beyond the existing limits of his personality and to become involved in a deep and emotionally satisfactory symbiosis. He can now give expression to more of his needs, be they infantile, adolescent, or adult, and can accept the response to and gratification of these needs and feelings with less guilt, shame, or sense of debt than before. He has found that he can emerge intact and with a new sense of his own worth and a deeper sense of his own integrity from such an experience. He has also discovered a greater sense of the integrity of others. The actual and specific content and framework of this therapeutic experience assumes less and less importance. He has gained the capacity to demand, obtain, and participate in a new experience. Therapy has gone beneath the cultural encrustation, and has biologically unshackled certain bound energy systems in the individual. The original function of these systems was the repair of the organism in its totality. The patient now brings this new capacity to bear upon his whole life experience. Most, if not all, of his specific conflicts and their genetic basis he then works through subsequent to professional therapy, and with individuals other than professional therapists. Therapy provides the patient with access to the whole gamut of therapeutic possibilities ordinarily available within every group and which the culture of each group has developed through many centuries. In short, the patient gets access to other human beings and, incidentally, enters the community as an adequate social therapist, no longer so concerned with himself that he cannot get and give therapy to others in a social setting.

10

The Process of Psychotherapy

Sail forth—steer for the deep waters only
. . . I with thee, and thou with me . . .
Walt Whitman

Introduction

Having discussed the motivations of the individuals involved in therapy and referred to the effective dynamics as revealed in the relationship of doctor and patient, we must identify the process of therapy. Traditionally, most psychotherapists do not identify the process of therapy as such, and some doubt that any identifiable and recurrent process typifies therapy. Usually, therapy is thought of in its relational sense, as providing a constant situation from and in which the patient can grow on the basis of his own unique needs. Ordinarily, therapy is assumed to have the characteristics of any social relationship; that is, it can be different things at different times, and has very little order or sequence. Are there sequential and recurrent phases in therapy which can be identified as the *process* of psychotherapy?

In most recent years, the analyst has come to speak of stages in the therapeutic relationship which imply such a sequence. He speaks of the beginnings of the therapeutic relationship, in which the patient responds to the therapist on a real level. He describes a second phase, in which the patient begins to project onto the therapist certain of his transference conflicts until he has displaced to, and condensed in, his relationship to the therapist all of his transference needs. The analyst then identifies a third phase, in which the patient expresses his conflicts within the framework of a transference neurosis. The penultimate phase consists in the development of negative transference and the gradual decathecting of the therapist's symbolic value to the patient. This last phase presages the actual termination of the analytical relationship.

These phases are not sharply delimited, and certainly a good number of analysts would quarrel with the above summary. Nevertheless, throughout the literature one finds repeated references to these phases. These "stages" are more descriptive than dynamic and, therefore, do not specifically refer to the process of therapy. They resemble standard cross-sections taken at various times in the anatomy of therapy. They suffer from the static quality of all cross-sections, and leave the relationship of one section to another to the imagination of the reader. The explanation for this static quality may lie in the perspective of some who look at the process primarily from the point of view of what happens in the patient.

Analysis of what happens in therapy necessitates broadening the perspective to include not only the dynamics of the patient, but also the dynamics of the therapist. The process uncovered may not be much different from the rather nebulous sequence which the analyst has outlined. Nevertheless, it may be a little more dynamic, and perhaps because of this, some of the more subtle aspects of the sequence can be identified. If the therapeutic process has a continuity and an identifiable pattern, it should be possible to discuss it in terms of the factors involved and of their functional relationship; that is, one should at least be able to outline the process, as such, in an operational manner.

There are two basic divisions: One, the process within the single interview with certain characteristics and certain variables, and two, the process of the therapeutic relationship as a whole. The identification of a general pattern in the whole therapeutic relationship presents less of a problem than uncovering orderly patterns within the single interview. It often appears as if the single interview telescopes the patterns which macroscopically unfold in the extended relationship. In a therapeutic relationship which endures over a period of time, the processes involved become more clear, yet in select cases, the process reveals itself with equal clarity within a single interview hour. Thus, therapy as an experience has the same timeless quality that characterizes all the functionings of the unconscious.

When, as therapists, the authors ask themselves how far along in therapy they have gone with a particular patient, the degree of their personal involvement in the relationship usually determines the answer. The factors which impair this must, of necessity, distort the timing of the process. Nonetheless, where personal involvement of both participants proceeds rapidly in the single interview, the process of therapy stands out as clearly as it does where equal involvement develops over twenty hours. If the process depends on such subjective factors, does it inevitably follow the same pattern and, if not, can we distinguish consistent variations in it?

Outline of the Natural Divisions of the Process of Therapy

Although the process is an integral whole, still three general segments can be distinguished within the over-all process. These are the Pre-Interview Segment, the Interview Segment, and the Post-Interview Segment.

In order to simplify the presentation of a process which has so many variables, we first have to present, in gross outline, the framework within which the total process falls. This, in turn, necessitates some discussion of the relationship of the process of psychotherapy to the culture, i.e., the manner in which the patient comes to the interview, and the ways in which the previous experiences of the patient reflect themselves in the interview. This is called the Pre-Interview Segment of the process, and it antedates the first interview with the professional therapist. It has no discernible stages within it, but is characterized by those qualities which were presented in Chapter 9.

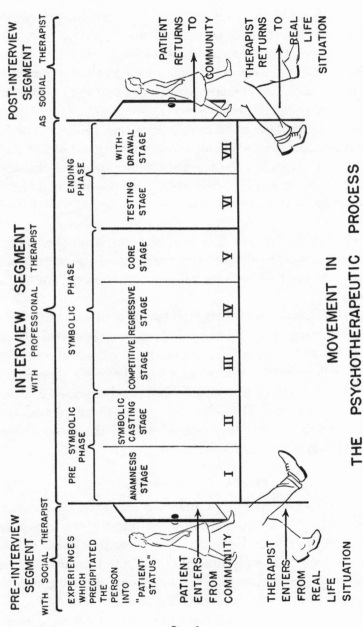

Fig. 1

The Interview Segment follows. This empirically involves only the contacts the patient has with the professional therapist. This segment seems to fall into three general phases: the pre-symbolic, the symbolic, and the post-symbolic (ending) phases.

The pre-symbolic phase involves the early interviews with the patient where the primary problem seems to be the transition of the patient into deep therapy. It includes two stages, the Anamnestic and Casting Stages.

The symbolic phase of therapy follows this. Its central problem is the resolution of symbolic or transference needs of the patient and, thus, it comprises the essence of the process of therapy. It appears to follow a rather definitive pattern which is designated in sequence as the Competitive, the Regressive, and the Core Stages.

The concluding phase is termed the post-symbolic (ending) phase, and involves primarily the transition of the patient out of therapy into the culture. This subsumes two stages, Testing and Withdrawal.

After the interviews are completed, the patient still has the problem of integrating the gains of therapy into his real life function within the culture. This occurs in the Post-Interview Segment, which seems to endure for only a definitive time, and the patient reaches a point at which we can say the process of therapy has been completed. The relationship of this completion to his further growth will be discussed as each of the above stages is discussed in greater operational detail.

PRE-INTERVIEW SEGMENT

At some specific point, an individual assumes the status of patient (Chapter 9), and begins the Pre-Interview Segment, which must be regarded as part of the over-all process. This segment may be a brief and minimal part of the total therapy, or it may be prolonged and include a greater proportion of the process usually described as the Interview Segment.

Many therapists have had the experience of having a contact with the patient which is therapeutic but in which the therapist contributes very little, since a great deal of the process has taken place before the actual contact with the therapist.

How much of the total process occurs in the Pre-Interview Segment cannot be assayed except in each individual case. It would be simple if the Pre-Interview Segment involved only those changes within the person which enable him to make a transition to a symbolic relationship. In fact, one might accept just such an operational definition and say that the Pre-Interview Segment of therapy antecedes therapeutic transferences. Since some patients come to the therapist further along in the process of therapy than others, the reader may object that these patients have already entered into therapeutic transferences. This is true, since social therapists can, and frequently do, function with the patient well into the Interview Segment of therapy. In fact, the patient may actually complete therapy with a social therapist. That is, the Interview Segment may occur with the social as well as the professional therapist. Usually, however, the process does not run its course with the social therapist, and the professional therapist begins his relationship with the patient at the level which the patient had already reached with a social therapist. By and large, the Pre-Interview process brings the patient up to, and facilitates his transition into, the symbolic segment of therapy.

The Pre-Interview Segment, as we have seen, does not require the patient's relationship to a professional therapist. This segment of therapy usually does not have qualities as easily distinguishable as those which characterize the next two segments. It comprises, essentially, the changes which occur intra-psychically in a person whose needs enable him to become a patient. These intra-psychic changes reflect, primarily, some upset in the minimal satisfactions of his real or his symbolic needs and usually arise from some limited gratification of these needs in his association with social therapists. This exact process remains, however, unclear, and does not have the isolative quality or the continuity which characterizes the Interview Segment. The Pre-Interview Segment plays an important part in the total process of therapy in that it enables a "person with needs" to become a patient and to gear himself to the more isolated and more fantastic relationship which obtains in the Interview Segment of therapy. Even so, the experience in the Pre-Interview Segment often extends over into the Interview Segment.

Thus, the first interview with the professional therapist is a summative experience for the patient (the Anamnestic Stage I). In a sense, he ends with his social therapists, covers in a condensed form his intra-psychic progress, and comes to the threshold of a symbolic experience with the therapist. (Regardless of the duration of this, which may extend over many years or may be very brief, it occupies only a small fraction of the patient's total relationship with the professional therapist.) This typifies the patients who come to therapy because of their own needs. By contrast, the patient who is directed into therapy administratively may devote many interview hours to working through the Pre-Interview Segment of therapy. The self-referred patient has already gone through this segment before he comes to the therapist. Even when this segment occurs in the interview situation, it entails primarily the development of a real, functioning patient-status in the patient (Casting Stage II). With the attainment of patient-status, the process of therapy crosses the outer threshold of a bilateral symbolic relationship. This symbolic phase occupies the major portion of the Interview Segment.

ANALYSIS OF INTERVIEW SEGMENT

Before presenting a more specific analysis of the Interview Segment of the process, it is necessary to define certain qualities peculiar to the professional relationship. These dimensions of the Interview Segment include a discussion of the role of the symbolic aspects and the real aspects of the relationship, and their interaction. There follows a discussion of the moot question about the location of the process itself. Further amplification of the dynamics of the process is included in a discussion of the energy exchange within the relationship and, finally, a section on the motivational vectors which keep the process moving. All this leads to a detailed operational description of the phases and stages in the processes. This, in turn, is preliminary to a presentation of the intra-psychic dynamics of each of the participants as they relate to themselves and to each other in the process.

THE SYMBOLIC AND THE REAL IN THERAPY (Figure 2). The Interview Segment develops only after both participants accept the preeminent importance of symbolism in their relationship. This phase brings into focus again the relationship of this symbolic involvement to the realities of both patient and therapist. Some systems of energy develop around the individual's pragmatic relationship with external realities; other systems of energy are linked with his relationship to himself and his inner experiences.

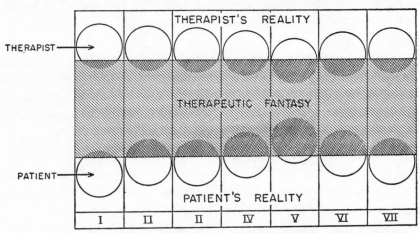

DEGREE OF FANTASY INVOLVEMENT OF THERAPIST AND PATIENT AT SUCCESSIVE STAGES OF THE INTERVIEW SEGMENT IN THE THERAPEUTIC PROCESS

Fig. 2

These latter are defined as symbolic. In this sense, even though quantities of energy may flow from one system to another, the living function has two general facets, one of which is realistic, while the other is essentially fantastic and symbolic. The energy systems in therapy are primarily those which are fantastic and symbolic.

One of the most effective dynamics of therapy relates to the patient's perception of the therapist as a "real" person. This implies that both therapist and patient participate in therapy with unconscious dynamics rather than via their more conscious or reality-oriented dynamics. The treatment relationship increases the patient's capacity to bring into the interview experience larger and larger areas of his symbolic component, and also expands the capacity of the therapist to respond to the patient with increasingly greater quantities of his own available energy. The interaction of the unconscious components of each determines the essential quality of the therapy. It will be shown, subsequently, how specific the variations are, and to what a great extent the involvement of each participant complements the other. The intensification of the joint symbolic dynamics varies, also, with the extent to which the reality component of the patient disappears from the therapeutic relationship. This reality component of the patient's daily life must remain outside the process of therapy. When it becomes part of therapy, it may even contaminate and hinder progress.

Deletion of the therapist's reality component presents a more delicate problem. Therapy would certainly be impossible if the therapist brought only his realities to answer the patient's symbolic needs. Indeed, he would be unable to function symbolically if, at the same time, he were overly concerned with also functioning realistically. However, the therapist must be responsible for maintaining some sure hold on reality, from which both individuals depart into this fantastic experience, and to which both return at the end of the symbolic experience.

In summary, the deletion of the reality of both patient and therapist from this experience, and the degree of symbolic involvement possible for the therapist produce a quality of clear-cut isolation: isolation from the reality of each person, and isolation from the physical, social, and cultural worlds which surround their relationship. This isolation, as one of the principal characteristics of therapy, was discussed in earlier chapters in more detail.

The process now looks fairly simple. We have two individuals, each responding to the other within a relationship, isolated from the real worlds of both. One of these persons has greater capacity for symbolic experience and unconscious functioning than the other. He is the therapist. The patient, even though he, too, has a large area of symbolic functioning, is not quite able to share with another the experience of these symbolic relationships. In general, the energies which impel his symbolic experiences are fettered by his inability to live them through to a different outcome, i.e., one which would free him as a person. By contrast, the energies of the therapist are free even in this symbolic experience, and the therapist differs, also, since he can better utilize these energies in his functioning as a real person.

THE LOCI OF THE PROCESS. The dynamics of the Pre-Interview Segment evolve chiefly within the patient, and only tangentially with his social therapists. Perhaps the chief difference between this earlier phase and the Interview Segment proper lies in an intensification of the motivations of the patient, brought about by the impact of the intra-psychic dynamics of the professional therapist.

One must still determine, more specifically, where the process of professional therapy takes place. As stated above, it does not take place within the interpersonal relationship. Although an interpersonal relationship is necessary, understanding this relationship does not provide one with an adequate operational explanation of therapy. It has also been said that therapy takes place within the patient as an intra-psychic process. This, too, seems only partially correct. The authors have already discussed the intra-psychic process in the patient in Chapter 9, and will discuss the intra-psychic process in the therapist in Chapter 12. The occurrence of each of these two components of the therapeutic process becomes possible only with the simultaneous occurrence of the other. To some degree, the means by which these two components come into being depends on communication between the therapist and the patient. The therapeutic process is, thus, intra-psychic in both the therapist and the patient, and only becomes possible through the interrelation between the two. This is not another way of saying that the therapeutic process resides in the interpersonal relationship. Therapy is possible only when such a relationship exists, but it specifically involves the unconscious dynamics of each of the participants. The really essential aspect of the relationship is simply the accessibility of the unconscious dynamics of both participants, each to the other. The therapy which occurs intrapsychically almost seems to be made possible by some special mode of communication. For example, the therapeutic impasse seems related to a modification of the communication in such a manner that the participants no longer have access to the intra-psychic dynamics of each other.

Intra-psychic dynamics mean, of course, essentially unconscious dynamics. Therapy involves an increasing accessibility of each participant's unconscious dynamics to the other. More specifically, the intra-psychic dynamics of the therapist involve his unconscious reactions to the patient as a projection of himself. The intra-psychic dynamics of the therapist demand, primarily, the integration of his current feelings into his total self (body-image problem) as these are specifically stimulated by the projected feelings of the patient. Together these force the therapist to precipitate himself into residues of his own transference feelings. In short, the therapist experiences both the dynamics of his own body-image integration, and the vestiges of his infantile familial experience as these continue to be present in residual as his "intra-psychic family." The intra-psychic dynamics of the patient involve, primarily, his reaction to the therapist as the latter provokes feelings specific to the functioning of the patient's transference needs where these have been previously internalized as his own intra-psychic family. The patient, in short, has an intra-psychic experience in which the therapist participates to a greater or lesser extent. In contrast, the therapist has an essentially nonfamilial and, primarily, personal experience which deals with the relationship of his various "parts" to his integrated wholeness.

Picture, then, the one individual, the therapist, struggling with the problem of integrating himself in a still deeper sense. Superimposed on this intra-psychic struggle are his feelings about the patient and his responses to the patient's feelings. Facing him is a person who lives through, on a very deep level, his infantile familial experience; this reliving arises because of his relationship with the therapist. This experience progressively alters and broadens the patient's perception of the feelings implicit in the therapist's participation, and this reciprocally deepens the experience. Only the accessibility of the experience of one participant to the other is essential for the broadening and deepening of the experiences of both.

There is no way of describing the type of communicability which underlies this relationship. It is certainly nonverbal, and involves massive proprioceptive and exteroceptive reactions on the part of each person to subliminal stimuli from the other. It is a communication reminiscent of the mother's sensations while feeding or holding her child, while singing a lullaby, or telling a story whose objective content may not be relevant to the kind of communication involved. It differs little from the kind of communication which occurs between lovers, whose verbalization is often inappropriate, and whose real communication may not even involve the use of words. An adequate definition of the character of the therapeutic process requires the exact clarification of the nature of this special kind of "communicability," which the authors prefer to call unconscious-to-unconscious communication.

DISEQUILIBRIUM DYNAMICS (Figure 3). Unfortunately, the process of therapy is not quite so simple as the therapist responding to obtunded areas in the patient. Some areas and energy systems within the professional therapist resemble those of the patient. Further, the patient also has systems of energy which can express themselves freely, and which are not bound. In other words, each individual participating in this relationship includes both a *patient vector* and a *therapist vector*. This duality of function prevents the establishment of any static equilibrium in the relationship. Whatever the specific process, the chief characteristic of therapy is its constant disequilibrium. The process of therapy itself involves successive, and perhaps sequential, resolutions of deeper and more pervasive states of disequilibrium. This formulation may seem to suggest that the locus of the process of therapy lies in the interpersonal relationship. Yet that is not the case.

What are the general dynamics of "movement" in the therapeutic process? Therapy "moves" whenever the character of the emotional relationship between the patient and therapist changes in some manner. An impasse in therapy exists whenever the emotional relationship becomes fixed, e.g., the therapist is unable to alter a transference projection of the patient. The various ways in which these transference projections emerge and then are altered can be spoken of as "disequilibrium dynamics." Through these the

infantile transferences are upset, or "disequilibriated." Utilizing
the kind of communication spoken of above, these dynamics involve affective stimuli from one person which bring about changes
in the intra-psychic experience of the other person. When integrated, these subsequently serve as stimuli which reciprocally
provoke additional changes in the first person. This is a constant
process. The stimuli may be minute or massive, and may be re-
acted to either with significant or with minute intra-psychic
changes in the other person.

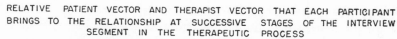

RELATIVE PATIENT VECTOR AND THERAPIST VECTOR THAT EACH PARTICIPANT
BRINGS TO THE RELATIONSHIP AT SUCCESSIVE STAGES OF THE INTERVIEW
SEGMENT IN THE THERAPEUTIC PROCESS

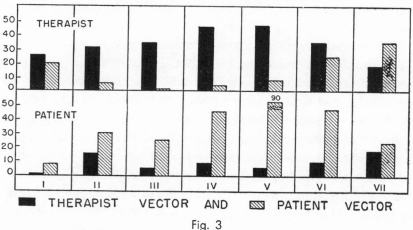

Fig. 3

Disequilibrium dynamics are significant only in an appropriate
setting. The isolative quality of the therapeutic process provides
this setting or culture. They depend, in addition, on an available
channel through which the stimuli and reactions can pass freely.
The type of communicability which we have outlined provides this
channel. Such communication seems to be an inherent capacity of
human beings. Once accepted by each person, it develops rapidly,
and errors of communication, or a breakdown in communication,
become increasingly minimal.

The disequilibrium dynamics manifest themselves in three general areas of the therapeutic process. (1) The least important area,
but one which nevertheless moves both participants into and
through transference experiences, involves rapid and sudden shifts

from the realities of the physical and cultural world to the fantasies of the unconscious world as either person crosses into or out of the isolation of therapy. Such shifts and migrations in and out of the therapeutic isolation frequently overcome a temporary impasse of the process as one or both of the participants respond to these shifts with intra-psychic changes.

(2) There are dual needs in both participants, since each has both patient and therapist vectors. The alternation between these functions acts as a very important disequilibrating force, and generally results in movement toward the ending phase and the resolution of the pathologic process. Once therapy begins, any movement toward ending means progress, and all movement is toward ending.

(3) The maturity of the person of the therapist and of the person of the patient upsets the repetitive character of the transference relationship and alters its outcome. This component has to do specifically with the therapist-vectors both in the patient and in the therapist. The intra-psychic dynamics of the patient involve a repetitive and compulsive living through of infantile experiences, always with the same unsatisfactory outcome. The intra-psychic family remains unaltered, and because of its persistent infantile character, the patient does not grow. He moves in a circle, repeating time and again the same effort at growth, followed by failure. This is but one way of formulating the principle of repetition-compulsion, which characterizes the neurotic process.

Now, however, this same patient-person relates to another human being, the therapist, in such a deep way that the latter replaces his symbolic family. The same internal, repetitious frustrations once more develop initially. The patient relives with the therapist his transference experiences in much the same way in which he lived them initially, and has been living them since, i.e., his repetition compulsions. This relationship, however, differs significantly. By virtue of greater therapist potential, this other person is a more adequate parent. This makes possible a different outcome to the transference experience resulting from better and deeper gratifications. This new parent responds more adequately to the patient's transference needs, adding the maturity of his person as a significant factor over and above the transference factor. The therapist, at first, serves simply as a symbolic screen for a projective repetition of the earlier parental experience. However, the therapist is also a real person and therefore more than, and different from, the sum of the patient's projections. The wholeness of him relates to the patient. Out of the therapist's maturity the patient constructs a more adequate and, finally, a truly satisfying internal parent. The patient certainly experiences the discrepancy between his projection and the maturity of the real person of the therapist and this may well constitute the most important disequilibrium dynamic. The transference repetition-compulsion is thus continually projected and altered until, either in massive or in splintered movement, the circular neurotic process breaks. Once the repetition-compulsion alters, the relationship can become more totally fantastic bilaterally, i.e., achieve a pre-transference level. This affords the patient a chance to regress to the pattern unconsciously directed toward the ultimate and complete satisfaction of those infantile needs which underlie self love (narcissism) and antecede love of others (transference). In this relationship, the patient achieves the gratification of certain infantile needs. This gratification leads toward a gradual dissolution of the patient's symbolic and neurotic processes. The patient's understanding of the character of his therapeutic transference relationships has little to do with the value of the experience. The actual child-parent gratification on a deep and meaningful level may or may not be understood. Growth, however, is always experience. No matter how this ensues, this gratification constitutes the effective force which shatters the neurotic process in the patient.

One other general aspect of therapy ought to be taken into account before examining the detailed phasic character of the process. We have spoken of a special relational communicability, and of the introjective involvement of each participant in the intrapsychic dynamics of the other. The authors will discuss the function of anxiety in therapy (Chapter 11), and wish only to point out its significance in this context.

Anxiety specifically expresses a breakdown in the relational communicability. When either of the participants becomes inaccessible to the other on an unconscious level, there results what amounts to a primitive form of separation. The separation engenders a specific type of anxiety. In this sense, all disequilibrium dynamics are motivated initially by anxiety. In other words, anxiety makes up the "stuff" which moves the process of therapy toward its completion.

Having described some of the components of disequilibrium dynamics, we hope to be able to delineate later some of the specific symbolic forms with which these dynamics of disequilibrium find an expression in therapy.

PHASES IN THE INTERVIEW SEGMENT (Figure 1). Understanding the general dynamics of the process and some of the factors involved, the phasic character of the process becomes more clear. The Pre-Interview Segment has been discussed in general terms. The present discussion will concern, therefore, the Interview Segment only. Thus, the reader will be less apt to be confused by concepts which overlap.

The Interview Segment can be divided into a pre-symbolic phase, a symbolic phase, and a post-symbolic phase. The pre-symbolic phase comprises the earliest relationship and one in which the patient makes a transition from the Pre-Interview Segment to a professional therapy. It includes the Anamnestic (I) and Casting (II) Stages of the Interview Segment.

The symbolic phase comprises the fantasy-transference experiences, and can be subdivided into more definitive stages. These are the Competitive (III), Regressive (IV), and Core (V) Stages.

The post-symbolic phase entails the transition out of the symbolic relationship into the Post-Interview Segment. It includes the Testing (VI) and Withdrawal (VII) Stages of the Interview Segment.

In its entirety, the symbolic phase has certain fairly specific qualities which set it off from other phases. The most obvious of these is indicated by the term "symbolic," which suggests that this phase involves transferences. The significance of the isolative quality of the symbolic phase lies in the increasing separation from the real world, and the consequent greater significance of the fantasy world within which the therapist and patient relate to each other.

Such a world of fantasy demands a kind of unconscious communication upon which depends the joint symbolic participation. It has been stressed that the therapeutic process is basically an unconscious one. The terms *psychotic involvement* and *therapeutic psychosis,* as used below, refer to these unconscious experiences, and are used in a special sense. Throughout this discussion, these terms will be used to describe the intra-psychic quality of either person's involvement. Finally, the symbolic phase involves not only the patient and his projections onto the professional therapist, but also onto the person of the therapist, since the dynamics of the latter are an important link in the process itself.

There are certain specific movements of these factors throughout the symbolic phase which can now be seen panoramically. The symbolic element in the relationship increases as the therapist and patient become more deeply related to each other and less concerned about the real world. This symbolic relationship begins to break up in the ending phase, as the patient's real world becomes more significant to him and the symbolic world ceases to overwhelm him.

The symbolic quality of the relationship gives rise to its isolative quality, which increases until almost complete isolation occurs in the core stage, and gradually disappears in the ending phase. The isolation, together with the symbolization processes, increases the mutual accessibility of the intra-psychic dynamics of both participants, and thus, their involvement with each other. These factors, too, reach a peak in the core stage where the patient and the therapist are more one, communication being at a maximum and anxiety at a minimum.

The *psychotic* or *unconscious quality* of that relationship, which has been increasing slowly during the earlier stages, now dominates the core stage. The patient rapidly represses this as the therapy goes through the ending phase. This re-repression emerges in the ending as the patient becomes more real in his total functioning. Its completeness in the patient, and partial character in the therapist, underlie some of the difficulties which the therapist has in his ending.

The principle of inertia may explain some aspects of the symbolic phase of therapy. The authors believe that once the patient makes the transition into the symbolic phase of therapy, he thereafter tends to proceed through acquired momentum to a satisfactory end, even though there may be recurrent minor distortions and interruptions due to the inadequacies of the therapist. Once a patient has begun therapy in a symbolic sense, although he may reach an impasse and may even change therapists, something has been precipitated within the patient which tends to acquire sufficient momentum to carry the patient through to an ending. The patient who sees the possibility of change within himself, and has made even the slightest beginnings toward effecting a change, develops dissatisfaction with every impasse in life, and so battles for more growth. The whole symbolic phase sometimes requires only a brief interval of time, and we have seen it completed in one interview. On the other hand, it may take years, and only at the end can one discern the over-all pattern of the process. The completion of the process seems to have very little to do with time.

In discussing communication and anxiety as movement factors in the symbolic phase, it was stated that the communication is at a maximum in the core stage, and anxiety at a minimum. Keep in mind, however, that since communication is so adequate, as in the pre-transference mother-infant relationship, separation in this phase, for whatever cause, has profound repercussions and results in a most intense and fundamental type of anxiety. Thus, although in the core stage the actual anxiety is minimal, the potential anxiety is maximal.

The exact dynamics of the Interview Segment can now be made more explicit although still not fully operational. The pre-symbolic phase has a mixture of qualities similar to those of the Pre-Interview Segment, and those qualities re-emerge as part of the Interview Segment. As indicated by its name, the pre-symbolic phase exhibits a relative paucity of symbolic factors. Neither the patient nor the therapist has extricated himself from the real world except to a limited degree. They relate to each other in a tenuous manner. The therapist, as a person, involves himself minimally. The patient now carefully protects his patient-needs from any relationship to the therapist, and functions on a rather conscious level. The whole relationship resembles the give and take of the patient and the social therapist, and frequently, recapitulates this in a very specific way.

In the movement from this phase into the symbolic relationship, the participants begin to isolate themselves from the real world. The therapist becomes more involved on a personal, unconscious level and, because of his greater maturity, takes the initiative. Reciprocally, the patient brings more of his patient-factors into the relationship, and increasingly separates the interview life from his outside life. The patient's anxiety increases now, and the unconscious communication between the two gradually becomes more adequate as they establish a deep symbolic relationship. During this phase, the therapist brings more initiative to the relationship but, as they near the core phase, the anxiety of each increases with the approach to the joint therapeutic psychosis.

In making the transition to the core stage, the therapist tips the scales by denying all reality, including even the realities of the interview situation and of words and behavior. He denies all the social aspects of the relationship, and all reference to the patient's outside life. He thus precipitates the patient into an acultural, deeply affective therapeutic psychosis which is usually nonverbal.

The core stage itself has such a degree of isolation and symbolic synchronization that communication becomes extremely exact and unequivocal. The fantasy component of the patient predominates as though there were little or no real world for him. The therapist, although not so deeply involved, has also separated himself from his real world to a large extent. This exclusion of reality enables the therapist to be maximally therapeutic and the patient to bring a maximum of his patient-factors into the relationship. Each now functions on a deep, unconscious level. The patient has long ago gone beyond the limits of his previous separation from reality, and the therapeutic benefit may well result partly from the therapist's ability to extend the limits (growing edge) of his own capacity in this respect, even though it be only to a slight degree. Thus, the therapist does, to a lesser extent, the very thing which the patient does. This affective synchronization, achieved by pushing the limits of one's emotional capacity, may well be one of the unique qualities of this phase. In other words, the patient functions on a maximally psychotic level and, in turn, the therapist also displays a certain amount of psychotic function. This phase tends to persist because it has a bilaterally satisfying character. The emergence from this core phase retraces, to some degree, the entrance into it. More specifically, it is initiated and precipitated by the patient himself who, as his need for the therapist decreases and as he becomes more and more capable of utilizing factors and persons other than the therapist for his own satisfaction, tends to emerge from the joint fantasy. This occurs sometimes in spite of the therapist's increasing tendency to bring his own patient-factors into focus.

The patient, though deeply anxious about doing so, emerges from the isolation of therapy into the real world. He has no essential need for the therapist and begins to re-repress the psychotic qualities of the relationship. The therapist's anxiety increases at the rejection implied by the patient's leaving. Simultaneously, the patterns of communication between them break down, due to the patient's re-repression of his psychotic functioning. The therapist may still strive for a resolution of his own patient-factors and the patient frequently ends by crudely rejecting him. A large amount of guilt and anxiety in the patient accompanies this rejection of the therapist, and reflects itself in a hesitation to end the therapy. This may not be as obvious in the ending phase of the symbolic relationship as in the Post-Interview Segment, e.g., when the therapist greets the ex-patient on the street two weeks later like a long-lost friend, and discovers that he is responded to only as a doctor.

So far, the general divisions of the therapeutic process, and the movement in the symbolic phase, and certain of the dynamics which characterize the total process, have been presented. It may be that, because of the telescoping quality of the process of therapy, only generalizations are possible, and more specific details may distort the picture. The definition of some of these more detailed steps in therapy, and of their relationship to each other, resists clarification. Furthermore many events in therapy recapitulate themselves. The total process may be identified in a single interview, a series of interviews, or a sample of nonrelated interviews with different patients. Yet the movement of the process appears multi-dimensional. The vagueness of the dimensions makes it difficult to see the detailed structure of the entire process. Focusing on such details emphasizes serial and chronological dimensions and becomes highly artificial. Despite these limitations, more specific description of the operation of therapy may be useful because it filters through the major movements, and orders them spatially and temporally. Such a description stems from the therapeutic experiences of the authors, both as patients and as therapists.

The movement in the process of therapy not only has specific dynamics, but also a recognizable direction. As a general principle, the movement, at different stages of the process of therapy, reflects the summative intensity of motivation in both the patient and therapist. More exactly, the movement functionally sums up both the intensity and the direction of the motivations of both participants. In most stages of the process, the patient's motivation remains greater and propels him specifically toward ending. In contrast, the therapist's motivations for ending may be minimal, and may be directed chiefly toward maintaining a symbolic relationship which begins to gratify him. By isolating some of the stages in the process, some of the characteristic shifts in the motivational vectors also become clearer.

In the pre-symbolic or beginning phase of therapy, the motivations of both therapist and patient are minimal. The intra-psychic needs of either patient or therapist may have little to do with this specific relationship. Pressures from his real, social world, rather than internal pressures, often push the patient into therapy. Sometimes, of course, he has a greater motivation, directed at a deep symbolic relationship, but these motivations usually result from a previous "orienting relationship" with an adequate social therapist. This latter patient comes to the therapeutic situation yearning for a deep experience, and enters immediately into the symbolic world of fantasy.

The motivations of the therapist are ordinarily minimal at first. In the mature therapist, they involve primarily the ego-satisfactions which lead him to accept the patient. The mature therapist may reject many *new* patients unconsciously to the extent that his motivations lead him away from any symbolic relationship. This therapist has satisfied his patient needs over a long period of time with many patients. His residual needs are profound and fairly specific. He responds to patients who have the kind of intra-psychic capacity, psychotic depth, and unconscious accessibility which resonate to his specific residual needs. For example, psy-chotherapists often say, "I am no longer interested now in treating patients with a neurotic problem." The authors, over the past two years, have noted a very distinct veering away from their desire to treat patients in general, and tend to treat certain kinds of patients. The enthusiasm and elation felt when contemplating the possi-bility that schizophrenic patients may be amenable to psycho-therapy may reflect a perception that some residual needs can perhaps be answered only in therapeutic experiences with the schizophrenic. These factors in the therapist influence the initial movement in therapy. Whether its direction is toward symbolic involvement or away from it depends on the degree to which this particular therapist has satisfied certain of his patient needs in previous experiences.

Thus, in the beginning phase, most of the movement comes from the patient, who responds primarily to external pressures. Begin-ning a therapeutic relationship in any symbolic sense is, therefore, a difficult task for the therapist since, compared to any other phase in the therapeutic process, his motivations are minimal at this point. This, of course, is a common experience. It is usually dif-ficult to establish a truly therapeutic relationship.

A surprising percentage of patients begin therapy, but never actually go on to satisfy any real needs. The above suggests that this may be due to poor motivation in the therapist. Two specific examples of this come to mind. As teachers in a medical school, the authors see the beginning therapist repeatedly deny his own patient-factors. He may see several patients who do not return for a second interview. Then some patient will propel the student into a deeper relationship. After this deep experience, few patients fail to return after the initial interview. In contrast, the mature therapist, even though his transference needs have been satisfied to a greater degree has, nonetheless, motivations towards developing a symbolic relationship on a deeper (body image) level. Because of this, he seldom has the problem of patients breaking off treatment in the early phases. This highlights the axiom that one cannot do psychotherapy on a conscious level. If the relationship is therapeutic, the therapist must always be deeply and pervasively involved.

A broad shift in these motivational vectors accompanies the transition into the symbolic phase of therapy. One sees in the patient the beginnings of internal pressures which seek to achieve the primitive, biological relationship of the infant, with the therapist as the primordial parent. This kind of relationship makes up the core of the therapeutic process. The direction of the motivation may be either toward, or away from, this type of relationship. The patient has within him the beginnings of this motivation, but again, they are minimal. Even so, they are directed at the core of the process. Once the patient enters this phase of therapy, a process begins within him which rarely stops or reverses itself.

The therapist, once he establishes a symbolic relationship with the patient, develops intense and positively directed motivations which, although complemented by those of the patient, supply most of the energy to carry the process forward. Nearing core stage, the motivations of the patient seem to become negative, and he retreats from the core experience. At this point, patients frequently say that they are afraid of losing their minds, or are afraid of just how crazy they might become. The motivation of the therapist overshadows this negative factor in the patient as they near the core experience. This results in movement toward the core experience, although to some extent minimized by the patient's negative vector. In no stage in the process of therapy are the motivations of the therapist more clear-cut than here.

The precipitation into the core experience entails a comparative shift in the vectors. The motivations in the core area are most difficult to describe, and they involve factors different from those in the initial, the transitional, and the ending phases. Generally, as in any other deep interpersonal experience, both participants have motivations to maintain the relationship. The patient has a deep need for this relationship, since he has finally achieved the type of parental response for which he has been searching. Once he finds such a relationship, the patient demands complete symbolic gratification. Within it, he also resolves those transference areas where previously the possibility of gratification was minimal. Thus, this pre-transference experience provides a basis for satisfying transference needs.

The therapist also seeks to maintain the relationship on this level. He functions parentally, but begins to intrude demands for a satisfaction of his own residual patient-factors. He does not test the relationship as much as he uses it. (See Testing Stage below.) This use of the relationship by the therapist sets up certain dynamics which finally move the process of therapy out of the core stage and into the ending phase. The patient's motivations force this transition, since the therapist seeks to remain at this level. The patient, in contrast, has satisfied some of his more fundamental infantile needs and begins to have more mature and real needs. Part of his testing of the relationship results from the loss of interest in a symbolic relationship and a demand for a real, adult relationship with the therapist. The mature therapist responds to this by a rejection of these real demands, leaving the patient with the need and opportunity to end the symbolic relationship constructively. This frees the patient to secure these gratifications in other areas. In the transition from the core stage to the ending phase, the motivations of the patient toward ending increase almost geometrically as he secures more and more satisfaction in his real-life experience. The need of the therapist to maintain the therapeutic relationship opposes this transition. Since, however, the motivations of the patient to end therapy dominate this stage, these overcome the inertia of the therapist, and the patient leaves.

As an over-all pattern, then, the motivations to preserve the core experience are those of the therapist, and the motivations for ending it come from the patient. The discussion of counter-transference will show that an understanding of these vectors clarifies the nature of the common types of impasse in the therapeutic process.

What is presented above is the ideal therapeutic process. In order to be specific and clear, it was necessary to make many compromises. Thus, although a chronological type of description has been attempted, such a chronological approach is an abstraction. The therapeutic process has been discussed in a cross-sectional manner when it must be obvious that it is at least three-dimensional. Actually, the authors merely have tried to indicate certain patterns which seem sufficiently valid and useful in their thinking, and which help organize, more accurately, the mass of experiences which they "live through" as therapists.

STAGES OF THE INTERVIEW SEGMENT AND THE INTRA-PSYCHIC REPRESENTATIONS IN THERAPIST AND PATIENT (Figure 4). So far, the process of therapy has been discussed from the point of view of its more gross qualities. These have included: (1) The relationship of professional interview therapy to Pre-Interview and Post-Interview growth in the patient. (2) The interaction of fantasy and reality in the process. (3) Symbolization. (4) The intra-psychic loci of the process. (5) The natural divisions of the process. (6) The motivational vectors. Here, with these as background, an attempt is made at a more refined definition of the intra-psychic "operations" of therapy as they occur in the successive stages of the Interview Segment. Each person has an intra-psychic representation of himself, which varies, albeit in a fluid manner, from the beginning to the end of therapy, and each person also has an intra-psychic representation of the other member of the therapeutic dyad.

THE PRE-INTERVIEW SEGMENT has been discussed at length (Chapter 9).

Anamnestic Stage (I). In the anamnestic stage (I) which is pre-symbolic, the therapist sees himself as a professional person endowed with certain functional potentialities and responsibilities. He tends to regard himself as a function, that is, as *The Therapist*, although he also retains his concept of himself as a person. In this initial period—which endures not a minute nor an interview but an indefinite period of time—the therapist sees the patient as an *Adult*, and shortly thereafter as a *Pseudo-Adult*. This latter term serves to indicate the adult who obviously lives behind a façade, e.g., the neurotic.

SYMBOLIC REPRESENTATION

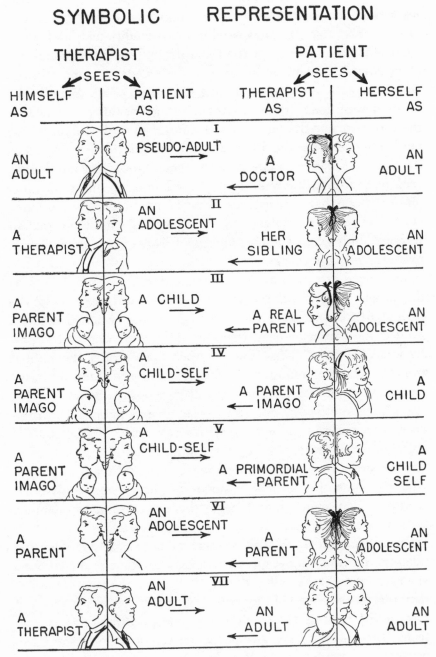

Fig. 4

In Stage I, the patient conceives of himself as *Adult*, and views his therapeutic need as less pervasive than an over-all modification of his personality. He arrives with a pre-conditioned, and somewhat objective, concept of the therapist and his professional role as *Doctor*. He assumes him to be an adult in the same sense in which the patient rationalizes himself to be an adult. As indicated in the description of the pre-symbolic stage, at this point, neither the therapist nor the patient feels himself to be "symbolic," and neither of them sees the other as "symbolic." In the first interview, the therapist may even talk with the patient on a very adult level, explaining to him the realities of the relationship and discussing, often at the patient's insistence, what he might expect in therapy and what therapy involves. The therapist talks as if the patient were an adult who will bring more and more of his immature self to subsequent interviews.

The above pattern is oversimplified and may be complicated by the patient factors in the therapist, the social transferences of the patient, and the extent to which the patient has obtained therapy, even though from a social therapist, before coming to the professional therapist. Thus, the therapist may propel the patient from the very beginning into a deep symbolic relationship based on his own fantasies of the patient. Again, either because of the importance of the "doctor stereotype" in the patient's transferences, or perhaps previous experiences with physicians, the patient's initial perception of the therapist may be replete with either positive or negative transference feeling. Finally, a patient who has gone through these stages of the process with other therapists may come in and begin therapy at some point much farther along in the process.

Casting Stage (II). With the development of early fantasy and bilateral intra-psychic representations, the therapeutic process emerges into what is called the symbolic casting stage (II). The therapist moves ahead of the patient, in that he pushes the patient toward the core of the therapeutic process. Strange as it may seem, this does not have any particular relationship to the intra-psychic representation in the developing process itself. Even though the patient holds back and resists the movement in the process, he is the one whose symbolization changes. The therapist in the second stage still sees himself in his professional functioning, as *Therapist*, although he becomes distinctly more of a person to himself, and becomes more free to relate in his own unique way. He may now see the patient intra-psychically not just as *Pseudo-adult*, but as *Adolescent*.

The patient, in the meantime, has gradually begun to perceive that he not only can obtain help with his functional complaint, but also, more pervasively, may find some of the gratifications which he had not obtained from his older sibling or the equivalent thereof. He, therefore, sees the therapist as an older *Sibling*, and thus represents himself intra-psychically as a younger *Sibling*. For example, the patient often becomes competitive at this stage and frequently describes in a somewhat belligerent manner his real and social achievements, and questions the therapist's professional capacity. As the relationship continues, the therapist sees the possibility of gratifying the symbolic needs of the patient, and the possibility of a deeper participation which will satisfy also his own needs. This marks the transition into the symbolic stages.

Competitive Stage (III). In the Competitive Stage (III), the therapist sees himself as *Parent-person*, and his perception of himself as a unique individual becomes less pervasive than it was before. He takes on, by means of this intra-psychic representation of himself, an unconscious parental responsibility for the patient. His representation of the patient within himself changes so that the patient becomes to him his own *Child-self*. At this stage the therapist feels protective, loses his identification with the culture, and becomes increasingly "warm." The patient, though still seeing himself as the younger *Sibling*, gradually changes during this stage until he begins to see the therapist more and more as *Parent-person*. This leads frequently to requests by the patient for factual answers to specific problems, for information about psycho-dynamics, and for an evaluative assessment of his behavior as "right or wrong," appropriate or inappropriate. Mistaking this demand for a close emotional relationship as a demand for content response may preclude the further development of the symbolic relationship. The inexperienced therapist is often seduced into reality precisely at this point, even while the patient moves toward an infantile, emotional dependence on the parental figure. An acceptance of this abortive effort (as expressed in demands for advice and "content" which he believes to represent the patient's ultimate need) prevents the development of this deeper parent-child relationship.

At this point, the therapist must provide an experience which negates the patient's fantastic conception of the therapist as omnipotent. The therapist must not accept the demands of the patient for advice and direction. Such acceptance of the validity of the patient's projections, as a reality, merely succeeds in making the therapist another episode in a repetition compulsion. There is no more blatant rejection of the patient on the part of the therapist than this. At the same time, nonetheless, he has to accept the projections of the patient within the relationship. The therapist must be able to tolerate the tensions provoked at this critical transition, particularly the tensions within himself which relate to his ambivalence about continuing therapy. Such tolerance includes the denial of any mechanism on his, or the patient's, part for temporarily reducing the anxiety. Progress depends on increasing rather than decreasing anxiety until the Core Stage is reached.

Regressive Stage (IV). As the therapeutic process approaches the Core Stage, the patient, secure in the therapist, conceives of himself as a *Child* and of the therapist as the *Primordial-Parent*. The therapist, in accepting this and in seeing himself as the *Primordial-Parent*, goes further in the denial of himself as a professional person, and sees the patient more completely as his own *Child-Self*. The manifestations of this phase are usually very overt and specific. The patient says, "I feel like a little baby," and most often the experienced therapist responds to this remark nonverbally by means of the most pervasive acceptance possible to him.

Core Stage (V). In the Core Stage (V), both the therapist and the patient see themselves in their true therapeutic roles—the therapist as *Parent* and the patient as *Child-Self*. Each of them introjects the other and regards the other as his whole intra-psychic "Society."

In this area the greatest therapeutic depth accrues. Only at this level do the bilateral symbolic relationships converge fully. The relationship involves only two symbolic roles, even though each is unique to the intra-psychic "Society" of the participants. This symbolic synchronization and complementary articulation increases the depth and extent of the symbolic participation because of the singleness of the vector, and because each sees himself in the very role in which he is seen by the other. Once such a symbolic relationship has been established, the patient has the capacity to develop other such relationships as a pattern through which segmental problems or conflicts can be worked out. The aim of Stage IV is the attainment of Stage V. The aim of V, however, is not VI. The Core Stage aims at an indefinite continuation of itself. It is the essential therapeutic relationship of and in itself. It is the relationship which, throughout the rest of therapy, and even subsequent to interview therapy, can be used by the patient in the attempt to work through his residual transference problems, and the problems of his emotional growth in general.

Testing Stage (VI). The Testing Stage (VI) does not necessarily evolve spontaneously from the use of the core experience. The symbolic emergence from Stages II or III to V is unitary; it is an emergent whole, the implicit aim of each level being the attainment of the succeeding level. If the process begins, and no new pathological factors intervene, it will naturally gravitate toward the Core Stage. This is apparently a primary quality of the symbolic relationship—it seems to seek the most primitive symbolism. The emergence, therefore, of Stages II to V is a by-product of the "symbolic need." In contrast, the movement of therapy from Stage V is a by-product not of symbolic need, but of reality and of social pressure, and presupposes a certain security gained from the experience of the core relationship. The break-out of the Core Stage into the Testing Stage resembles the battle for status between the mature adolescent and the parent.

The Testing Stage marks the beginning of new patterns of intra-psychic representation both on the part of the therapist and of the patient. The therapist still functions as a *Parent-Person*, but in a somewhat different sense, for out of the synchronous fantasy of

Stage V has come an increasing awareness of his own separateness from the patient. Although still a parent, he is also more of a person. He now sees the patient as a real person, whose immaturities are fading away, i.e., he sees him as a potential adult.

Typical of this phase is the therapist's delight in the story of how the patient "told off" the man next door. The patient conceives of himself as an *Adolescent* much as the therapist sees him, but with the added sense of power so typical of the adolescent. This also entails an incipient awareness of the therapist's inadequacies. The patient's concept of the therapist now becomes much less specifically parental, and comes closer to the benign tolerance which the maturing adolescent shows toward his "aging" parent. It recapitulates the adolescent's belief that his parents belong to a different and passing generation, which has very little appreciation of the realities of his own life experience and which, in a sense, is doomed to be left behind, alone with its memories of the earlier family life.

Thus, this stage reveals the growing rejection of the therapist as a symbolic parent, and the development of the patient's concept of himself as an adult. He has increasing sureness that adulthood is possible for him, too, and that he can bring it into being.

Withdrawal Stage (VII). The mechanism of the growth process appears in the Withdrawal Stage, with the patient beginning to see his *Child-Self* in the therapist, and to obtain a glimpse of the first realities of his own integrated adultness. The therapist now loses his pervasive parental quality. He becomes just a professional means wherewith the patient can round out his own capacity to carry on therapy as an intra-psychic process, and without direct participation by a professional therapist. The final ending occurs when the therapist loses his intra-psychic representation of the patient as his own *Adult-Self*. The patient sees himself now as real and *Adult*, with a growing perception of his uniqueness as a person. He even begins to see the therapist as a *Pseudo-Adult*, in much the same way in which the therapist had previously seen the patient. Stage VII parallels the manner in which, in real life, the young man resolves his relationship to his parent. It involves a rejection of the parent in his symbolic role, and an acceptance, on the part of both, of the autonomous adult status of himself and of the other.

Endings of Therapy

The ending of therapy, which we have discussed in terms of the interview process, deserves a more extensive discussion. Earlier it was said that the patient needs help initially because he cannot "end" with the members of his intra-psychic family. Just so, the process of ending with his therapist attains utmost significance, and may well be the decisive factor in determining whether the therapy has been effective. In medical and psychiatric circles, the doctor assumes responsibility for telling the patient both when to come back and when not to return because the "cure" has been completed. Some people have talked about "ending" as being something that happens within the relationship. The authors regard ending as occurring within the patient. Most specifically, it is related to his extrusion of the symbolic parent-person. This, however, assumes the fact that the therapist also goes through a somewhat similar ending. These ending processes are not synchronous. Thus, the problem arises of differentiating between these two endings, especially in terms of the practical difficulties which arise. Before going into a description of kinds of endings, we should like to suggest that throughout this discussion, the analogy of the adolescent leaving home be held in mind, because the general categories and possible variations in ending are all very similar to this model process.

There seem to be three general types of endings. First is the so-called positive ending, in which both the therapist and the patient have emotionally accepted the termination of the relationship, and their capacity to live separately. Each implicitly recognizes the contribution of the other to his own living, and separation feelings on both sides are, therefore, minimal. This ending parallels the going away to college of a boy who thereby becomes independent of the family; yet both he and the family have accepted the right to separateness. There is, of course, always a minimal bilateral feeling of rejection. Coincidentally with this, the boy accepts the fact that he has gotten all the parents have to give him and has given to the parents all that he is capable of giving. The parents accept the fact that the boy's leaving will not be too grievous a loss to them, and that what residual needs they have will have to be satisfied in other ways.

Second is the negative ending. It may be as clear-cut as the positive one, with the patient leaving the therapist aggressively or defiantly, and with the therapist nurturing minor feelings of rejection. The case of the young man whom his family has educated, and who then decides, over the parents' protest, to get married and to lead a life of his own, exemplifies this type of ending. Firmly, and with fairly mature aggression, he insists on having a life of his own, despite the pressures and lamentations of his parents. The parents characteristically say they feel that the boy deserts them "after they have worked their fingers to the bone." Returning again to the therapeutic situation, it may be easier now to see how the therapist, like the parent, is himself looking for a parent. This is often the real, i.e., unconscious, affective meaning of the statement made by many therapists about patients who leave precipitously, to the effect that "they have not finished in therapy and really don't know what is best for themselves." The bitterness of many therapists toward patients who end negatively reflects an underlying feeling that the patient has rejected the therapist. The above remarks may even help us understand why certain therapists have a predominance of negative endings. For instance, the therapist who needs less help would be apt to end positively most of the time; the therapist who is less insistent upon satisfying his patient-needs will more likely have casual endings; while the therapist who has many unsatisfied patient-vectors, or strives for more satisfaction, would be apt to have many negative endings.

The third and most unsatisfactory of all endings seems to us to be the most common ending in contemporary psychiatry. The therapist compromises the ending phase, and this results in a dependency relationship of the patient to himself, so that the therapist never has to face directly the fact of his rejection by the patient. This post-therapeutic relationship becomes further complicated by dynamics similar to those apparent in the boy who stays at home all his life. Thus, we find patients who will end their own appointments by means of a fatalistic withdrawal. In others, the therapist terminates the bilateral tension state on an administrative level. Sometimes both drag out the relationship for many years, during which the therapist continues as an introject so that the patient suffers from a persistent transference neurosis. Certainly, a most difficult problem of contemporary psychotherapy is the resolution of the transference neurosis.

With some patients the ending is specific, but ambivalent. This reflects a mild type of therapeutic impasse, and relates to factors many of which are still unknown. It may be that the therapist has not been able to establish clearly his dual status. For example, the therapist may have become a powerful symbolic figure to the patient, but may have been unable to develop or retain his status as a separate person. Consequently, his insistence upon the resolution of his own patient-factors may bind the patient to him by a feeling of guilt for not having answered the therapist's patient-needs. In that case, the process of ending becomes a repeated effort on the part of the patient to "pay the therapist off" either by actually being therapist in turn, or by trying to force the therapist to accept the patient's rejection of him. These patients characteristically resolve their guilt and ambivalence about leaving the therapist by returning to him for subsequent interviews, in which they present complaints about their failures to function adequately in real situations, and question the effectiveness of the therapy. Usually, the therapist senses the "pseudoness" of these complaints and that, in a sense, the patients are asking the therapist whether he now recognizes that underneath their hollow complaints they are actually more adequate as a result of having begun their growth in the therapy. The therapist's acceptance of their new adequacy, and his denial of the meaningfulness of these temporary setbacks, confronts the patient with the more fundamental reason for his return, i.e., the fact that he has returned in order to help the erstwhile therapist. The explicit recognition of this fact usually suffices to resolve the former patient's guilt and ambivalence about leaving. It now appears less a rejection, and involves the same dynamics as the mother's explicit recognition of the child's sexual feeling toward her, which frequently suffices to resolve the child's guilt and ambivalence about his sexuality.

Any reluctance to accept the patient's impulse to terminate the relationship constitutes a most serious error. In fact, the authors have come to believe that whenever an adequate therapeutic relationship has been established, an early ending is preferable, if one leaves the final decision to the patient.

The patient's impulses to separate from the therapist seem to arise in three general areas: (1) from an implicit denial on the part of the patient of his patient status; (2) from his new insistence upon his status as a separate person both in the interview and outside; (3) from some, usually subtle, acceptance by the patient of his new therapeutic role. As cues, the patient may describe himself as functioning as counselor to a neighbor or to his wife, may offer to set the therapist straight on some aspect of their relationship, or may offer the therapist a social relationship, or again describe the satisfactions of his life outside the interview situation. He may, in retrospect, deny the fantastic relationship of the therapeutic interview by being implicitly indifferent to the interview itself, or offer another patient to the therapist. It is significant that cues for this ending phase are as specific in young children as they are in the adult patient.

Post-Interview Segment

The process of therapy does not terminate with the Interview Segment. On the contrary, from the point of view of time, most of the realistic therapeutic gain occurs in the Post-Interview Segment. An adequate ending of the relationship does not completely resolve the transference neurosis, but rather, provides the impetus which begins the resolution of this neurosis. The final resolution of the transference needs occurs in the Post-Interview Segment of therapy. This segment involves, primarily, an increase in the importance of the patient's real needs, and in his capacity to gratify them as they become fused with his fantasy needs, which he is able now to gratify outside of his relationship to the therapist. The fantasy-reality ratio swings toward the real. The patient leaves, not free of intra-psychic obligations, but now confronted with the introject of the therapist, as it has come to replace the "intra-psychic family" during the process of therapy. Patients frequently refer to the fact that after the interviews have ended, they carry the therapist around within them for some time as a dynamic part of their functioning in their social and real relationships. The difference in the quality of the introject of the therapist, as compared with that of the original parents, resembles the difference between the introject of the parent in the infant or child and the introject in the adolescent, who has had an adequate relationship with his parents earlier, but still retains some symbolic relationship to them which he gradually displaces and extrudes in his transition from adolescence to adulthood. The restrictive and compulsive quality of the infantile introject is what overwhelms the patient. The child may succumb to this powerful introject, primarily because of his dependence upon the parent for vital satisfactions. The introject in the adequate adolescent differs significantly. It is, in the first place, the introject of a parent who was a satisfying parent and, therefore, its compulsive and restrictive qualities are not very intense. In this case, the dynamics of the adolescent's growth and of the person of the adolescent are more powerful than the introject. He no longer depends on the parent for the satisfaction of any of his fundamental or vital needs, yet because of his earlier pervasive relationship to his parents, he reluctantly extrudes the introject as time and deep satisfactions in real adult life finally replace the introject.

The parent-introject may never be completely extruded, but it loses its repressive and compulsive quality. One of the factors in the patient's new ability to extrude the introject of the therapist and to resolve the transference neurosis, as against his previous inability to resolve the infantile neurosis, may be the lesser importance of reality factors in the introject of the therapist. The personal inadequacies and immaturities of the therapist in his real relationships with other individuals have not been made a part of the therapeutic relationship and, therefore, do not contaminate and distort the symbolic introject of the therapist in the patient. Thus, the patient develops an increasing capacity to obtain real gratification even in the presence of the residuals of the transference neurosis. As these real satisfactions accumulate, the transference neurosis fades until, finally, the patient has completely extruded the introject of the therapist. Much as the process of therapy, once begun, has an inherent movement of its own which carries it to termination, so the Post-Interview phase of transference-neurosis resolution has an inherent movement, and seems to "carry itself" to a successful termination, although different patients require different periods of time for this and work it through differently.

An attempt by the therapist to intrude himself into the Post-Interview phase may contaminate this on a personal level, thereby upsetting the ratio between the real and the fantastic by an intensification of the importance of the fantastic relationship. This difficulty arises invariably when the therapist and the patient have not only a professional relationship, but also a social relationship. One sees this most vividly when one attempts therapy with colleagues or close friends.

The patient makes these transitions in the Post-Interview Segment better if social therapists, external to the interview situation, are readily available. The patient uses these individuals in this phase with about equal emphasis on the real and on the symbolic. In the relationship with the social therapist, fantasy needs do not overwhelm the patient as readily, and he expands the real areas of his living in a relationship with persons who have some awareness of his fantasy need. There seems to be a point at which the patient finally extrudes the therapist, and a more gratifying balance between real and fantastic satisfaction obtains.

This point is usually followed by a new swing in the patient toward his fantasy gratifications. He is no longer afraid of his fantasy experiences, and therefore, no longer has as deep a need for "flight into reality." The patient obtains greater real satisfactions, and also shows a capacity for more fantasy satisfactions, with a fusion between the two which represents the most functional balance possible for that particular patient. This continues as a process of growth.

THE FUNCTION OF RE-REPRESSION IN ENDING. The successful termination of therapy, as described above, involves extensive re-

repression. It has always seemed paradoxical that the psychiatrist deliberately breaks through repressions in the neurotic person to bring to consciousness unconscious fantasies, while he, at the same time, diagnoses as refractory or incurable those individuals who have almost all of their unconscious available to awareness and expression, that is, the schizophrenic. It is not far wrong to say that many of the individuals who have had extensive, but incomplete, psychiatric treatment have, in a sense, been made somewhat "schizophrenic." At any rate, the community consistently expresses such an idea in characterizing the post-depth therapy patient as one who never simply eats food without, at the same time, being conscious of his introjective dynamics and the cannibalistic implications of the simple process of eating.

A person concerned with the mechanisms of breathing and of heart action is less apt to breathe well and more apt to have cardiac difficulties. Like those primitive biological systems with diencephalic representations, the unconscious functions best when we are unaware of its functioning. The restoration of this unawareness subsequent to the interview phase occurs during the Post-Interview phase of therapy, sic, re-repression. The dynamics of this type of re-repression are so radically different from those of the original repressions that perhaps even the use of the term re-repression is ill-advised. The re-repression discussed here occurs not out of guilt or fear, but rather, in order to raise the level of homeostatic functioning in the individual. In this sense, it may be likened to one facet of the original repression, i.e., that facet which involves repression not from guilt or shame (interpersonal factors), but for the sake of personal well-being. Whatever the dynamics of the re-repression, fundamentally, it occurs simply because this constitutes the best way for the organism to function.

As a therapist, one does not aim at creating a cult of therapeutized persons who are different from, and can expect to be isolated within, our total culture. On the contrary, the individual should be better able to return to his culture, to become part of it, to contribute to it, and to obtain maximum gratification within it. This involves a certain submission to the cultural structure for the economy of the culture as a whole. It demands a re-repression of certain aspects of fantasy existence, and the acceptance of the need for a certain amount of conformity and realism. This is not an index of immaturity, but a quality of maturity in the patient. In this way, the cultural pressures which operated initially to bring about repression also operate in the Post-Interview patient to bring about re-repression. The critical difference is that now the individual accepts these cultural restrictions for their positive value, and only to the extent that they do not interfere with his vital needs and with his new-found image of himself as a unique individual who has a status even more profound than that with which the culture can provide him.

11

Anxiety and Psychotherapy

I saw and heard, and knew at last
The How and Why of all things, past,
And present, and forevermore.
The Universe, cleft to the core,
Lay open to my probing sense,
That sickening, I would fain pluck thence
But could not, —Nay? but needs much suck
At the great wound, and could not pluck
My lips away till I had drawn
All venom out.

*Millay**

Bilaterality of Affect in Psychotherapy

Psychotherapy in its most elemental form represents an interchange of affect between two people. A traditional concept that the affect resides solely in the patient and that the therapist simply perceives and evaluates this affect objectively does not cover the full range of this interpersonal relationship. Nor does the therapist simply reflect or resonate to the affective state of the patient in order to enable the patient to better accept his own feelings. The actual experience of the working therapist is neither objective nor impersonal. Beyond his professional involvement, the therapist also participates personally in this relationship with all the affect and personal feeling that he would ordinarily have in a comparable interpersonal relationship of a nonprofessional character. Therapy cannot be understood if psychiatry persists in placing primary emphasis upon the patient and his feelings. In contrast, when the element of bilaterality is visible, many of the

*Lines from "Renascence," in RENASCENCE AND OTHER POEMS, published by Harper & Brothers, Copyright, 1912, 1940, by Edna St. Vincent Millay.

problems of therapy become clear. The very process of therapy has its foundations in the duality of the affective participation of both individuals. Without the affective participation of the therapist, therapy is not possible. This participation goes beyond simple empathy with the patient's feelings, goes beyond a vicarious experience of feeling in response to the patient's feelings and, when analyzed, appears as a rapid alternation in feeling in both participants, each responding to the other with different feelings, the totality of which moves the process of therapy along toward its conclusion.

Therapy as defined by the authors occurs only if the therapist becomes so personally involved that he pushes his own growing edge and inherits a little more of his own potential energy. Whatever the specific expression of affect in therapy, the orienting concept presents therapy as a bilateral interchange of affect. The affect in either participant relates both quantitatively and qualitatively to the affect of the other participant. In any particular instance, the feelings in both may be identical or they may be more or less related; but often they are diametrically opposed. In all instances, the depth of feeling in either participant varies directly with the depth of feeling in the other. Were it possible to plot the changing intensity of feeling in both, one would find that intensity in each grows, throughout the process of therapy, with the intensity of feeling in the other.

Anxiety in Psychotherapy

The problem of psychotherapy, in many ways, centers around the dynamics of anxiety. Other affective states present themselves, but have therapeutic import primarily in their relationship to anxiety. Understanding of the role of anxiety in the process of psychotherapy should then clarify many of the problems of affective interpersonal dynamics. The reader's awareness of the role of anxiety in psychopathology is assumed, and the following discussion deals exclusively with its place in psychotherapy.

Anxiety as used in this chapter differs in some ways from the term as used currently in psychiatric literature. Anxiety, to the authors, represents the most primitive form which affect, or feel-

ing, can take in the human being. As such, anxiety represents unorganized affect. This affect has both subjective and expressive
components. It differs from other affects, however, in that both
subjectively, and in its motor and biochemical expressions, the
quality of disorganization predominates. In this sense, it represents
the basic, or most primitive, affect seen in the infant. Out of the
matrix of the anxiety experienced by the child soon after birth,
other affects or feeling tones differentiate, i.e., become organized.
Thus ego development in the child correlates directly with an
increasing organization of affective states out of unorganized
energy or affect, i.e., out of anxiety. The structuring of personality
occurs around the organization of affect (anxiety). This organization occurs, of course, in the multiple, ever-expanding interpersonal relationships of the child. The final organization of affect, for
example, the sentiment of love and the capacity to love, is intrapersonal, but as initially experienced it occurs in the parent-child
relationship. The intrapersonal affective organization is preceded
by, and reflects, an interpersonal experience emerging from the
organization of complex feelings derived from anxiety.

The implications of this for psychotherapy can be clarified. In
the infant, anxiety arises whenever the supporting interpersonal
relationship fails, since there is as yet no firm intrapersonal organization of affect. In the adult, anxiety as defined above arises
whenever the organization of affect in the individual breaks down,
i.e., whenever his ego breaks down. Likewise the adult, like a
child, may organize his affect, not intrapersonally, but around
interpersonal relationships. An adult whose relationship to another
adult supports his infantile need will respond with anxiety whenever that interpersonal relationship collapses. This peculiarly
intimate and dynamic relationship between interpersonal and intrapersonal organization of affect finds its clearest expression in psychotherapy. The process of psychotherapy represents an effort to
better structure the personality through the organization of affect
intrapersonally in the patient as a result of the adequacy of the
interpersonal organization of affect between patient and therapist.

Whenever the intrapersonal organization of affect breaks down
(disintegration of the ego), or where an inadequate, infantile

adult loses security in an interpersonal relationship, the result is anxiety. Here, the anxiety has a *negative* quality. It is associated with inadequacy and, as such, is a direct expression of the pathology of the patient. Such negative anxiety provides much of the motivation of the patient seeking psychotherapy. It pervades the initial phases of the process of psychotherapy, and the outcome depends largely on the capacity of the therapist to convert this to more constructive drives.

In this chapter, reference will also be made to *positive* anxiety. This differs from negative anxiety in its dynamic origins. In contrast to negative anxiety, which arises out of psychopathology, positive anxiety occurs in an individual who finds himself in an interpersonal relationship within the matrix of which he perceives the possibility of better organizing his affect (growing). In these instances, new and unorganized affect becomes mobilized for growth. Thus, the mobilization of potential for growth also takes the form of anxiety in therapeutic relationships. Because anxiety promotes growth in these instances, it is termed positive anxiety. Whether the anxiety stems from pathology in the intrapersonal organization of affect, or from the mobilization of affect for growth, in either instance it antecedes the development of capacity to utilize feeling in interpersonal relationships. Looked at from this perspective, anxiety assumes central importance in the whole therapeutic process. The therapist deals with anxiety both in the disorganization and in the reorganization of the personality within his interpersonal relationship to the patient. Anxiety accompanies the most fundamental biological processes of growth, integration, and differentiation, as these occur in psychotherapy. With regression or differentiation, the anxiety expressed is usually of a *negative* quality. When the process involves integration, the anxiety expressed has a more positive aim and function.*

Negative and positive anxiety not only differ in origin and function, but also are subjectively distinguished by the patient. Where the anxiety centers around increasing integration, tenseness

---

* Soren Kierkegaard talks about the despair of not being a person and the despair of being a person (since one can never be all the person one yearns to be).

and expectancy predominate over panic and apprehensiveness. Where the anxiety stems from a breakdown of defensive mechanisms, panic and apprehensiveness assume threatening proportions. Patient and therapist each experience these differences in the process of psychotherapy.

In this sense, then, anxiety accompanies all movement in therapy. Whenever they are present, one can be sure that the interpersonal relationship is moving, or changing in some respect. The anxiety may be in either patient or therapist, as each separately perceives the possibility of more adequate integration in response to the feeling potential in the other person. On the other hand, it may represent a breakdown in a previously rigid and pathological organization of affect in either the patient or the therapist. The movement or change has value in either instance. Negative anxiety associated with a breakdown of the patient's or therapist's defenses usually antecedes positive anxiety associated with the onset of a more healthy organization of affect within the matrix of this relationship. In many cases, however, the opposite is true, and the anxiety first experienced has positive qualities. This is particularly true where the patient seeking help has a great deal of maturity and adequacy, with minimal psychopathology. Such a patient seeks further development of his own potential. The anxiety of the mature therapist likewise has positive aims. Having worked through most of his gross psychopathology, he seeks better integration and organization of his own affect intrapersonally through his relationship with each patient. He has anxiety commensurate with his intuition of the potential depth of the interpersonal relationship with a particular patient. This presages growth for him. The growing pains are the anxiety. The resolution of the anxiety, whether negative or positive, reflects successful growth and better integration in either or both participants.

A great deal could be said of the relationship of anxiety to various psychiatric diseases dealt with in therapy. Such a consideration, however, would take us far afield into the implications of a therapeutic approach to the whole problem of psychopathology. It has been the experience of the authors that psychotic patients present a problem because of the inability of the therapist to empathize with their unorganized affective responses. This makes the development of a therapeutic relationship with the psychotic a more difficult task. Nonetheless, the therapist who attempts therapy with psychotics may rapidly develop a certain amount of positive anxiety because of the primitive quality of the psychotic's personal demands. On this basis, the therapist can develop the relationship, provided he can tolerate his own anxiety.

In contrast, therapy with a neurotic initially demands very little of the therapist since the anxiety in the neurotic is largely organized around a pathological symptom or syndrome. The therapist aims at breaking through this syndrome, creating negative anxiety so that the therapeutic process can continue. Therapy with the neurotic proceeds after the defensive patterns are breached, releasing negative anxiety. Therapy with the psychotic proceeds after enough of the patient's positive anxiety becomes organized to serve as a motivation force for deeper emotional participation. In either case, anxiety becomes the psychological drive which serves as the basis for growth in the patient. In much the same way that growth in other areas depends on stress, so emotional growth originates in stress, one aspect of which is anxiety.

Anxiety in psychotherapy has a specific relationship to the process of symbolization. Symbolization ordinarily binds anxiety, and in the therapeutic process, the patient symbolizes the therapist as a specific method of binding the emerging anxiety within the interpersonal relationship between him and the therapist. This enables the patient to tolerate an increasing amount of affect and to release energy previously bound in neurotic mechanisms. Anxiety also arises in the symbolized therapist, although this ordinarily has a positive quality in direct proportion to the intensity of the negative anxiety in the patient.

Not only does anxiety motivate the important process of symbolization in therapy, but it provides the necessary energy for the other dynamics of therapy. Thus, the transferences of the patient arise out of the anxiety he feels in his relationship with the therapist. Transference does not arise in the beginning phases of therapy where the patient has minimal anxiety in the interpersonal relationship. After the patient develops a symbolic relationship with the therapist, the transference phenomenon occurs primarily as a way of containing the increasing negative anxiety which the patient feels. In the same manner, counter-transference in the therapist arises when the patient's relationship to him provokes infantilism or threatens his defensive mechanisms. His counter-transference contains the resultant negative anxiety. In contrast, where his feelings, including anxiety, are positive in character, the dynamics which these engender in him make up his therapist vector, or what has been referred to in earlier chapters as his "mature counter-transference." All of the psychodynamics which obtain in therapy arise out of, and are motivated by, anxiety in some measure. Introjection, fantasy, projection, etc. arise out of the same matrix. Whether the dynamic is expressed interpersonally or is therapeutically functional depends in each instance on whether it arises out of negative anxiety or positive anxiety. When it arises out of the former, the psychodynamic expressed is that of a patient; when it arises out of the latter, the psychodynamic expressed interpersonally is that of a therapist. This is so whether the therapist-vector or patient-vector be present in either participant at any given time. When the anxiety felt in any relationship is positive in both participants, the relationship can be said to be mature in character. This also defines a mature constructive social interpersonal relationship.

ANXIETY ALTERATIONS IN THE PROCESS OF PSYCHOTHERAPY

The isolation necessary in psychotherapy augments the development of anxiety in the patient in the beginning phases of therapy by removing some of the supports which obtain in the real world. With the isolation comes an increasing awareness by the patient of the possibility for direct satisfaction of his unconscious needs. With the removal of these cultural controls, anxiety, as defined earlier in this chapter, increases in intensity. This makes more sense when one looks upon cultural patterns as acceptable ways of organizing interpersonal affect. The break through out of these interpersonal patterns leaves the affect in the patient relatively disorganized, assuming, of course, no well-integrated intrapersonal organization of affect. Faced with the loss of predetermined patterns of behavior, the patient has little to which to retreat, being insufficiently integrated to organize and express his affect maturely.

As the relationship develops, however, anxiety gradually diminishes in intensity, by becoming organized around the therapist in this relatively acultural but more symbolic relationship. In this matrix, unconscious need and primitive affect slowly organize to express the needs of the patient. Free of many parentally imposed and culturally reinforced patterns of relating, underlying needs are expressed directly. Toward the end of therapy, as the patient turns more and more affectively to the cultural situations, anxiety seems to increase as he once again makes the transition from the relative safety of the therapeutic interpersonal organization of affect to the stress of living in the real community. Anxiety

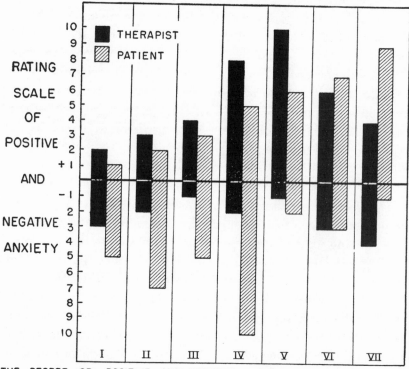

THE DEGREE OF POSITIVE AND NEGATIVE ANXIETY IN PATIENT AND IN THERAPIST AT SUCCESSIVE STAGES OF THE INTERVIEW SEGMENT IN THE THERAPEUTIC PROCESS

Fig. 5

in the ending phase, however, does not have the threatening quality, nor the intensity, of the anxiety which developed as the patient entered the symbolic relationship with the therapist. At that point when the therapeutic process moved into the area of regression, the anxiety of the patient developed in direct proportion to the increasing capacity of the therapist to see the potential in the patient. The therapist's capacity to assay this potential correlates directly with his own positive anxiety, i.e., the gradual recognition of the possibility of his finding new capacities in himself. Thus, at every point, the therapist's increasing positive anxiety buffers the patient's negative anxiety.

The deeper the regression associated with the more primitive transferences the greater is the affective on the part of each participant. The therapist tends to push farther into the therapeutic relationship than does the patient. This precipitates more anxiety in the patient. In the latter part of the regressive phase, and as the therapeutic process approaches the core phase, the patient's negative anxiety amounts to veritable panic. He says, "I feel as though I am going crazy. I'm afraid I'll never come back again." The therapist at this point must assume the responsibility for overwhelming the defensive dynamics of the patient so that the homeostatic state between them becomes bilaterally supportive. The negative anxiety of the patient and the positive anxiety of the therapist are summated then to make an interpersonal homeostasis which enables the patient to go on into the core phase of therapy.

ANXIETY AND COMMUNICATION

The relationship of anxiety to the important problem of communication in psychotherapy presents interesting facets. Like any other form of behavior, communication is based on need, i.e., it is motivated. The deeper the level of communication the more profound the motivation needed for such communication. The needs which motivate such communication may be, first, the need to transmit affect to another and/or the need to understand affect which is perceived only partially. In this sense, communication on an affective, usually nonverbal level almost always follows anxiety in one or both participants. The actual communication represents an interpersonal resolution of shared anxiety. It represents an interpersonal organization of primitive affect into a more economical, less threatening form. Although communication is anteceded by anxiety, the experience of communicating itself is startlingly free of anxiety, and accompanied ordinarily by other more gratifying affective or feeling tones. There comes a sudden increase in anxiety whenever the patient and therapist fail to communicate, i.e., whenever their interpersonal organization of affect has broken down. If the failure to communicate is profound enough, the resulting anxiety may assume almost catastrophic proportions or intensities. The anxiety indicates the breakdown in communication. The above refers essentially to nonverbal affective communication. Anxiety also interferes with verbal ideational communication, but this does not present a problem of any moment in psychotherapy.

Apparently, anxiety also serves as a measure of the quality of the therapeutic process. Actually, the authors believe that the degree of the patient's anxiety in the regressive phase of therapy can be taken as a direct measure of the amount of energy brought to the therapeutic process. Thus the degree of positive anxiety in the therapist, based upon his hope of inducing certain body-image changes in himself, is the limiting factor in the degree of negative anxiety possible for the patient. In the ending phase of therapy, the therapist becomes concerned with integrating the changes brought about in him by this therapeutic experience. The patient's withdrawal thus occasions some anxiety. This places the patient in the role of a therapist. The therapist then becomes, for a moment, the patient to his own patient. This dynamic also enables the patient to see his own potential, and helps effect the termination of the professional-therapeutic relationship.

FUNCTIONS OF ANXIETY FOR THE THERAPIST

The above analysis suggests that the adequate therapist could use his anxiety as an important asset to the psychotherapeutic process. He gauges the movement of the relationship in terms of his perception of the intensity and quality of the patient's anxiety together with the subjective experience of his own anxiety. When the process lags, movement is augmented by those techniques which serve to increase his own positive anxiety or the patient's negative anxiety. Stimulation of anxiety then becomes an over-all procedure for pushing the process of psychotherapy along toward termination. This does not imply, of course, the indiscriminate and insensitive provocation of anxiety in the patient whenever the process has reached an impasse or whenever the therapist feels inadequate. It only implies such provocation as the therapist professionally and personally feels his relationship can adequately organize. On occasion, the therapist, though unsure of the adequacy of his relationship with the patient, may provoke anxiety with the hope of breaking through an enduring impasse. Such calculated risk-taking becomes necessary at times, even though he remains uncertain that the primitive affect so released will take acceptable form.

Anxiety functions for the therapist in a number of specific ways. (1) It antecedes meaningful communication, indicating to the therapist areas of need in the patient and, more significantly, his own areas of emotional blindness. To facilitate this communication, partial regressions in him may serve to establish some resonance with the psychotic segment of the patient. These partial regressions are ordinarily accompanied by anxiety—the anxiety of a temporary disorganization. (2) Apart from communication, development of negative anxiety in the therapist always presages his assumption of patient status. (3) Anxiety also arises whenever the therapist's residual pathology is touched. This provides a basic element in the motivation for pushing his own growing edge and achieving greater personal capacity in his own experiences with patients. The negative anxiety which accompanies any highlighting of his residual pathology usually has another aspect. Growth beyond this point stimulates, in the therapist, a great deal of positive anxiety which he then makes available to the patient. Without such positive anxiety he would be unable to carry the patient through certain critical transitions in the over-all process of treatment. As long as the therapist remains comfortable with his anxiety experiences, and still senses their potential usefulness, he can share these experiences with the patient. When such is not the case, anxiety in the therapist becomes a serious detriment to the process of therapy and sets up a counter-transference impasse.

Repression of affect in either the therapist or the patient has a characteristic action on the therapeutic process as such. Repression in the patient at the onset of treatment produces the recurrent problems faced by every therapist. The release of this repression is brought about by the amount of communicated affect from the therapist. Repression by the therapist, on the other hand, presents quite a different problem. This originates from his response to the patient and involves anxiety aroused by the specific area into which the patient is pushing with his transference. Confronted with repression in the therapist, the patient retreats only to offer to the therapist another facet of his pathology in the effort to establish a therapeutic relationship. Repression in the therapist may take many forms, e.g., a flight into consciousness (interpretation). At times, nonetheless, the therapist's tolerance of the repressions of the patient reassures the patient of the therapist's respect for his individuality and integrity. The limitations of time and the realities of their personal and professional lives effectively govern the repression necessary in the subtle balance of reality and transference. Thus, each one knowing the time limit of the interview can push the limits of his tolerance for anxiety with the sureness of their reality-bound separation at the end of the interview.

Tolerance for anxiety increases as the participants communicate more adequately, in addition to being proportional to the wellness of each. It decreases when the reality limitations of the relationship become uncertain, as well as when the pathology of the therapist dovetails with that of the patient. When either participant's tolerance for anxiety is exceeded, repression occurs. This may reveal itself as increased resistance, symptom formation, anxiety-binding techniques, and flight into consciousness. In any event, the manner in which anxiety arises, is tolerated, or is compromised reflects not only disturbance in the patient, but more significantly the adequacy or inadequacy of his relationship to the therapist.

Repression has a very clear cut relationship to the communication of affect in therapy. The patient, wanting to know the quality of affect in the therapist, represses a certain amount of affect in himself and assays the anxiety developed in the therapist. The therapist, with affective feeling tones about the patient or anxiety about his own participation, unconsciously perceives the patient's response to his repressions. His own participation varies with these unconscious perceptions. When repression in one produces anxiety in the other, the therapeutic process moves along, with assurance in each of the bilateral emotional involvement. To recapitulate, we can define several generalizations. (1) The therapist's denial of the patient's negative anxiety elicits repression in the patient. This is equally true whichever participant expresses patient vectors. (2) Whenever affect in one of the participants induces repressed affect in the other, then the repression spills over to the process itself, with a resultant therapeutic impasse. (3) Repression in the therapist results in a feeling of rejection or feelings of separation in the patient. This separation produces anxiety.

There are technical cues to the presence of repression. Exhaustion of the therapist after an interview indicates his repression during the interview itself. The fatigue arises out of the repression of affect. Along the same line, elation or depression in the therapist ordinarily indicates approaching ending in the relationship. A feeling of urgency or expectancy and of being stimulated ordinarily indicates progress into the core phase of therapy. Intellectualization and theoretical reminiscing about the interview, or expressions of tolerance by the therapist with what has occurred during the interview, are strong evidence of an impasse.

The relationship of anxiety to the impasse can be stated very briefly. An impasse exists whenever one of two situations obtain: (1) where there is an absence of affect in one or both participants over a period of time; (2) where there is a single affect which characterizes the relationship over a period of time. In this latter case, the irreversibility of the persistent feeling is ordinarily based in an impasse. In a more fundamental sense, an impasse exists when both participants are simultaneously patients, both having persistent negative anxiety with no positive anxiety. In such cases, resolution of the impasse almost always produces a rapid increase in the amount of anxiety which then pervades the relationship. This usually originates in an increase in the intensity of the negative anxiety bilaterally which, in turn, gives rise to some positive anxiety in one of the two participants. This provides the necessary motivation for movement out of the impasse into a successive phase of the therapeutic process.

ANXIETY AND AGGRESSION

The specific patterns of interpersonal exchange of feeling which emerge out of anxiety in one of the participants are infinite. These depend on the personality of both participants—their needs, defensive mechanisms, and maturity. Fundamentally, however, anxiety usually eventuates in either repression or aggression. If, because of the quality of the relationship, the anxiety cannot be interpersonally channeled, intrapersonal organization of the anxiety results, i.e., repression, and/or the resultant defense mechanisms associated with repression. In contrast, when the interpersonal relationship has a therapeutic quality so that the anxiety in one of the participants can be organized within it, then the most primitive interpersonal organization of anxiety takes the form of aggression.

Aggression then becomes an important affect channel in the organization of the patient's anxiety into more security-providing behavior. Such a concept of aggression as a necessary affect in psychotherapy needs further clarification. Expression of hostility in the therapeutic relationship is fraught with danger. Because of this, therapists ordinarily hesitate to express any aggressive feelings toward the patient. They even limit the amount of aggression the patient can express. When the primary emphasis centers on the negative qualities of aggression, then these precautions are probably warranted. If the aggression expressed aims at the destruction of the object against which it is directed, then such aggression does serious damage in psychotherapy. Reconsideration, however, of the origin of aggression in the infant provides a clear rationale for its use in psychotherapy. Here, the emphasis lies more on its positive qualities. Anxiety in the infant gives rise first to diffuse motor responses which, when organized and directed against an object in the environment, are called aggressive. Such aggression in infants aims initially not at the destruction of the object, but at securing a relationship with that object necessary for the satisfaction of a need in the infant, usually hunger. Only in the later development of the child when the problem of ambivalence arises does aggression take on a specifically hostile quality. The same sequence holds true in psychotherapy. Anxiety, as primitive unorganized affect in one participant, finds expression within the relationship as an effort to obtain from the other participant the responses necessary to the satisfaction of his needs and the alleviation of his anxiety. This primitive outgoing effort at need satisfaction provides the core of healthy aggression.

Whether or not aggression has a positive aim depends directly on the quality of the anxiety which motivates it. When positive anxiety arises out of the therapist's awareness of the difference between what the patient could be and what the patient is, the resultant aggression has a positive, therapeutic aim. When the therapist introjects the patient and develops a fantasy relationship within himself to the introject, the difference between this relationship and the actual relationship may give rise to severe positive anxiety about their interpersonal relationship. This positive anxiety again gives rise to therapeutic aggression.

When, in contrast, the aggression arises out of negative anxiety in either participant because of a threat to their defense mechanisms, the aggression has a more destructive aim. This has no place in psychotherapy except to precipitate the therapist into doing something about himself.

From positive aggression other more complex affects emerge. These include the varied expressions of love, e.g., parental feelings, sexual response, respect, tenderness, sympathy, and other more complex sentiments. The interpersonal experience of organizing positive aggression and then love out of the same matrix, resolves for the patient, experientially, the core problem of ambivalence. This provides the patient with a behavioral basis for expanding his interpersonal relationship into one compatible with the cultural pattern.

Therapeutic aggression as defined above, when directed against repression in the patient, leads to an increase in the patient's negative anxiety. In contrast, when therapeutic aggression is directed against an area in the patient which had been worked through previously, the aggression elicits a mature response, leading to an increase in positive anxiety. In either instance, in addition to the development of more mature interpersonal affects, aggression in therapy invariably leads to some increase in positive anxiety. After the core phase has been reached, and an adequate relationship between patient and therapist has been established, aggression on the part of the therapist may be inappropriate, and usually signifies the therapist's premonition of ending. Even so, it is usually motivated by positive anxiety and has a positive aim. More complex feelings, with repressive origins like guilt and shame, in the therapist, may mask aggression which has a negative aim.

Summary

This discussion of anxiety has endeavored to clarify its importance in therapy. The concepts of negative and positive anxiety aid in this clarification. The presence of each in the patient and therapist gives rise to specific dynamic changes in the process itself. The functions of anxiety are discussed, including its value as a motivational factor and its organization as a means of developing more adequate interpersonal relationships. The results of repression, aggression, and certain secondary affects are indicated, as well as the significance of anxiety in relation to the problem of the therapeutic impasse.

Through all of this, the role of the therapist as a person becomes increasingly evident. His own dynamics and the anxiety developed in him are regarded as essential vectors; both their origin and the clarification of their role in psychotherapy must be taken up in greater detail. This will be the purpose of the following chapter.

12

The Therapist as a Person

What, after all,
Is a halo? It's only one more thing to keep clean.
Fry, "The Lady's Not for Burning"

In a general sense, persons who deal with psychiatric patients fall into two groups, the nontherapists and the therapists. *Nontherapist*, as a term, should be restricted to the person who either functions only in a custodial sense to patients in a psychiatric hospital, or who serves in a similar way to care for ambulatory psychiatric patients. Included in this group would be the professional administrator and the psychiatrist whose relationship to patients is a business one. The nontherapeutic psychiatrist seldom reacts to the child in his patients; he does not really accept them in terms of their potential capacity. His artificial role-playing contributes little to the patient's growth, though it may make significant contributions to their current adjustment. He denies his own patient needs, does not identify with patients in any but the most superficial sense, and has never had any adequate therapy himself. The nontherapist has access to his own fantasy life, but is unable to make that part of his life available to other people. One of the most conspicuous examples in this category is the psychiatrist who has had an incomplete psychotherapeutic experience, and is thereby categorically determined to keep himself from any entangling alliances.

In contrast, the *Social Therapist* forces growth in persons around him. He accepts his own patient need and his fantasy life. He thereby can identify with patients and their needs and can go with the patient into the symbolic experience of a therapeutic relationship. In the course of this, he accepts their projections upon him, reacts positively to the child in the other person, and carries the person into "therapy," although in ordinary circumstances, not through the *core* phase of therapy. Because he has satisfied his own patient needs, he knows his own limitations and will frequently refer patients who need deeper therapy to a professional therapist. This is the usual role taken by an adequately treated patient, or by a therapist who is still immature but functioning in an honestly therapeutic way.

Like the social therapist, the *Professional Depth Therapist* has been a patient, and has resolved the major portion of his infantile transference needs. He can identify with his patients in the specific sense of seeing the patient as his child self while he is critically aware of his limitations in the therapeutic sense. As a professional, he learns to separate his therapeutic function from his real life. His motivations have to do with his own efforts at reconstructing his body image, and he thereby accepts the therapist-vector in the patient as a specific dynamic in the therapeutic process. He can take patients through the therapeutic experience, help them constructively with the symbolic relationship and also with their relationship to him as a person. By virtue of his personal motivations in the therapeutic relationship, he goes to sufficient depth with each patient to gain from the therapeutic potential of the patient. In thus being patient to his patient, he strengthens the patient's capacity to become a separate, growing person.

It is not difficult from the above to visualize the *Ideal Therapist* as one who is able to function as a professional depth therapist to any patient. Rarely, someone develops this degree of maturity; but if he does, he usually becomes so out of synchrony with the culture that he is unacceptable in it. If psychiatry could offer the young therapist adequate enough treatment for himself, he might become so mature that he could live beyond and above this rejection by the culture.

The dynamics of psychotherapy are intra-psychic to the therapist; therefore, an inquiry into the motivations and growth of a professional therapist has practical significance. Responsibility for the development of social therapists on any planned basis has not been accepted by our society. In contrast, the discipline of psychotherapy has been advanced through improved selection and better training programs for professional psychotherapists. Psychiatry must continue to be particularly concerned with those aspects of the therapist as a person which seem most relevant to his professional effectiveness, yet each therapist has a professional, a personal, and a social life, all of which contribute to his capacity as a psychotherapist.

Community and the Therapist

Inasmuch as the therapist emerges from the community which imbues him with certain of its qualities, his therapeutic efforts reflect some of the dynamics of this interrelationship. The community ordinarily pictures the therapist, and to some degree the doctor, as a stereotype, so that he is seldom seen as a person. For example, the community finds it difficult to think of a doctor as becoming ill. Sickness temporarily excludes him from the profession in their minds. By the same token, they are firm in their belief that the doctor will not become infected even when exposed to the same bacteria which they assume can infect them. These feelings, of course, are part of their projection of the doctor as omnipotent.

More recently, the doctor has come to be regarded also as an impersonal scientist, more interested in the illness than in himself or the patient. This fantasy picture exerts considerable pressure, not only on the community itself, but also on the doctor's picture of himself. Since the doctor cannot modify the community's projection, he must develop a healthy relationship with the community in spite of these problems. Failing in this, he automatically becomes less of a person, and may become an almost pure symbol to the community. These projections from the community onto the physician are significant to the professional therapist as a person, since his function as a professional therapist depends on his access to the community as a real person.

Not only does the community project qualities onto the therapist and make of him more a symbol than a person, but psychiatrists themselves tend to accept the validity of these projections as they operate within the psychotherapeutic relationship. Such an acceptance of projections underlies the acceptance in psychiatry of the importance of roles within the therapeutic relationship. Until very recently, many psychotherapists felt that they provided a neutral screen on which the patient projected certain roles. The projected role presumably motivated their participation so that the patient's transference became the sole motivation in the continuing therapeutic relationship. Some psychiatrists ascribe to psychotherapy the unreality of drama. Each participant presents himself in a role which has meaning in terms of his past experience, but which, in some measure, is inappropriate to his total person. Role-playing based on the unconscious fantasies of either patient or therapist is certainly a valid and effective dynamic in psychotherapy. This has been well documented through the technique of psychodrama, which uses roles and dramatization extensively. The acting out of roles has validity in that such role-playing often provides rapid and effective ways of developing a deep bilateral unconscious relationship. The danger lies in the misconception that psychotherapy is only role-playing.

The demands made on the professional psychotherapist as a person give rise to some of the common difficulties encountered in psychotherapy. Ideally, the major part of the therapist's life is private and personal, to which is attached a small, well-separated professional life; this interferes only minimally with his private living. The ideal is more readily realized by most other professional people than it is by the therapist. His person constitutes the major tool of his profession. The point at which his private life begins and his professional life ends is always uncertain, changes constantly, and provokes a great deal of anxiety in him and in his intimate associates. The authors, in discussing the use of deep feeling on the part of the therapist, have repeatedly heard an experienced psychiatrist say, "I used my own deep feeling responses in therapy early in my life as a therapist, but found that such constant, deep involvement with patients disrupted my personal life and family to such an extent that I have had to give it up even though I felt it was worth while." A rigid separation of the therapist's personal from his professional life often ensues. This division detracts from his integrity, and ways should be found to enable the therapist to function on a deep level while at the same time not jeopardizing his personal life. A presentation of some of the major aspects of the therapist's life may serve as a frame of reference within which this dilemma can be resolved.

The therapist has three distinct aspects as a person: *the professional person, the social person,* and *the individual person.* As a professional person, he is cast in a number of separate and sometimes confusing roles which overlap. He most often is a physician, frequently an administrator, often a scientist, and, of course, also a therapist. Because of his training as a physician, he feels responsibilities, not only for the emotional well-being of the patient, but also for the physical health, and at times, the social effectiveness of the patient. These latter responsibilities may interfere seriously with the more limited role of a therapist. His being a physician contributes to his capacity to see the person as a whole, but at the same time, his training may make it difficult for him to be an effective therapist who demands that the patient accept responsibilities which ordinarily are assumed by the physician.

In his role as an administrator, he must be objective, direct in action, and decisive in real matters. This differs from his therapeutic orientation. Furthermore, his administrative role may bring certain satisfactions and certain changes in the therapist's relationship to patients so that his professional therapeutic function seems less important. Administrators who maintain their capacity as therapists, do so by separating the two roles so that they can partake in the satisfactions of each. The therapist who faces a difficult patient may retreat from this emotional responsibility by becoming the administrator. One successful way to resolve this ambivalence is to function in a group setting where he can be administrator to one patient and therapist to another. The relationship of the administrator to the community as a whole creates additional problems. He endeavors to make himself part of this community, see its needs and contribute as he can. This may make it more difficult for him to see the patient as a unit as well as part of the community.

Administrative responsibilities for the patient of another therapist commonly include arrangements for custody of the patient; assurances to the patient, so that he will continue in therapy despite temporary difficulties with the therapist; mediation of the family's control of the patient; a buffering of the family's feelings about the patient and his therapy as these feelings are intensified in the process of therapy; and adjudication of the community's reality demands about the patient's behavior during and after therapy.

A fundamental principle of therapy involves isolation of the therapeutic relationship from the real world of the patient. If the doctor tries to assume both therapeutic and administrative responsibilities, he compromises seriously his therapeutic effectiveness. Some psychiatric hospitals have found that division of these two responsibilities has appreciably increased the effectiveness of therapy and reduced the time required for its completion. The separation of psychiatric management from treatment promises to be a major advance in psychiatric effectiveness. Research in this area could bring about more effective coordination and separation of these two functions, since this seems to augment the patient's recovery.

The interest of the therapist as a professional person ordinarily includes the effort to expand the knowledge within his field. Increasingly, therapists are doing investigative work. The methodology of the scientist, together with the use of recording and measuring instruments, carries with it responsibilities for an objective relationship to patients which often works to the disadvantage of the individual patient who has a need for subjective participation on the part of the therapist. Scientific interest often interferes with perception of and response to a particular patient. An interest in generalizations usually interferes with the highly individual needs of the patient. Scientific investigations and constant experimentation tend to distort the spontaneity necessary in the therapeutic relationship. In the therapist who is also a scientist, this overlapping and distortion cannot be completely resolved. One will always partially compromise the patient whose treatment is undertaken with the added aim of investigation. Such distortion can best be limited where the therapist-scientist works in a group setting. Here, the misuse of his investigative objective as a retreat from his therapeutic responsibilities can be controlled, to some extent, by his colleagues. Separation of the scientific function from the therapeutic can be achieved in much the same manner as therapy and administration are separated, but to a lesser degree. As a therapist, his responsibilities are singularly limited. He acts as catalyst to the growth potential in patients. This precludes concern with discreet physical problems, custodial problems, or research problems. His is a transient, highly emotional, subjective relationship with a unique individual in a sharply limited situation. This isolated and limited participation on the part of the therapist is most effective when denuded of administrative and investigative contaminants. Some overlapping and contamination is unavoidable. Nevertheless, his value to patients increases as he minimizes these distortions as far as possible and the use of group practice appears to be the most advantageous procedure available for the accomplishment of this.

The Professional Therapist as a Social Self

The therapist becomes symbolic to many people in the community who, because they overreact to the significance of his professional role, make his social relations difficult. In his social living and associations, he lives under the constant shadow of this symbolic role. He is symbolic to his neighbors and to many of his professional associates. The therapist can't spend a social evening without facing the recurrent problem of an acquaintance or friend expressing his patient-needs. No matter how mature the therapist may be, his therapeutic response in this setting is always circumscribed and inadequate.

His dilemma approximates that of the general practitioner whose friends demand curbstone consultations without physical examination. This precludes the therapist from obtaining those natural, gratifying, social relationships so necessary for his continued well-being. The therapist needs normal social gratifications as buffers for the intense and circumscribed interpersonal relationships demanded by his professional job. Without them, he tends to withdraw from diverse and natural social contacts. This withdrawal predisposes toward the development among therapists of a sub-culture of their own. Such limited social living can never be as satisfying as nonstructured contacts with various neighbors and friends who present no psychiatric claims. The development of a subgroup of therapists can never fully fill his social life. The constant demand for his therapist function in social situations continues to occur in the subgroup of therapists. He must cultivate a group of people who have satisfied their therapeutic needs or who have long since become so fatalistic about their own growing that they see a psychotherapist as they see a carpenter or a plumber. This group could become as satisfactory for a therapist as for the others. It becomes a source of great satisfaction to a therapist to enter a social situation where other persons respond to him as a person and not as a therapist, yet the therapist will only cultivate such a group when his own therapeutic needs have been satisfied.

The Development of the Therapist

There is no exact point at which an individual ceases to be either a patient or a nontherapist, and suddenly, because of training or experience, becomes a professional therapist. Certain events occur which mark his development to professional maturity. These include his maturation as an individual, unique person; his experience as a patient, whether with a social therapist, or with a professional therapist, or both; his experience as a therapist both socially and professionally; and his professional training. At any given time, he presents a summation of these four factors. A therapist may be well trained professionally, but have limited experience as a patient; or he may be very mature as an individual, very experienced as a therapist, and still have limited training. Distortions appear where there are marked discrepancies between his relative development in these different areas. For example, it is not unusual to see a professional therapist who, because of experience and because of satisfying his patient needs in his work with patients, becomes an adequate therapist with no treatment from a training therapist. Similarly, we find therapists who have had adequate therapy for their own patient-needs, followed by extensive experience as a therapist, but are still limited in their effectiveness. Ordinarily, the various dimensions of professional maturity expand simultaneously.

The development of the therapist has a natural history. Every person has certain therapeutic capacities which he utilizes almost from birth. His experiences, both as therapist and as patient, mark many of the critical areas of his own growth as a person. These experiences provide the substrata out of which the professional therapist develops. In this sense, the nontherapist is an individual who has reached a plateau in his growth so early that his therapeutic potential remains unavailable to himself or others.

The experience of being a patient marks the beginning of professional growth as a therapist. The evolution of patient status has been discussed in an earlier chapter. The dynamics which occur in the ordinary patient hold true in his development also. He has certain dissatisfactions with his life experience along with a need to develop his person so that he obtains more satisfaction either internally or socially. He becomes a patient first in a nonprofessional situation. This arises out of his multiple experiences with social therapists in his ordinary living. From this he precipitates himself into a professional therapeutic situation and emerges from that to become a social therapist, that is, the therapist who brings to his social contacts both the capacity to utilize reality and the capacity to utilize the fantasy component existent in all interpersonal relationships. Having developed his own maturity in the context of these experiences as a patient, and on the basis of his beginning experiences as a therapist in a social situation, he then becomes a neophyte professional therapist. The problem at this stage becomes one of expanding his experiences as a therapist and simultaneously obtaining professional training to reinforce his professional growth. The neophyte therapist often finds it necessary, because of this therapeutic inadequacy, to return to the status of patient and obtain deeper experience as a patient. Through this, implemented by growing experience as a therapist, and by professional training, he may develop into a mature therapist.

The mature therapist, thus, has attained a certain maturity as a person; has had a deep patient experience so that he is no longer burdened with transference problems; has had experience in a therapist role with many patients; and has had some professional training. He becomes ready, at this point, to integrate technical auxiliaries with his therapist capacity. He may develop a specific technique to some considerable degree, but as he becomes more mature, he becomes less dependent on techniques and brings to the therapeutic situation his maturity in such a way that technical means become less important.

In summary, the development of the therapist follows a recognizable pattern. Beginning as a nontherapist, he successively becomes a patient in a social situation, then a patient in a professional situation, a therapist in a social context, the neophyte professional therapist, and the mature therapist. Finally he becomes an experienced therapist, who can bring his therapeutic capacity quickly and deeply to any patient without circumscribing this capacity by the techniques and paraphernalia of the professional person. This continuum involves the progressive development of four facets of the person: his experience as a patient, his maturation as a person, his experience as a therapist, and his professional training.

MOTIVATIONS OF THE THERAPIST. The need which originates the decision on the part of a physician to specialize in psychotherapy differs little from that need which originally motivated him to become a doctor. He senses that in this type of professional role he can best find the satisfactions which seem necessary to him. Here too, he finds a suitable environment for the partial expression of his pathological facets, while at the same time protecting himself from social censure.

There is little need to discuss the motivations which urge the young man into the practice of medicine. Certainly, in addition to the pathological motivations, e.g., grandiosity, belief in the magical, noncensured sexual fantasies, missionary zeal, there are real and mature motivations stemming from the applicant's perception of the satisfactions and security to be obtained in the medical profession.

Whatever the needs which originate the decision to become a psychotherapist, the process of his development as a therapist carries him beyond them. His patient experience so alters these motivations that the needs originating the decision to become a therapist are seldom the needs or motivations which promote his continuing as a professional therapist. The decision, however, usually centers around his perception that here is a profession in which he can consistently and constructively push the "growing edge" (limits) of his own maturity.

TRAINING. Having made the decision (primarily an unconscious one) to become a professional psychotherapist, the individual enters a new phase of development. In the ordinary course of events, and on the basis of his previous experience in medicine, he decides to implement his decision by appropriate didactic training. This implementation may, in some ways, be unfortunate. The needs to become a psychotherapist stem from deeply personal and emotional drives within the person of the applicant. The contrast between the academic, didactic atmosphere and the highly subjective motivations which send him into training, frequently lead to disillusionment. This results from his failure to obtain, at this critical time, full satisfaction of the needs which originated his decision. It may be that the objectivity of the training causes him to utilize objectivity as a method of isolating and holding in suppression his personal therapeutic motivations. The disillusionment may even eventuate in his abandoning professional training prematurely. More often, however, it leads to an abandonment of his psychotherapeutic impulses. He develops a series of reaction-formations as a means for tolerating the discrepancy between his patient-need and the necessarily impersonal quality of professional training. He takes on, in the course of his training, a basic conceptual framework about personality which may extend into his concept of himself and become a limiting factor in his growth, both as a person and as a therapist. His intellectual comprehension of the dynamics of behavior and of pathology then become pegs on which he hangs, or categorizes, his deeply personal needs. The striking differences in the value of professional training to this person and to the individual who has already had a deep patient experience, and some therapist experience, is tremendous. To this latter person, the didactic training does not constitute a rejection of his personal needs. Nor does he come out of it with any implicit conviction that the patient cannot get well. He has grown as a person. He has been in the patient's chair, felt the need and anxiety which the patient feels, and finally, has had some experience with the demands made upon a therapist by patients and some supervision in his work with patients. With this background of experience, he can assimilate the didactic training more realistically. Psychodynamics, psychopathology, psychiatric nosology, and even theoretical principles about psychotherapy are accepted or rejected on the basis of his own experience. His evaluation of his own professional training is realistic. Each part of it becomes integrated into a whole which has personal significance and which is related to the fundamental purpose of the psychotherapist.

On the basis of the above considerations, training in psychiatry, particularly of the psychotherapist, should be delayed until such a time as the trainee has had sufficient patient and therapist experience to provide a resilient basis upon which the academic training can build. This, in essence, is no different from the general pattern in industry. It is not wise to make an individual an executive until he has had some experience as a workman and as a participant in the basic function of the industry as such. Some other precautions seem to be indicated. It is impossible to train a psychotherapist didactically. The capacity of a psychotherapist evolves only with his experience in the therapeutic relationship both as patient and therapist. Didactic training, prior to such experience, is not only of limited worth, but may even be a serious detriment to his further growth as a psychotherapist and, in many instances, makes more certain his continuing as a nontherapist. This is particularly true when didactic training follows immediately the decision to become a psychotherapist. In this instance, such training stultifies the growth which would naturally have followed, if the personal needs which originated the decision had been gratified in a therapeutic context. Results in education come from handling felt needs.

Therefore, training in psychiatry, in following this same principle, should be brought to the young therapist at a time when he is successful with some patients and struggling to be more successful with his patients. Then he is reaching out for something and help with the problem becomes personal, deeply significant, and rapidly integrated into his own functioning.

Implicit in what has been said is a belief that training for the psychotherapist must be secondary to his personal involvement in the therapeutic process. Many people going into psychotherapy as a profession after three years of professional training have learned to dissociate themselves and their feelings from their contact with patients. This means that no matter how adequate their technical ability, their contact with patients will be superficial, and actually one would be straining a point to call them therapists. They are really trained psychiatrists functioning as diagnosticians. But since they do not believe that therapy can be anything for them, personally, they can be of only limited value to most of the patients they see. Implicitly they have decided that, as patients, they themselves are hopeless.

A partial answer to this problem lies in requiring didactic therapy early in the training of the psychotherapist. This may suffice to answer the needs which originate the applicant's decision to become a psychotherapist. Even if therapy results in his abandoning his training, each will have gained. There are, however, some very serious deficiencies in this type of training program. It is even unfortunate that such therapy is considered didactic. One of the major defects in such a training program stems from the inadequate relating of the neophyte therapist to many and varied patients during the period when he himself is in treatment. Didactic therapy for the applicant assumes greater significance to the trainee if, at the same time, he functions as a therapist. This latter experience provides the type of stress needed so that his so-called didactic experience can become deeply personal. By didactic therapy, in this sense, is meant the interviews demanded of a trainee as part of an integrated training program in psychiatry and psychotherapy. Often, such therapy begins didactically but becomes deeply personal, and the benefit which the patient-trainee obtains from it resembles that which would ordinarily accrue from therapy with any patient. He has, however, an additional problem. In addition to the utilization in his personal life of the growth which he obtains from therapy, he must bring the emotional learning which occurs in therapy to his function as a therapist. This latter development is catalyzed better if, while undergoing a didactic therapy, he is, at the same time, confronted with the stresses of being a therapist, including the demands of patients and the constant recognition of his own inadequacies as a therapist. It has been shown that his choice of patients during the time will indicate some of his own needs, and may even catalyze the interviews with his own therapist. Whatever the procedure followed, the general principle needs emphasis. A therapist needs deep and pervasive personal psychotherapy as a beginning step in his own development as a psychotherapist. It constitutes the primary requirement for becoming a psychotherapist. Its aim should be the resolution of all major transference problems in the neophyte therapist. Until this aim is achieved, the psychotherapist, to complete his growth, should be compelled to continue as a patient.

Surprisingly, the young therapist frequently has very good results with patients. He brings to his patient, not only his maturity and his wellness, but also, a certain amount of his immaturity. His transference needs emerge so often that the supervisor finds it difficult to decide who has helped whom. In other words, the young therapist becomes the patient frequently during the interviews. Although the willingness of the young therapist to share his immaturities seems to be an effective dynamic in helping the patient, nonetheless, it involves serious dangers which demand close supervision by a mature therapist with active intervention when necessary. If working alone, the young trainee would be liable to gross transference problems which would limit both his effectiveness and maturation. Supervision in this phase of the training requires intimate personal contact supplemented by free interchange among a group of trainees. They work out their impasses with their patients jointly, and catalyze each other. Even after didactic training has provided the trainee with both professional understanding and an opportunity for a deep personal therapeutic experience, there follows an interim maturation from the status of a neophyte therapist to that of a mature therapist. The interim growth involves the deepening of his patient and therapist experience as each of these erupts in his professional functioning. His experience as therapist highlights his problem areas and expands his "growing edge." During this interim period, he will repeatedly find himself inadequate to different patients and to varying needs. He will develop anxieties which, after a period of time, will center around certain specific aspects of the therapist-patient relationship. Patients, in many instances, will delineate his limitations in these areas.

GROWTH IN TREATING PATIENTS. Being a therapist offers many types of satisfaction, including its contribution to personal growth. The importance of the latter is reflected in the oft-repeated notion that parents grow up by raising their children. The continued challenge of the patient's demands for greater integration on the part of the therapist, for his deeper participation in their own suffering, and for help in their struggle with their world and with themselves, inevitably produce personal growth in the therapist. In an even more significant way, the patient who has thus involved the therapist as a person contributes to his personal growth in the process of ending the therapeutic experience. Just as the adolescent can challenge his parent and sometimes offer him significant insights, the patient who is about to leave the therapist is free to challenge the inadequacies of the therapist as a person. Simultaneously, of course, the patient reinforces his integration by expressing the deep satisfactions of the relationship, either directly or indirectly, and by the very fact of leaving. Some of the implicit stresses created in the therapist are even more powerful. For example, the fact of the patient getting better and, as it were, growing past him, pushes him toward increased growth.

The patient's capacity to mature the therapist is, of course, limited. The patient rarely offers the therapist a full experience, but merely challenges him and points up his need for greater adequacy in certain areas and for further personal therapy. Most therapists accept the fact that they get help from their patients, as well as from their colleagues. This help may come under the guise of supervision or in professional discussion of a patient. At other times, the therapist may develop a close colleague relationship so that the latter makes a more direct, substantial contribution to his personal growth. In the event that the therapist feels uncertain in his relationship to colleagues, as so often happens, then he seeks professional help elsewhere with more formal arrangements. Group experience with colleagues has a limited value and, in certain situations, even the mature therapist suffers if his professional and personal reservations prevent him from taking up deep personal needs with the same depth and purpose and straightforwardness that characterized his original therapeutic experience. No therapist has approached the limits of maturity and all therapists tend to protect their vested interest and professional isolation to their own detriment.

CONTINUING MOTIVATIONS OF THE DEPTH THERAPIST. Repeated reference has been made, in previous chapters, to the motivations which impel individuals to become physicians or psychotherapists. Some generalizations have been made, but specific motivations are unique to each individual. Work as a professional person can answer many and varied personal needs. Some of these are admittedly immature, while others are mature. This section deals only with those needs and motivations which impel the practicing psychotherapist to continue doing therapy. If the original infantile motivations persist in the therapist, he remains immature. The motivations discussed here are primarily those of the mature therapist who has, by virtue of his own therapy and continued experience with patients and colleagues, matured to a point where new motivations arise. As is true in any form of behavior, the drives in the mature therapist are overdetermined. Ego satisfactions, economic security, social status, and other reality satisfactions probably represent a good part of his motive power. Beneath these ego motivations, unconscious motivations are at work. Only by virtue of the satisfactions of these deep unconscious drives can he persist in his exhausting role.

The first of these can be termed *residuals*. No individual ever completely loses his infantile fantasies. This is true even when infantile needs are most adequately satisfied in deep psychotherapy. The remaining or residual affective tones determine the persistent identity of his character structure. This generalization is as true of the psychotherapist as of other individuals. In the ordinary mature individual, the affective memory of his transference fantasies plays a relatively unimportant role in his total behavior and comes to the forefront only in situations where the person has to resonate to the pathology of others in order to communicate adequately in social relationships. These residuals underlie his appreciation and enjoyment of those areas of our cultural living which are based on unconscious fantasies, e.g., esthetics, drama, and mythology. In the professional therapist, however, the residuals assume greater importance. In continued deep therapy, where the fantastic component dominates, his residuals are constantly stimulated and assume relatively greater importance in his motivations. The capacity of psychiatric patients not only to demand the maximum strength of the therapist, but just as often to seek out his areas of greatest weakness, pinpoint these residuals. Their greatest value as a motivating factor in the therapist lies in their providing him a means of effectively articulating with the unconscious fantasies of his patients.

The second motivational area is that of *slivers* which remain after the major transference problems have been adequately worked through. Many areas of *minor transference difficulties* are not worked through in psychotherapy. Again, in the ordinary person, these are unimportant interpersonally since they do not involve critical areas. To the professional therapist, however, because of the multiplicity of his therapeutic relationships, they give rise to frequent and varied interpersonal impasses. During therapy, these are continually being worked through by the therapist-vector in the patient, and they represent a major source of satisfaction to the therapist. Each time an impasse is resolved, such a sliver problem has probably been resolved in the process. Together, these make up the "growing edge" of the therapist's maturity which he constantly expands in his professional function.

The third area of motivations reflects *reparative or remedial needs* originating in his own therapy. Certain aspects of his intrapsychic structure are destroyed in his own adequate therapy. This necessitates reconstruction in order to provide the therapist with maximum integration of his own personality. One could say that depth therapy effectively destroys the child's introject of the omnipotent punitive parent, and in the process of extruding this introject, the loving parent is always, to some extent, destroyed. This destruction of the introject leaves the personality of the therapist wanting. His growth necessitates the image of a parent in order to cement more adequately the structure of his own person. He does this by being an adequate parent to his patients, who, as has been seen, represent on a very deep level his own child-self. This continued parental function provides major satisfactions to the therapist, primarily in that it is accompanied by a slow but effective reconstruction within himself of a parent image. Maximum economy of the person necessitates some effective superego component. With the reconstruction of the parent through his therapeutic activity, he redevelops within himself a nonpunitive, flexible, but effective superego. The importance of this reflects itself in the increasing satisfactions the therapist obtains from feeling that he is a part of the culture and capable of being better integrated in the society within which he lives. His motivations for expanding his participation in social and cultural areas assume increasing significance the longer he does therapy. Because of the cultural tendency to isolate the therapist, together with the positive satisfactions he finds in community living, his needs for such participation become cumulatively more intense. The psychological contrasts between the area of his major participation, i.e., fantasies in therapy, and the relative isolation of his extra-therapeutic life, creates a deep need for constant reinforcement from reality and participation in acceptable cultural living. Psychotherapy is, by nature, somewhat acultural, and at times, seems anticultural. The feelings which arise in the therapist because of this demand constant reassurance that he is, and can be, an integral part of the various communities within which he lives.

The very deepest motivation which impels the therapist to continue to do therapy arises in the satisfaction of his most primitive needs. The outcome of the most adequate therapy is essentially the clarification of one's relationships to others as these are specifically determined in early life. The individual emerges with a mature freedom to participate realistically in many interpersonal relationships, free of the transference inhibitions and defenses which circumscribed his relationships prior to the therapy. This maturity with reference to others is further augmented in the mature therapist by the satisfactions obtained in "sliver growth" and the other minor areas of motivation presented above. In a broader sense, his work with patients subsequent to therapy ordinarily succeeds in integrating him successfully with his culture and his community. The ultimate outcome, then, is satisfactory maturity with reference to other individuals, and a comfortable acceptance of his cultural status.

There remains one relationship, however, which is not touched significantly by his initial therapeutic experience. This involves his relationship to himself. More specifically, it involves the relationship of his adult self to a series of selves which have crystallized intra-psychically throughout the years. The integration of his self component, so that he is as free in his relationship to himself as he is in his relationship to others, represents one of the most fundamental needs of the therapist as, indeed, of any person. The motive toward obtaining this self-integration assumes paramount importance in the psychotherapist, as distinguished from other individuals. In the mature person, the relationship of the self to the self constantly alters, usually toward increasing integration. This results from the fact of his maturity in the relationship of the self to other selves and to reality. This is true of any mature person in whom integrity accrues by virtue of his maturity. The problem of integrity assumes critical significance to those individuals who do psychotherapy. Sometimes it is distressing to encounter an individual whose adequacy and maturity in interpersonal relationships and reality function are very obvious, but whose intrapersonal relationship of his various selves to each other, i.e., his integrity, is lamentable. From this point of view, his functioning as a therapist represents a concerted effort on his part to obtain increasing intrapersonal integrity by virtue of his use of the patient as a projective self which he integrates with the nonprojective selves he uses therapeutically. Through his projection onto the patient, whom he may alternately see as any one of his multiple selves, he succeeds in getting (psychologically) an intrapersonal experience from a series of interpersonal experiences. It can't be said too frequently that his projection of any one of his multiple selves onto the patient is not pathological, since they are not transference projections, but represent mature efforts on his part to extend the boundaries of his own person to include, by introjection, the needs and growth potential of each patient. He responds to the patient because the patient has come to be one part of him.

The togetherness between him and the patient is the residual of successful integration of one part of the therapist with the rest of his person. In this very specific way, each time the therapist succeeds with a patient, he has increased his own integrity in some measure, and has clarified some aspect of the relationship of his various selves to each other.

BODY IMAGE. The efforts to reconstruct the parent within the mature therapist, together with the effort to reconstruct the superego, and in an over-all sense, reintegrate the segments of the person, i.e., the need for the development of a well-integrated self, all represent motivations toward increasing self unity, or increasing the integrity of the self. The locus of such reintegration, particularly in the primitive aspects of the personal self, is the body schema. The psychological concept of self is central in any mature person, and expresses itself and its constant change in what has been referred to in the literature as the Body Image. Diseases of the self are spoken of as representing fragmentations of the body. Thus, the terms "falling apart," "nervous break-down," "loosing his head," "up in arms," "beside himself," "has himself in hand," "all torn up," and a thousand other expressions, reflect the primacy of one's concept of one's own body as the locus of his concept of himself.

Fragmentations of the body image are produced in any physical illness. These alterations in the body image produced by pain, fever, etc., are always accompanied by some disturbance in the psychological component of the body image. This intimate relationship provides one workable basis for an understanding of psychosomatic medicine. In physical disease where trauma, amputation, either surgical or accidental, occur, the distortion produced in the body image with its emotional overtones is most marked, e.g., phantom limb. In these instances, compensatory psychological mechanisms are at work to repair the body image as rapidly as possible, sometimes involving even hallucinations in an otherwise mature person. The central point to be inferred from all of this is the fundamental significance of the body image as the locus of the personality and of disease of the personality. The maintenance of its integrity is probably the central aim of homeostatic mechanisms in psychological areas.

The concept of body image, although fundamentally psychological, can be defined more specifically in terms of the central nervous system. The evidence for such a persisting body schema as an organizing principle in behavior of the individual becomes primary in psychiatric patients. The most specific evidence, however, is seen in the phantom limb syndrome, and less clearly in physical illnesses where the patient's experience of his body is altered.

Affective attitudes in the normal person are often accompanied by changes in posture, in body muscle tone, and in the felt experience of the body. The depressed person walks differently, stands differently, and feels his body in a different way from the elated individual. Primitive feelings are accompanied by specific changes in posture or muscle tone and in the central perception of one's body. Much evidence has accumulated indicating that these postural changes not only are specific to different feelings in the same individual, but also may be similar in all individuals. Anger, for example, involves autonomic activity, but in addition is accompanied by changes in body position and body sensation. Confirmation of the universality of body image experience accompanying a specific feeling is the fact of their communication. In the normal individual, feeling is thus ordinarily communicated with more accuracy than is possible through language. The autonomic changes accompanying any emotion are fairly nonspecific, for example, in fear and anger. Nonetheless, other individuals easily distinguish fear from anger. The observer can differentiate emotions with ease. The differential factor in many emotions may well be these body image changes. These observations supplement our understanding of the manner in which the child first develops his concept of reality. His perception of stimuli are closely interrelated with the response, usually muscular, which he makes. The efferent response itself is the significant part of the perception, rather than the sensory stimuli. This, at any rate, is true in the very earliest stages of growth. In a sense, he learns to perceive the outer world through his perception of his body responses to the outer world. This response occurs essentially in his muscular-skeletal system so that the proprioceptive systems are most primitively involved in these earliest perceptions. One can almost make perceptions of the outer world interchangeable on this level with the perceptions of one's own body. It may be that our responses to the outer world in later life, and our conception of reality, has an ever-changing but persistent representation within the person, localized essentially in the muscle system. This, in addition to those areas in the central nervous system where muscle tone and posture are experienced and integrated, make up the body image.

Therapy radically alters the body image, correcting distortions that were produced in it by infantile fantasies. Subsequent to therapy, the patient's growth depends on his better integration of the body schema. Depth therapy itself represents an assault of some severity on the body image. Like a surgical assault, it is necessary and constructive. Nonetheless, depth therapy invariably leaves secondary sequelae in body image distortions which motivate the individual post-therapeutically. These are more important in the psychotherapist, since he continually exposes his body image to minor fragmentations associated with his therapeutic relationship with patients. Because of this, the reconstruction of the body image assumes greater importance as a basic need in the therapist. Initially, the growth of the body image arises out of the child's early interpersonal relationships. It assumes its underlying structure when the child first succeeds in demarcating himself from the rest of reality. This demarcation develops around the intra-psychic image of his own body. As his interpersonal relationships expand and reality makes its impressions more vigorously, this image takes on more definite form. The psychopathology which results from early relationships carries through life as distortions of the body image. Alterations in the patient's image of his body accompany any regression in adult life. Psychotherapy, since it involves regression, is associated ultimately with an alteration of the body image. When successful, these pathological distortions are corrected. The problem of arriving at a new integration after the original distortions are altered by therapy, in addition to the temporary imbalance produced by the therapeutic impact on the body image, are both worked through by the patient in his growth subsequent to therapy. Reintegration on the basis of extended experience is always necessary. Successful therapy results in such security in the self that ordinary stresses do not fragment his body image (his integrity). The effort to secure further integration of the body image appears as a significant, and probably the most fundamental, unconscious motivation of the therapist. This amounts to a deep need for better personal integration, and greater capacity to utilize one's total self in all behavior. These needs are satisfied fragmentarily in every successful therapeutic relationship the therapist establishes. The exact manner in which adequate treatment of the patient results in some change toward better integration in the therapist remains unknown to date. The fact of this occurring, however, has been affirmed frequently in the experience of the authors and their colleagues.

The same phenomenon occurs when parents achieve greater adequacy by virtue of having been successful parents. More specifically, successful participation in any intense interpersonal situation brings strength to the individuals for subsequent adequacy in similar situations. In some manner, these experiences increase the integration of the participant personalities. This the therapist seeks in his professional experiences.

Summary

This chapter has reviewed the personal life of the therapist as it influences his professional activity and is modified by the tensions and satisfactions of his profession. Some effort was made to present a working classification of therapists. This involved a review of the factors which distinguish the nontherapist from the therapist, the most central of which is that the therapist have adequate and deep psychotherapy for himself. A division was made between the social therapist and the professional therapist, and the characteristics of each were presented in some detail.

The problem of the therapist's integration in the community was reviewed. He was seen to have status in three areas. He is, first, the therapist as an individual, unique person, with both maturity and immaturity; second, the therapist as a social person who is both rejected by, and given status in, the community; third, the therapist as a professional person, with his varied and sometimes conflicting roles of investigator, administrator, and therapist. Some of the conflicts arising out of these different roles were presented.

An effort was made to present the development of a mature therapist from the immature nontherapist, discussing in turn, the needs which originated the initial decision, the contribution of medical and psychiatric training to his growth, the importance of therapy for himself, and the growth which accrues through his relationship with patients and colleagues. The motivations which provide the basis for his continuing to function as a depth therapist were presented as being distinct from those which initiated the original decision. These motivations were classified as residuals, sliver growth, the post-therapeutic need to reconstruct a parental image and a more adequate superego, and the need to participate in ever broadening social and cultural areas. Beneath these persistent motivations were seen to lie the most primitive drives which impel the therapist to do therapy. These drives were said to center, essentially, around the need to better integrate his body image and to increase his integrity. This was said to occur, primarily, through projection of part of himself onto the patient in therapy, with resultant intrapersonal integration.

The following chapter will discuss the distortions in therapy which result from unresolved patient-vectors in the therapist.

13

Patient-Vectors in the Therapist

... Go to your bosom
Knock there, and ask your heart what it doth know.
"Measure for Measure" II:2

The Concept of Counter-transference

The meaning of the term "counter-transference" has changed in general usage over the years and has been, at any one time, subject to various interpretations. The term is used universally, probably because it not only explains a dynamic pattern, but also answers a defensive need. The prefix "counter" confuses unless one accepts literally that the term seeks to differentiate between the "normal" transference feelings in the therapist and his "counter-transference" feelings. In our own usage, the term "counter-transference" refers literally to those transference problems of the therapist that are specifically related to and elicited by the transference problems of the patient. In this sense, certain "transference" problems of the therapist simply "counter" the effort of the patient to work out his own transference problems, and deflect the patient from his objectives by an intrusion of the therapist's infantile response to the patient's transference feelings.

159

The prefix "counter" has several meanings. It means to work against, to render ineffectual, to offset. In this sense, "counter-transference" refers to those feelings of the therapist that make the transference feelings of the patient ineffectual. That is to say, the "countering" blocks the patient's transference, so that "counter-transference" is operationally definable as the act which renders ineffectual the transference of the patient in that it disallows or distorts his projections. One way in which this may occur is when the therapist *complements* the patient's pathological father-transference by an equally pathological or immature child-transference. This, as Deutsch has stressed, blocks even the progress of an otherwise well-conducted analysis.

The authors, however, are dissatisfied with the term as it was discussed above, and therefore have endeavored to formulate the transference needs of the therapist in a more specific way. This attempt originally failed, since the term transference is ordinarily reserved for the infantile feelings of the patient, just as counter-transference is used as a definitive term for unresolved and uncontrolled pathological disturbances within the therapist himself. Our first efforts led to the attempt to use contrasting terms "pathological" and "mature" to describe the two poles of transference feelings in the therapist, since we felt that the dynamics of therapy are determined primarily by the affective reactions of the therapist to the patient's transference needs. The question remained: What term are we to use for this affective and therapeutic reaction on the part of the therapist? At first, and in a somewhat offhand way, we used the term "mature counter-transference." At this, some of our colleagues accused us rather humorously of using upside-down words. Nevertheless, spontaneously, at least, it seemed a most appropriate term, since it referred to those feelings of the therapist which "counter" or respond to the transferences of the patient, though not in an inconsidered and infantile manner. The term, used in this way, seemed appropriate, since we know that the therapist has certain transference needs which, when uncontrolled and unconscious, do seriously interfere with therapy. Yet real clarity about this matter only seemed possible if one defined "counter-transference" in definite operational terms.

Patient-Vectors and Therapist-Vectors

There was no simple way of doing this, except by reformulating the problem in terms of the belief that, in any therapeutic relationship, the therapist functions most often as a therapist, but sometimes also as a patient. Conversely, while the patient functions most frequently as a patient, he, at times, also acts as a therapist. In brief, each person involved in a therapeutic interpersonal relationship operates both as therapist and as patient. When one of these persons functions as the therapist, he responds on a more mature level and with more mature motivations and feelings to the needs of the one who, at that time, becomes the patient. He responds much as the parent responds to the needs of the immature child. The totality of these "responses" may be called the *therapist-vectors*.

In contrast, when either person in the relationship satisfies his immature transference needs, he is demanding of the other person a feeling response, much as the hungry child demands a response from his parent. These "demands" we refer to as *patient-vectors*. Those of the therapist's patient-vectors which seriously interfere with the process of helping the patient constitute what are historically and currently referred to as "counter-transference" factors. Yet the term patient-vectors has an even more pervasive meaning to us. It includes, in addition to the therapist's serious (infantile transference) involvements, also certain affective "sliver" involvements. These, in our opinion, are a necessary ingredient in the process of psychotherapy and occur whenever these minimal patient-vectors interact with the therapist-vectors in the other person involved in the therapeutic situation. We must emphatically stress that, since at a given moment the patient-vectors may be those of the professional therapist or those of the patient, the term "patient-vector" is not synonymous with the conventional term "counter-transference." This chapter discusses, primarily, those major patient-vectors in the therapist which lead to an impasse in therapy. We will give only brief mention to those motivating patient-vectors which are fundamental to the normal process of psychotherapy itself, since these latter have already been dealt with in earlier chapters.

We have stated that some patient-vectors in the therapist inhibit the therapeutic process. The character of transference needs, their genesis, the mechanisms or dynamics of their expression, and the role they play in therapy have been quite adequately covered in the literature and need not be discussed in detail at this juncture. The time seems ripe for making certain general distinctions and for offering a working classification of the patient-vectors in the therapist. Such an approach to the problem of counter-transference might help clear the board for a better understanding of the pathology of the therapeutic process.

Any discussion of the pathological aspects of the therapeutic process must begin with an examination of certain well-defined, generally-recognized disturbances, brought about by pathological needs in the persons involved in the therapy.

Certain general principles related to this concept of therapy are directly pertinent to any understanding of the problems of counter-transference. We feel that the therapeutic process, regardless of whether it is seen from the side of the patient or from that of the therapist, is an intra-psychic one. We can go even further and specify that the *pathology of the therapeutic process is determined primarily by the pathology of the intra-psychic functioning of the therapist,* i.e., the "person" of the therapist. The patient himself never "pathologizes" the therapeutic process; he can however unconsciously precipitate a certain change in the intra-psychic forces of the therapist which renders the latter therapeutically ineffectual. Theoretically then, any patient who has a therapist adequate to his needs will get well by virtue of the intra-psychic dynamics of the patient himself. We mean, by such an adequate therapist, a person whose dynamics provoke constructive intra-psychic changes in that patient. The therapeutic process is disturbed, retarded, or precluded only when the dynamics of the therapist render him ineffectual and unavailable to the growth-needs of the patient. Stated another way, the patient will get well if the intra-psychic needs (patient-vectors) of the therapist do not implicitly make excessive demands on the patient's therapist-vectors. These latter are of course present to some degree in every patient.

The above considerations seem heterodox only because they are not formulated in psychoanalytic language. The autotherapeutic significance of the act of analyzing a patient is generally recognized by analysts who, while analyzing their patients, also concurrently engage in self-analysis, and often obtain new insights into themselves by these means, i.e., secondary to some remark made by the patient. The analyst also knows how shrewdly the paranoid patient especially can touch upon the analyst's own tender spots and unresolved conflicts. From this insight to the inference that some of the patient's remarks actually constitute an expression of his therapist-vectors, i.e., of his therapeutic impulses toward the analyst, is but a short step, which even the most cautious could take, be it only for heuristic reasons.

As regards the fact that the therapist's major patient-vectors can interfere with, and may even inhibit, therapy altogether, there is little disagreement.* In fact, the principal purpose of didactic analysis is to reduce to a minimum the counter-transference (or gross patient-vector) needs of the analyst-to-be, since the analyst is not supposed to demand any gratification whatsoever from his patient, possibly not even the gratification of getting him cured.

The above considerations led us to conclude that if anything goes wrong, it is directly traceable to an inadequacy of the therapist, i.e., to some of his patient-vectors. To phrase this positively, we feel that, given an adequate, mature therapist, any patient will be sufficiently freed to grow a fuller potential within the framework of his relationship to this ideal therapist.

The pathology of the therapeutic process is, then, always caused by the pathology of the therapist. We believe that such remarks as "The patient isn't really interested in therapy," or "The patient is sick in an area which he finds difficult to handle," or "The

---

* We are indebted to Dr. George Devereux for the information that several analysts, including Freud, Deutsch, Hollos, Hitschmann, and Hann-Kende, implied that "telepathic" communication between analyst and analysand often occurs only when the analyst is deviating from the analytic ideal, i.e., when he gives free rein to his subjective or counter-transference needs.

patient isn't ready," etc. are only rationalizations which seek to disguise our own inadequacy in the handling of our own psychological conflicts. We have found it necessary to assume the validity of this principle for a successful battle to resolve a therapeutic impasse. We have also found that many impasses in therapy may be resolved by bringing to the patient our feeling of responsibility for the current failure of the therapeutic process and our acceptance of the fact that the therapist has patient-vectors.

A second principle, a direct inference from the first, states that the patient does not require a completely adequate therapist for effective therapy. What he does demand is that the therapist should make available to him all the adequacies which the therapist has available to himself. The patient demands also that the therapist should expand the frontiers of his own personal growth by what he emotionally gives to the patient. In brief, the patient demands the total participation of the therapist, including even the latter's immaturities. The patient feels rejected whenever there is a discrepancy between what the therapist gives to the patient and what the patient perceives in the therapist and views as potentially obtainable. Thus, the authors were surprised by the therapeutic successes of the medical students they were teaching. The students had many personal limitations and many of them had gross immaturities. Yet their motivation to help the patient was so intense that they brought to the clinic patient as much of their maturity as they had available at that time. In addition, they also brought to him even their immaturities. By contrast, we have seen professional therapists who, for various reasons, brought less than their maximal adequacy to their patients. The latter thereby felt rejected and got less from their therapy than did the patients of the relatively immature medical students. This therapeutic principle reflects also a more fundamental principle underlying the feelings of rejection in children. *We believe that the child feels rejected only when he senses a difference between what the parent could be as a person and what he actually is.* The child of an inadequate parent does not feel rejected by the parent simply because of the latter's immaturities. The child's relationship to the parent may be quite satisfactory if the parent can give what maturity he has, and dare also to share some of his immaturities with the child. This may be true even though to the observer the parent may seem to be grossly childish.

Bilateral Character of Therapy and Patient-Vectors

The concept that the bilateral character of therapy constitutes its most effective dynamic basis was discussed in the previous chapter and has some very definite implications for the problem of the therapeutic impasse. In the best therapeutic relationship, the therapist recurrently brings his own patient-vectors to the patient. The resolving of these factors materially advances the process of treating the patient-vectors of the real patient, probably because the relationship is thereby bilateral. The therapist's patient-vectors help establish this bilateral quality of the relationship. This we term a "sliver type" of involvement on the part of the therapist. No therapist matures enough to be free of all patient-vectors in himself. The acceptance of such limitations in therapy provides, in fact, a realistic basis for growth. Moreover, the therapist's patient-vectors are, in themselves, an effective dynamic element in the process of good therapy. Indeed, a therapeutic impasse can often be resolved only by the therapist's willingness to bring his patient-vectors to the patient quite overtly. This principle implies that were the therapist free of all patient-vectors, he would be no therapist at all.

What significance has the single therapeutic interview as a unit in the total process? Contemporary thought defines therapy as a process possessing a distinct time dimension. Therapists tend to view therapy as a continuing relationship manifesting certain linear and temporal sequences. Thus, many analysts believe that what happens in the twentieth interview is determined by what took place in the second interview, or that the meaning of the material presented during the first part of the hour may be apparent only by its relationship to feelings expressed at the end of the hour. We have been impressed with the patients' tolerance for the lack of continuity characteristic of brief therapy. They never seem to question the lack of a rational relationship between one aspect of the interview and any other or even the relationship of the beginning of the hour to the middle of the hour. Each hour of therapy is a unit in itself within which as much therapy occurs as the bilateral depth of the interpersonal relationship will permit. In fact, this seems theoretically true, also, for any fraction of the hour of therapy. As regards the therapeutic impasse, a therapist is only as good as his own therapy. His negative feelings about the growth he obtained from and subsequent to his own therapy, fundamentally define his relationship to his patient. As one surveys the therapist's patient-factors, one is repeatedly confronted with the fact that many of these manifest themselves as ways of handling his negative feelings about his own therapy. The previous chapters stressed the importance of the therapist's ability to introject the patient psychically, a capacity intimately related to his own experience as patient. He must have had the experience of being introjected and then extrojected. Only in this way can he introject various facets of his patient without guilt, or flight into projection. It is not at all surprising that the inadequacies of the therapist's own therapy will result in certain limitations, which in a sense, are genetic. Indeed, the therapist is inadequate in just those areas in which therapy did not make his own unconscious processes functional for him.

Categories of Patient-Vectors

There are some differences between the function of the inexperienced therapist and that of the mature person who is adequate to the needs of a large percentage of his patients. It would be a functional blindness to suggest that a therapist can become so mature that he will have no pathological involvement with any of his patients. In the previous chapter, this was denoted as a sliver type of transference, implying that (a) it is not deeply rooted, (b) it is fairly easily broken, and (c) it is not grossly disturbing to the therapeutic process. This sliver type contrasts with the gross pathological patient-vectors of the immature therapist.

Some classification of patient-vectors in the immature therapist seems necessary. The logical basis for such a classification would seem to be provided by the various kinds of personal involvement by the therapist in the therapeutic process, and their pathology.

At first, it seemed possible to classify these disturbances in relationship to their time of occurrence in therapy. However, as already indicated in a previous chapter (Chapter 10), the time element in therapy is an artifact since therapy, like the unconscious, has no temporal dimension. The involvement at any phase of therapy may be recapitulated at any other phase. This made it impossible to discuss patient-vectors in the therapist from the point of view of time.

Dynamically, the first large category of patient-vectors in the therapist stems from the need of the therapist to include the real, or conversely, his need to exclude the symbolic from the therapy. Even after one excludes the "real," the possibility continues to exist that the nature of the symbolic relationship itself may be pathological. This constitutes the second category of countertransference problems.

Avoidance of Therapeutic Relationship as a Category of Patient-Vector

Let us now examine those patient-factors which determine the therapist's inclusion of the patient's "real" in the therapeutic relationship. The therapeutic process is always symbolic and never "real." Thus, to the extent that the therapist accepts any aspect of the real as important in the therapeutic matrix, he slows down and distorts the process of therapy. The traditional taboos against the psychotherapist treating his social acquaintances, or close colleagues, or members of his own family group implies recognition of this general principle. Reality impedes therapy insofar as it deletes the symbolic from the relationship. The therapist who takes on the real problems of the patient introduces into the therapy a serious patient-factor in himself. Such a therapist asks for the reality problems of the patient because they are personally symbolic to him even though they are real to the patient. The discrepancy between the manner in which the two respond to these data causes the patient to feel that his realities are symbolic to the therapist. This, in turn, leads the patient to sense that what is symbolic to him (and therefore crucial to the therapeutic process) has been rejected by the therapist. The therapist who takes over the reality management of the patient attempts to be the foster parent at the same time and only projects his own needs into the therapeutic process, thus impairing the symbolic gratification of the patient.

The same general pathological result occurs when the therapist fails to keep separate his therapeutic and administrative functions. His failure to keep therapy as essentially an irrational emotional process will deter him from becoming involved on the personal level at which he must be involved if the patient is to obtain full therapeutic gain. This separateness of therapeutic and administrative functions is an extremely important principle. Physicians in general, and many psychiatrists as well, have, for years, carried out both of these functions, and in spite of this dual role are able to promote the growth of the patient through their role as the good parent. However, modern psychotherapy must go beyond this clinical method. When one dares to refine his relationship to the patient by the elimination of administrative responsibilities and real decisions—in fact, of all functions pertaining to the patient's outside life, and of specific decisions about the reality factors in the therapeutic relationship—this precipitates deeper emotional involvement. The initial experience of this sort may elicit in the therapist considerable anxiety, since it limits the therapist's role to such an extent that it resembles a rejection of the patient. It is amazing, however, that the insecure, immature, inadequate patient, who initially demands most pathetically just this type of direction, seems to stumble only momentarily and then take up, with increasing satisfaction, the lines of his own living. This, in turn, enables him to make even greater demands on the therapist. At times, it helps the therapist if someone else takes over the administrative function. Then the patient cannot use real needs to gain more affect from the therapist. Later in therapy, administration usually becomes relatively unimportant. Such an approach undoubtedly puts increasing demands upon the therapist for deeper participation on an emotional level. Actually, this may explain why one often finds it difficult to accept hints the patients give about the need for such a change.

So patient-vectors in the therapist are introduced into the therapy whenever the therapist gives consideration to aspects of the patient's real life. There is, however, another side to this picture, which consists in the introduction of the reality of the therapist's life into the therapeutic relationship. For the time being, discussion of what might motivate these various patient-factors will be postponed. Suffice it to say that frequently a disturbance in the therapist's real-life situation is projected onto the therapeutic relationship and to the detriment of the patient. The therapist is essentially a participant in an isolated fantasy experience, and by making himself real to the patient, he impairs the possibility of greater depth in the fantastic relationship. Indeed, this is one common way of sidestepping the deep emotional demands made by the patient.

Up to this point, only those patient-vectors implicit in the inclusion of reality into the therapeutic relationship have been presented. The second group of patient-vectors which interfere with the process of therapy are due to the therapist's exclusion of the symbolic aspects of therapy. This occurs when the therapist cannot accept his symbolic status and interferes with the patient's efforts to relate himself to the therapist unconsciously. The therapist just stays therapist-doctor.

Before discussing this further, it seems necessary to dispose of the problem of confusing content with affect. It has long been thought that if the psychiatrist could accept the patient's content, he thereby also accepted the patient, and that the therapist who denied the content presented by the patient also denied the patient himself. The authors feel that this is not generally true. The therapist can reject the patient and deny the affective relationship, while only accepting the content presented to him. He may do so either because it interests him, or because he assumes that whatever seems symbolic to him is symbolic also to the patient. On the other hand, we know that, in some therapies, all symbolic content is denied, at least overtly. Another group, the psychobiological, accepts symbolic content and feels that by this means, the patient and his affect are also accepted. In fact, one's affective relationship with the patient may have direct relationship, an inverse relationship, or no relationship at all to the content material. Subsequent discussion will pertain to the affective relationship between the therapist and the patient, and take up the therapist's patient-vectors which are conducive to a disturbed affective relationship.

One of the most specific problems of counter-transference, especially in modern-day psychiatry, is not ordinarily thought of as pertaining to counter-transference. The pioneers of psychotherapy became personally involved with their patients, and found it necessary to utilize deliberately a defensive "objectivity." The term and the practice in question have long since been debunked in the literature. It seems very difficult, however, to get past the safety-factor—past the security derived from maintaining a cold and distant relationship with a warm, hungry patient. Certainly, a schizophrenic withdrawal is the most universal mechanism for adapting oneself to the anxieties elicited when one is precipitated into deeply symbolic human relationships. Further, the schizoid personality is admittedly quite prevalent in the profession of medicine, and particularly in psychiatry. Hence, it is not at all surprising that some individuals should seek to handle the anxiety which arises in the course of their therapeutic efforts by means of their habitual defense. Another very common form of excluding affect utilizes constant, impersonal interpretations which place the therapist outside the relationship, and lead the patient to complain that the therapist treats him out of a book. Compulsive objectivity is as serious a counter-transference problem as is intense subjectivity.

We should like to call attention, also, to the dynamic aspects of an objectivity exercised in the therapeutic relationship. The picture of the patient asking for a warm, parental person and meeting instead a cold, intellectual, withdrawn person is obviously a specific type of rejection, reinforced by its synchronization with our culture, which places a premium upon withdrawal. The similarity of this to his childhood rejection increases the patient's need of a symbolic parent. More specifically, objectivity can dominate the relationship under various guises. The most conspicuous of these masks deals with the patient only as an administrative problem. These psychiatrists interest themselves in the pathology of the patient on a content level, and use the routine case history as a means of relating themselves to the patient in an impersonal manner. Next, one finds the psychiatrist whose interest in his patient goes somewhat deeper, but only in the sense that he sees him as a member of society and related in a social relationship, and does what he can by way of helping the patient manipulate the environment. There are those who go beyond this and whose interest in the patient becomes personal, but only to the level of an interest in the symptomatology. We have already discussed the general function of real-life situations and their pertinence as patient-vectors, which can now be seen, also, as a devious method of attaining objectivity. Further, there are those therapists who give themselves in a partial sense, only to deny later the pertinence of their feelings for the patient. Last of all, the immature therapist may become so convinced of the patient's maturity that he denies him access to his therapist-vectors.

Every therapeutic relationship works on at least two levels: the level of the apparent relationship and the level of the unconscious relationship. Hence, the mere presence of the above factors may be a serious deterrent to adequate therapy. The converse may also be true: beneath the crust of any of these "objective" techniques the psychiatrist may have a quite adequate unconscious relationship with the patient.

Transference as a Patient-Vector in the Therapist

One of the effective means through which the therapist's patient-vectors exclude a symbolic relationship stems from the therapist's emotional denial of the possibilities of the therapeutic process itself. In effect, for one reason or another, he denies the possibility of therapy as an unconscious process and seems specifically to express, among other things, the inadequacies of his own treatment. The therapist who denies the patient's symbolic affect because of the development of anxiety within himself does so because of his feeling that he will be overwhelmed by his own irrational participation. This may be true, in general, or may be related to a specific patient and to the symbolic use he seeks to make of this therapist. The immature therapist may be able to tolerate certain symbolic roles, for example, the mother role and the father role, and yet be panicked if he suddenly finds himself symbolized as a homosexual partner. Thus, he may find himself again precluding the patient's fantasy by the dovetailing of his own projections with those of the patient, even though no real or overt acting out occurs. The above examples seem to form a continuum pertaining to the therapist's ability and freedom to participate in the irrational affect of the patient, to the extent to which the patient leads him. Certainly nothing tries the therapist more than the patient's demand that they "go crazy together," regardless of whether he is asking on the superficial level of the therapist's listening to the patient's recitation of irrational ideas, or in terms of a demand for actual participation in psychotic behavior. To put it another way, it takes a certain amount of maturity to tolerate the patient's affect when it becomes irrational. It takes even more maturity to participate with one's own irrational affect, because there always looms the fear that, in the final state of the bilateral synchronization of psychotic feeling-tone, there lies a "nether world" from which the therapist himself may be unable to return. And, as if this were not enough, he is constantly tempted by his interest in the completely fantastic living of the patient.

We have tried to formulate here some general concept of the factors which prevent the therapist from fully answering the demands of the patient, and to which he responds essentially by preventing the development of a relationship which is deeply symbolic.

The therapist must have certain emotional involvements with the patient if the therapy is to succeed. This, in turn, raises the possibility that his involvement may become pathological, which would therefore decrease the effectiveness of therapy, or even preclude its possibility. Such patient-vectors reflect the fact that certain of the therapist's transference needs have been stimulated by a particular patient, and that these revived needs have interfered with his function as a therapist. This presumably occurs whenever a patient becomes symbolic to the therapist. We have seen, however, that the symbolic value of the patient for the therapist provides much of even the mature therapist's motivation. What then is the specific quality of the "counter-transference" which disturbs the therapeutic effectiveness of the relationship?

Probably the most subtle patient-vector operative in ordinary psychotherapy is the therapist's involvement with the patient on a simple transference level. The motivations of the mature therapist still involve his symbolic use of the patient. The mature therapist, however, relates to the patient on such a level that his symbolization of the patient involves only the person of the therapist himself. He projects onto the patient only the image of his own child-self. In our introductory statements, we presented the concept that the intra-psychic family is the product of the normal accretion of growth. The problem in maturing and, therefore, the problem in therapy as well, is essentially a "working through" process which resolves gross fantasies about the intra-psychic family. Whenever the therapist's response to the patient involves the patient symbolically as a member of the therapist's intra-psychic family, the process of therapy reverses. The therapist's patient-vector becomes predominant, and impells the patient to respond with his own therapist-vectors. If the patient responds adequately to this particular patient-factor within the therapist, the distortion is temporary, i.e., of the sliver type, and the process soon reverses again, the therapist functioning once more as a therapist to the patient. If, however, the patient's therapist-vectors are not adequate to the specific need of the therapist in this symbolic situation, a serious impasse in therapy occurs. The most severe distortion of the therapeutic process arises when the therapist sees the patient symbolically as his mother or father or brother, and brings this specific patient-vector to bear in the relationship. The seriousness of this type of patient-vector results primarily from the attendant inability of the therapist to utilize his therapist-factor unconsciously while so grossly overwhelmed with his patient-projections. Later in the chapter, some of the dynamics through which this kind of impasse is resolved will be elucidated.

There are more common forms of this patient-vector. Generally speaking, these patient-vectors are precisely those which the patient also brings to the therapist initially. In a sense, this includes the whole gamut of psychopathology. The ways in which his transference needs express themselves in the therapist during therapy are, however, fairly specific. A common one is simply an accentuation of the normal motivations found in every therapist who identifies the patient as the means of satisfying his own infantile needs. Despite the fact that he frequently achieves good therapeutic results, he invariably ends up with an unresolved transference cure: "You go now; you are well. (I am well in your being well.) But you aren't you. You are always my child (me). You can't grow. The most you can do is keep what you have now." This type of symbolic identification with one's child-self in the patient makes impossible an adequate termination of the therapeutic relation. It is the transference cure *par excellence*. It effectively eliminates the possibility of there being a post-interview phase in the therapeutic process.

The most common expression of this patient-vector in the therapist is simply an intense transference relationship to the patient. Most patients have enough of a therapist-vector to handle the therapist's sibling transferences, while others can even handle the therapist's maternal and paternal transference needs. However, few are adequate enough to respond as the primordial parent to the therapist's deepest needs. These transference phenomena are so common and so well understood that there is little need to explain them in detail. The situation becomes more difficult, however, when these transference needs are presented on the level of secondary projections, a very common patient-vector among therapists. It usually involves the therapist's continuing to work through his own relationship with his original therapist in the matrix of this current therapeutic relationship. He seeks to work through the unresolved transference needs, which he carries over from his own inadequate therapy. His work has, however, a compulsive quality, in that he responds by projecting himself onto the patient with the same feelings which he sensed in his own therapist. Unless the patient has enough of a therapist-vector to break through this cycle, the whole therapeutic process comes to a halt.

Another form of this patient-factor involves dissociation by symbolic displacement, the economy of which is not clear. It takes the form of the therapist's assuming a symbolic role—one which he feels or thinks the patient wants the therapist to assume or that he believes the patient should have. The discrepancy between his assumed role and his real self amounts to a serious rejection of the patient, whose symbolic needs he implicitly denies in favor of his own symbolic needs. Within the therapist, the assumed symbolic role represents nothing more than wish-fulfillment on his part. It probably represents an intra-psychic condensation of a desired relationship between himself and a member of his intra-psychic family. Such a therapist seems unwilling even to take the chance of overtly expressing his symbolic needs to the patient.

Still another type of this patient-vector in therapy involves the therapist's expression of his resentment and feeling of hopelessness over ever finding an adequate symbolic parent. He begins a transference relationship with the therapist-vector in the patient, but expresses it negatively. He says in essence, "I'd like you to be my mother, but I know you aren't adequate, because no one could ever be adequate." The patient may get well in spite of this, although more often any "cure" has the quality of a transference cure. The therapist says "I never will get well. No one can help me. I know you really don't love me." To which the patient responds, "If you're hopeless; if your well-being is sheer fantasy, then my well-being must depend on my continued relationship with you, so I can't live as a separate person."

Non-Transference (Sliver) Patient-Vectors in the Therapist

Although most of the therapist's patient-vectors come within the scope of reversed transference involvements, the authors have also observed in themselves certain additional non-transference patient-vectors. Thus, one interview carries over into our relationship with another patient in a succeeding interview, in some cases to such an extent that responses to the second patient were largely irrelevant. This involves "acting out," a resolution of the depth of the participation in the preceding interview. The therapeutic process is distorted by bringing to it some of the realities of the therapist, the reality here being his emotional involvement with another patient. In this area, some of the more general classes of patient-vectors discussed above seem to converge.

Not only are the therapeutic realities pertaining to other patients distorting, but professional and research realities can also distort the therapeutic process in much the same way. For example, one of the authors became interested in bottle feeding as a therapeutic technique, and found himself pushing patients in therapy toward this kind of experience, sometimes with little regard for the patient's integrity. This happened, also, with three or four other therapeutic techniques which interested the authors, and it seems that our preoccupation with these techniques, at any given time, represented a patient-vector in ourselves. Luckily, the technical form within which therapy is presented seems to be relatively unimportant to the patient. Inappropriate use of technique or content gives rise to temporary impasses which resolve rather quickly. When the carry-over is either from another patient or from our personal life, involving acting out even though of a sliver character, the resolution becomes difficult.

In the previous chapter, the motivations of the mature therapist for continued activity were presented. The accentuation or under-development of the therapist's normal motivations frequently distort the therapeutic process. Such poor motivation can be a genuine patient-vector. An immature therapist's therapeutic drive may be so personal that he cannot handle adequately the necessary reality aspects of his professional function. This results in an increasing tendency toward ever deeper identification with the patient as his adult-self. Thus, overly motivated the therapist decreases his real satisfactions in living outside of his therapeutic world. This imbalance seems to be cumulative, and more and more of the therapist's person becomes involved in what is initially but a facet of his whole life. This may result in either pushing the patients beyond the level of their immediate needs, or in making ending very difficult, if not impossible.

In contrast, some therapists have not developed adequate, normal motivations. Paradoxically, this may be due to the absence of sufficient sliver patient-vectors in the therapist. The best examples of such therapists are those who, at some time in their professional career, seem to lose interest in therapy and find it increasingly difficult to spend time in doing therapy. These persons were very adequate and mature therapists but, for some reason, gradually seemed to lose the necessary motivation for this type of work. This may eventuate from their having worked through most of their own patient-vectors during the years when they were doing therapy. To some extent, this occurs in every mature therapist, since over the years they find, in their growth, that some types of patients no longer interest them. These patients apparently offer less of a challenge. This inference involves certain implications pertaining to the operational factors in the motivation of the mature therapist. More specifically, it involves the concept that a therapist's motivation with each patient stems from his inner effort to work through certain slivers of pathological disturbance in his own personality, and that these patient-vectors keep him active as a therapist.

We have examined the character of the therapist's various involvements in previous chapters, and there discussed some aspects of his pathological involvement with certain patients. We found that one can be a therapist only by deep participation in the interpersonal relationship, even though this may arise from patient-vectors in himself. Such an involvement of the therapist can take place only when the patient himself has developed a fairly deep transference. However, whenever the therapist's more pervasive patient-vectors come to the front in the therapeutic relationship, there occurs an impasse, sometimes called the transference-counter-transference jam. This leads us to the empiric problem of what the therapist can do to resolve such an impasse. Much of what has already been written on this subject pertains to the concepts of supervision, to controlled analyses, and to therapy for the therapist.

Resolution of the Impasse

It has been gradually driven home to us that the therapeutic aspects of any interpersonal relationship, like the maturing factors of a child's life at home, become fully available only after the interpersonal relationship has been successfully terminated. In fact, any relationship has therapeutic value limited by its depth, no matter what the character of its termination. This implies that in the ending phase of a relationship, rejection of the patient cannot occur. Ending at this phase, even though forced by the therapist, constitutes an affirmation of the patient's wellness.

Any impasse or jam, of necessity, implies a problem pertaining to the ending phase of a relationship. One wonders whether the difference between an adequate therapeutic relationship and an impasse problem reflects the varying capacity of the therapist and patient to resolve their relationship. From this perspective, the whole discussion of counter-tranference can be considered as a discussion of problems of ending.

The possible factors involved in efforts to resolve the impasse present a continuum ranging from the more usual, superficial efforts to the more pervasive and radical methods. Such a discussion presupposes a recognition of any immature professional therapist's obvious need to have had a therapeutic experience adequate for the resolving of his major transference needs. Some of the subsequent discussion, however, also seems applicable to those therapists who have not had such an experience. The usual effort on the part of the therapist to break up the impasse is via introspection or self-analysis. It seems almost trite to say that the therapist should be aware that any effort to resolve the impasse necessitates a greater involvement in the therapeutic relationship, and that no actual resolution ever comes from withdrawal. The therapist's introspection at a free-association level succeeds only when he manages to carry his fantasy to its limits. However, the resolution of any deep relationship seldom occurs on this basis alone. The most obvious person who can be involved, and can help the therapist to break up the patient-vector in himself, is the patient. Because the latter may not be the easiest person for the therapist to enlist as an aid, he may prefer to resort to supervisory conferences with someone with whom he has a relationship deep enough to make possible at least the sliver type of therapeutic gain. By this we mean the resolution of a limited facet of the therapist's own pathological involvement. His free-association may suggest the most appropriate method of utilizing such a person just as it may help resolve his panic with the patient. Successful resolution of any impasse necessitates a straightforward struggle with the problem of ending. Real success comes to the therapist who dares to push to the limit his own tolerance for ending. Such ending may be imminent whether or not the therapist can see its reality. Usually the denial of ending itself reflects some unsolved impasse problem. By such denial, the therapist maintains the possibility of satisfying his own patient needs. For a therapist to face his patient-vectors in his own fantasy is hard enough; to call himself a patient to a colleague is even more difficult; but to call himself the patient to the person across the desk is most difficult. This holds true since the sliver usually involved has been resistant enough to previous resolution to have been retained in spite of his own struggles as a person.

A still more difficult procedure crosses the very matrix of therapeutic orthodoxy. This involves the use of a colleague as a catalyst, and so exposes the relationship to the participation of a third person. This means that the patient and the therapist must face squarely not only the impasse, but all of their joint inadequacies at its resolution, and make the decision to ask for help with their impasse. It is desirable, of course, that the patient and the therapist should both be anxious and ready for this step. However, often the patient denies the anxiety of the impasse. In that case, it becomes the duty of the therapist to assume total responsibility for such a step. Not infrequently, the patient does assume such a responsibility and resolves it by changing therapists. More often, the therapist assumes such responsibility and demands that the patient accept a colleague as therapist to their relationship. The fact that it is rarely necessary that the second therapist be present for more than one hour reflects the effectiveness of such a procedure.

The resolution of the impasse situation in therapy, no matter what form such a resolution takes, always involves, in some manner, an adequate satisfaction of the therapist's patient-vector which is currently jamming the relationship. This is true because the origin of the impasse is rooted in the therapist's denial of his own patient-vectors.

Fig. 6A. *For Example:*

I.

The therapist dreams about the patient.

The therapist fears the patient's ability to hurt him.

The therapist becomes dependent on the patient, the dependence being expressed as concern that the therapy continue.

The therapist idealizes the patient.

II.

The therapist dominates the patient because of insecurity over his professional status.

The therapist over-protects the patient to compensate for his own inadequacy as a father in his real life situation.

The therapist sexualizes the therapeutic situation because of his own unsatisfactory marital situation.

III.

The therapist plays golf or has lunch with the patient.

The therapist provokes the patient to an excessive reaction to someone in the patient's environment.

The therapist marries the patient.

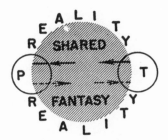

MAJOR PATIENT VECTOR ⟵——————   ⟵—————— MAJOR THERAPIST VECTOR

MINOR THERAPIST VECTOR ----⟶   ----⟶--- MINOR PATIENT VECTOR

Normal Therapeutic Transference Relationship

Diagrams Illustrating ABNORMAL THERAPEUTIC RELATIONSHIP

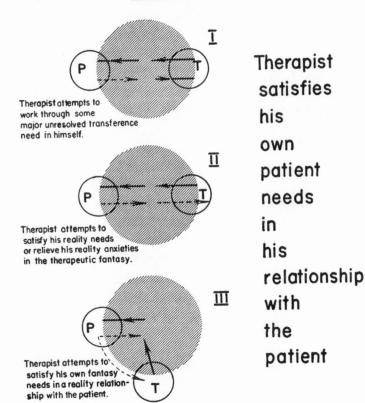

I

Therapist attempts to work through some major unresolved transference need in himself.

II

Therapist attempts to satisfy his reality needs or relieve his reality anxieties in the therapeutic fantasy.

III

Therapist attempts to satisfy his own fantasy needs in a reality relationship with the patient.

Therapist
satisfies
his
own
patient
needs
in
his
relationship
with
the
patient

Fig. 6A

Fig. 6B. *For Example:*

IV.

The therapist withdraws from the relationship for fear of personal involvement, and utilizes learned procedures or formalized techniques, e.g., interpretation, in a compulsive manner.
The therapist is preoccupied with content to the exclusion of affect.

V.

The therapist responds to the patient's symbolization by discussing his own
personal responses to similar stresses.
The therapist discusses his successes or failures in the treatment of previous
patients with similar problems.

VI.

The therapist tries to satisfy the patient by giving advice, by environmental
manipulation, or by reassurance.
The therapist protects the patient from anxiety by extra appointments,
hospitalization, medication, or manipulation of patient's real life situation.

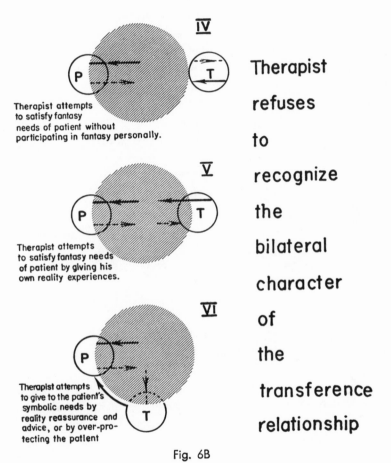

Therapist attempts
to satisfy fantasy
needs of patient without
participating in fantasy personally.

Therapist attempts
to satisfy fantasy needs
of patient by giving his
own reality experiences.

Therapist attempts
to give to the patient's
symbolic needs by
reality reassurance and
advice, or by over-pro-
tecting the patient

Therapist
refuses
to
recognize
the
bilateral
character
of
the
transference
relationship

Fig. 6B

Fig. 6C. *For Example:*

VII.

The therapist ends the relationship before it becomes symbolic.
The therapist transfers the patient to another therapist.
The therapist says, "This patient is not ready for psychotherapy."
The therapist says, "This patient is adjusting pretty well and therapy might upset her."

VIII.

The therapist acts as a screen to reflect the patient's feelings back to him.
The therapist refuses to accept the relevance of any criticism from the patient and insists that the patient not act as therapist even minimally.
The therapist denies that the patient has contributed anything to the therapist's personal growth.

IX.

The therapist expresses doubt concerning, or refuses to accept the validity of, the patient's successes in real living.
The therapist always sees the immature aspect of the patient's expanding social relations.
The therapist counsels against the patient's setting up in business or getting married because of disbelief in the patient's adequacy.

X.

The therapist counsels the patient to change the reality situations which previously induced stress, e.g., husband, job, religion.
The therapist insists that only fantasy relationships can be satisfying, and infers that the patient's real life relationships will always be shallow.
The therapist pushes the patient to sublimate his affects.

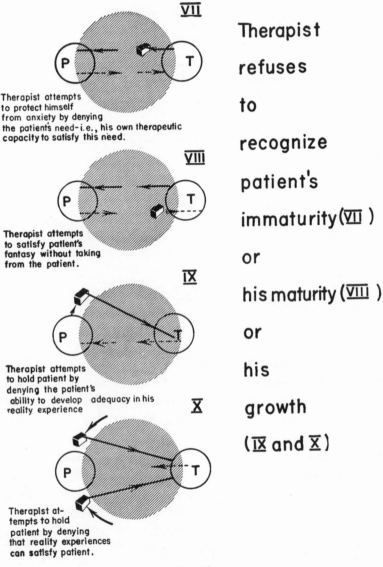

VII

Therapist attempts
to protect himself
from anxiety by denying
the patient's need- i.e., his own therapeutic
capacity to satisfy this need.

VIII

Therapist attempts
to satisfy patient's
fantasy without taking
from the patient.

IX

Therapist attempts
to hold patient by
denying the patient's
ability to develop adequacy in his
reality experience

X

Therapist at-
tempts to hold
patient by denying
that reality experiences
can satisfy patient.

Therapist

refuses

to

recognize

patient's

immaturity (VII)

or

his maturity (VIII)

or

his

growth

(IX and X)

Fig. 6C

14

Restatement of the Problem
of Psychotherapy

Tseking asked, "Is there one single word that can serve as a
principle of conduct for life?"
Confucius replied, "Perhaps the word reciprocity will do."
"The Wisdom of Confucius"

The concept that psychotherapy begins and ends with the professional relationship of the patient to the therapist artificially re-
stricts our horizons. When one examines the process of therapy, it
becomes apparent that a good deal of therapy takes place prior to
the first interview and that more occurs subsequent to the last
interview. Indeed, every human relationship involves an effort to
resolve tensions. Any definition should seek to differentiate implicit therapy, which takes place in any social relationship, from
psychotherapy, defined as a special, isolated relationship, within
which deep symbolic needs are gratified. Nonetheless, it appears
that the interview relationship constitutes but a segment of a process which begins some time prior to seeing the therapist. In the
beginning and ending phases, the transitions take place through a
utilization of the available social therapeutic mechanisms. The
pre-phase originates out of the intra-psychic symbolic compro-

186

mises with personal tension systems and these compromises result in symptoms. In the interview segment, the patient resolves his tensions within an interpersonal, but still symbolic, relationship. Out of this experience emerges the capacity to resolve tensions on an interpersonal, but less symbolic level, which one can call the post-interview segment. An understanding of the total process of therapy requires insight into the nature of these phases and of their relationship to the professional interview segment in particular. An attempt has been made to describe the sequence and dynamics of the critical transitional phases.

These transitions bring about a change in the relative importance of fantasy and reality in the motivation of the patient. Before therapy, the patient confuses the fantastic and the real, the result being an endless vacillation between the two. Specifically, there results a gratification of neither fantasy needs nor of real needs. Somewhere along the line, the patient either feels that additional fantastic gratifications are possible, or else more of his real needs are gratified, so that the possibility of a direct gratification of one set of needs can be envisioned by him. At this point, therapy in its restricted, non-social sense begins. In the interview segment, there gradually develops a primarily fantastic or symbolic relationship. In this relationship, characterized by an increasing exclusion of reality, the patient finds the greatest opportunity for the realization of fantasies.

The transition to the post-interview segment reverses the above balance, in that the patient endeavors to satisfy real needs concomitant with a progressive obliteration of the fantastic therapeutic relationship. At this point, the patient may deny almost in toto the fantastic relationship implicit in psychotherapy. Therapy terminates with the beginning of a fusion between the real and the symbolic in a system of unitary functioning, i.e., with the restoration of the patient's biological integrity.

Thus, the therapeutic process has a definite, total gestalt quality. The pre-phase of therapy originates in the dynamic change which takes place within the patient. It lead to the interview relationship, in which the patient transforms the therapist into an amalgam of his own intra-psychic capacities and of the cultural forces which impinge upon him. Subsequent to the interview phase, he increasingly utilizes cultural forces for his continued growth. Thus, in this sense, the phases merge inseparably into each other and the whole therapeutic process fuses into the cultural processes.

We are, of course, primarily interested in the interview segment. Obviously, therapy occurs within the framework of an interpersonal relationship, or is itself an interpersonal relationship. At the same time, however, it becomes more than an interpersonal relationship, since the therapist purposively utilizes some basic convictions about growth arising out of his own experience and training.

Three such principles of human behavior seem to be fundamental. First of these is man's inherent *growth capacity*, which is as relentless in the psychological as in the biological sphere, where it manifests itself, e.g., in the area of cell division, tissue differentiation, and repair of organ structure after trauma. One often sees in the psychiatric patient a type of emotional malnutrition which makes it necessary for the total organism "to take the situation in hand" in a very special sense. In the presence of emotional deprivation, the organism will make endless efforts to satisfy its needs. It may even adjust itself with maximum economy to a perpetual state of deprivation. The "break-through" out of this neurotic compromise is most often, and most effectively, triggered by appropriate stimuli from the environment. Sometimes these stimuli are rejected in much the same manner as a starving man may vomit a large meal. At other times these stimuli are accepted, whereupon the organism develops a state of emotional hunger which, for a time, can be satisfied by the minor gratifications available in social situations. However, pressure increases and accelerates the process to the point where the patient actively seeks deeper relationships and more stimulation toward growth.

Second, we assume that psychotherapy augments growth and becomes a real experience in living. This implies, in turn, that the effort to superimpose a historical framework on this process destroys its unity and integrity. The essential dynamics of psychotherapy unfold themselves within a current experience. This current experience modifies the relationship of other current experiences to each other, and integrates the biological effects of past experiences on the organization of current experience. Such a therapy might appropriately be labelled as *experiential*. It is essentially non-genetic, ahistorical, atemporal and therapist-activated, and deals essentially with Id processes. This distinguishes it from ego-level therapy, with the latter's analytical, genetic, temporal, historical, and causal emphasis.

The genetic approach in the area of psychopathology has been our most rewarding research technique. However, since research differs from therapy, as analysis differs from synthesis, the genetic approach brings about dynamic changes in the organism, only to the extent that it also involves a therapeutic experience as defined above.

Third, we assume that the organism, which so beautifully protects itself by homeostatic measures in the biochemical and physiological spheres, has the same capacity for self-protection also in the psychological sphere. In the therapeutic process, the patient can protect himself not only from the inadequacies of the technique, but often, also from the pathological counter-transference of the therapist. Belief in this principle frees the therapist for more total participation, even to the extent of accepting temporarily his own patient-needs, present even in the mature therapist. He brings to the interview all of the motivational factors pertaining to his professional function which are, in turn, reducible to deeper personal motivations and needs.

The energy which the therapist uses in his continuing therapeutic effort stems from his need to resolve those residual problems of his own, which apparently center around the reintegration of his concept of himself, i.e., of his body image. This objective can be attained only after the resolution within the therapy of the intrapsychic counter-transference problems which arise out of his infantile experiences with his own parents. His relationship to the patient involves a personal gratification, in that the patient functions as a projection of the therapist, thus making possible a gradual resolution of the therapist's body image needs. The therapist, thus, has at his disposal, a highly specific and deeply rooted segment of motivation, which enables him to relate himself to the patient with a great deal of affective intensity. This is re-enforced by his empirical conviction that therapy has been of maturing value to him as a person and that, therefore, the patient can grow within the therapeutic relationship. The need of the patient to grow as a person can be significant for the therapist only if the therapist also gets fragmentary therapy from the patient, although on quite a different level. It appears that the therapist has to get the patient well, in order that the patient can function for him and on his behalf in just this way, i.e., he unconsciously sees the patient as a possible therapist who could satisfy and resolve certain of his own basic needs. These needs of the therapist, which motivate him in doing effective therapy, are intra-personal needs, which seek to achieve a better integration of the therapist's own self. At the same time, the mature therapist has a few residual and deep interpersonal needs, particularly unconscious, infantile transference needs associated with unresolved child-parent relationships. Whenever the therapist uses the patient for the purpose of gratifying this latter type of need, he is involved in a pathological counter-transference, which may cause the therapist to be relatively ineffectual in helping the patient. In other words, when the patient symbolizes for the therapist someone else other than the child-self of the therapist, the character of the therapist's own need will preclude his effectiveness in a professional role. If, on the other hand, the therapist sees the patient as a symbol of his child-self, then, even though this reflects a deep, unconscious need, it does not seriously interfere with the therapist's ability to function for the patient. On the contrary, it will motivate him to function more effectively as a therapist. Hence, when the therapist first sees the patient, he brings to the patient a very powerful and specific vector of feeling and motivation. This initiates a process of mutual induction resulting in a gradual deepening of the unconscious relationship between the therapist and the patient. If the therapist can function in a manner compatible with the needs of this particular patient, he then enters into the process of therapy which has already begun in the patient. He becomes part of it, and remains in the relationship, until the patient's fantasy needs are fulfilled.

The character of the therapist's motivation gives the therapeutic relationship a quality of isolation. It is really an externalized intra-personal relationship, in the sense that everything happens as though there were but one person—the therapist and a projection of himself. This isolation relieves the patient of some of the responsibility for playing the real roles which society ascribes to him. He is, therefore, capable of realizing in the interview those fantastic roles which he ascribes to himself and to the therapist, and is for the first time not held socially and interpersonally accountable in the usual sense. In this isolation, the relationship takes on a dream-like quality so that the depth of the experience, and its unconscious components, are correspondingly greater. This isolation implies a momentary rejection of other realities for the sake of this one person. This, in turn, justifies the further isolation of himself and a new acceptance, on the part of the patient, of his own impending right to be isolated even from his therapist—(ending).

The patient brings to the therapist all of his transference needs. He relates himself to the therapist on a symbolic level, much as he would relate himself socially to any person, e.g., teacher, minister, or employer, but with the added factors present in the cultural stereotype of doctor-therapist. From the beginning, the patient is disposed to enter into a deep symbolic relationship with the therapist. This stems from the patient's unconscious concept of the therapist-role, from conscious experiences, and from ruminations about what the therapist might be or how he might function. It arises, primarily, out of the patient's unconscious disposition to view the therapist as the potentially good parent, who is the fantasy representative of his own parent as the patient saw him a few times in his life, and from whom he received the momentary gratifications which made his initial growth possible. He thus sees the therapist symbolically in terms of his infantile transference, with the overtone that the therapist stereotype is also a possible good parent.

The process then involves the circular deepening of affect on the part of both patient and therapist. The therapist next brings to bear upon the patient those of his own past motivations and feelings which he perceives as positive, and which he associates with the potentially good parent. Yet he can do this only if he himself is a mature person. This enables the patient to deepen his symbolic involvement with the therapist, and increases the fragment of affect mobilized by the symbolic presence of the good parent. This deepening of involvement entails, also, the unconscious recognition by the therapist of the patient as himself. This, in turn, implies a greater urgency to accelerate the growth of the patient (positive anxiety). In this manner, the therapist hopes to satisfy his own deeper integrative needs. This results in a seesaw of feeling, each swing increasing the common core of the relationship, until finally both are involved, on a functional level, to the very depths of their personal capacity and need. The limit of this depth is generally set by the limitations of the therapist rather than by those of the patient since, presumably, the therapist has a greater capacity for unconscious emotional involvement.

At some point the quality of the unconscious relationship of the therapist to the patient minimizes conscious factors, and the relationship becomes maximally isolative in the sense referred to above. Somewhere at this level, the patient recognizes unconsciously the real character of the therapist's involvement, and perceives that the therapist himself works toward a greater personal self-integration and growth in this relationship. The therapist, on the other hand, now has a maximal unconscious awareness of the patient's needs. Each of the two maximally responds to the unconscious of the other. The level of communication is primitive, being essentially one of mass body sensations, particularly of the autonomic, proprioceptive, and somaesthetic type. This stage may be thought of as the joint fantasy experience. By fantasy, we mean a pervasive experiencing of the unconscious in its totality which, by definition, remains non-verbal and organic. In the matrix of this level of his relating himself to the therapist, maximal therapeutic benefits accrue to the patient.

The ways in which this kind of relating facilitates therapeutic growth can be summed up as follows:

1. The patient's acceptance of his own fantasies and unconscious experiences, because he has them in the presence of one who implicitly participates in them, and thereby accepts them. The therapist, thus, not only symbolizes the parent who forbade these fantasies earlier in life, but also represents the total culture.

2. The development of a greater continuity between consciousness and unconsciousness; the experiential breakdown of the boundaries resulting from this total experience, and involving the conviction that one can be fantastic while, at the same time, retaining a very adequate reality capacity.

3. The increasing capacity for the realization of one's fundamental biological needs. This implies the ability to accept, use, and alter reality in such a way as to get maximal gratification and growth in the continuity of one's separate life experiences, with but a minimal interference from the fantastic, compulsive repetitions in the relation of the self to the non-self.

The problem of ending differs essentially from the rest of the therapeutic process in that it is almost exclusively a function of the patient. The dynamics of ending are basically intra-psychic to the patient. In this phase of therapy, the therapist becomes more obviously the patient, and selfishly tries to retain the patient in the fantasy relationship. The patient, having grown up in that relationship, now insists upon a less fantastic relationship. He demands that the therapist become a real (social) person if the relationship is to continue. Denied this, the patient transfers his affect to real relationships occurring in his life outside the therapist's office, and the therapist is left to nurse his rejection and to transfer his affect to the next patient, with the recurring hope of finding the perfect therapist.

15

Some Techniques in Brief Psychotherapy

A mind all logic is like a knife all blade.
It makes the hand bleed that uses it.
Tagore

Psychotherapy has many similarities to the fine arts, not the least among these being the tendency of its practitioner to emphasize either the expression of his inner self or techniques. The authors' emphasis, up to this point, has been largely on the affective aspects of psychotherapy and the persons involved. This chapter outlines more specifically some technical aspects of the therapeutic process. To some extent, this does violence to the orientation of the authors. A concern with technique could distract the young therapist and distort any deeper understanding of his function. Nonetheless, techniques, when used by a mature therapist, make the difference between good therapy and the most adequate therapy possible. Thereby this chapter becomes important.

An interest in the technical aspects of psychotherapy serves several purposes. Most specifically, it develops the therapist's professional adequacy. His deeper motivations are catalyzed and polished by the development of certain technical patterns which guide his perception of how therapy can be improved, and keep him in a framework of scientific thinking. Yet the deliberate use of technique demands certain safeguards. The therapist must be mature and experienced enough to maintain his personal affect despite the deliberateness involved in technical procedures. Certainly, any technical procedure which becomes devoid of personal feeling and participation has little meaning. It may also damage the deeper relationship between the therapist and the patient. Patients can always see beneath the therapist's technical skill, and if this is artificial, it becomes another barrier placed between the patient and the person of the therapist.

Specific techniques grow out of the uniquely personal way in which an individual therapist relates to his patients. They reflect the dominant character motifs of the person who develops them. Communicated from one therapist to another, they may lose much of their usefulness to the second therapist because they are not consistent with his personality.

Out of his inexperience and need to learn, the beginning psychotherapist tends to overemphasize techniques as such, using them to avoid the depth of relationship necessary for good therapy. There is still a further problem in talking about techniques. Certain technical patterns have pertinence to one phase of therapy, but if utilized in another phase, they quite automatically become sterile, nonpertinent, and even damaging to the relationship. For example, certain technical patterns of response to lead questions in the beginning phase of therapy make for a deeper relationship. These same responses to identical questions in the testing stage would tend to precipitate an impasse.

In the interest of integrity, the authors must limit their discussion to specific techniques utilized in their own work. Many of these are orthodox techniques, others vary significantly from the more standard procedures. All, however, have personal meaning for the authors, having been utilized repeatedly to develop deeper feeling in the relationship with a patient. Since much of the basic operation of therapy might be considered technical, the need for a specific definition of technique is apparent.

A technique is an *interpersonal operation deliberately used by the therapist, the function of which is to transpose social, latent affect in both participants into deeper, manifest affect in order to catalyze the affective and symbolic process of psychotherapy.* Technique so defined implies an underlying unconscious set (disposition to feel) on the part of the therapist; and further, it suggests that the affect he has at that point is less deep than what is implied by his behavior. The basic dynamics involved in a technique are similar to those in dream work, i.e., condensation, undoing, dramatization and symbolization. Unlike dream work, the major transposition here is not of content, but rather of affect, although some psychotherapists continue to approach the patient through content. A technique is effective if it induces personal and deep feeling in the relationship, producing relatedness which is no longer deliberate and conscious, but spontaneous and integrated. Techniques, then, are deliberate interpersonal operations which begin with minimum affect on the part of the therapist, and ideally result in spontaneous and deep affect bilaterally. Techniques apply specifically whenever the therapeutic relationship lacks motivating affects or is jammed by persisting unresolved affects (impasse). Techniques, therefore, are most pertinent in the beginning and ending phases of psychotherapy. They have little pertinence in the core stage of therapy where deep affect takes over. Techniques tend to develop appropriate affect in the other person. This is then calculated to stimulate real affect in the therapist. The mature therapist by this technical inauguration precipitates an honest, deep affect in himself.

Where a technique provides a means of avoiding deep affect in the therapist, it becomes a patient-vector in the therapist. Real affect precipitated in the therapist and patient by the deliberate efforts of the therapist has been repeatedly observed by the authors. Patients report that they recognize the deliberate quality of this initiation to a new phase in the relationship, but at the same time, they accept the depth and sincerity of the affect which results.

Techniques of Administration in Therapy

Psychotherapists have recently tended to isolate their therapeutic functioning from the realities of the patient's life and from their own extra-professional living. The therapist may not only isolate his experience with the patient, but also, establish limits to his administrative responsibilities. One method of management is to utilize a second person as an administrator. The administrator may be someone who naturally assumes this role within the culture, for example, the parent or the referring physician. It may be a designated administrator whose function is more carefully defined and more effective in many cases, e.g., a social worker. This person takes the responsibility for alleviating anxiety in the patient's family, for seeing that the patient continues in therapy, and for talking with the referring physician, the patient's boss, or other responsible persons concerning the real problems which come up in the patient's everyday world. The administrator may take further responsibility. He may, for example, be responsible for planning the patient's treatment in the beginning with the patient himself. He may, at that time, or at a later date, refer other members of the family for psychotherapy. Should the patient need medical treatment, he refers the patient to an internist. He also signs commitment papers if the patient has to be hospitalized. It may even be desirable during the therapeutic process to involve the administrator in a more direct and personal way. For example, he may be asked into the interview itself to make certain demands upon both the therapist and the patient. In the closed ward, the administrator might well meet with the patient and his therapist to face them with the fact that the patient can only stay in the hospital one week more, or that the patient will have to be moved to another ward if his behavior remains as disturbed as it has been. He thus confronts them with their failure, and demands greater efforts of each. He could also be asked to take responsibility for limiting the therapist's time with any patient, or to take up with the patient reality problems which bear upon the two of them in their therapeutic job.

The administrator actually facilitates the patient's fantastic involvement with the therapist and helps them proceed more rapidly and with less contamination. Freed of certain reality responsibilities and demands, the therapist can push on into the therapeutic relationship with fewer restrictions on his own functioning and greater freedom for affective involvement.

When it is not feasible to have somebody else assume an advisory relationship to the family and an advisory role to the seriously ill patient, it may be necessary for the therapist himself to function in these two roles. This is difficult with very sick patients, since the therapist himself may confuse his administrative role by behavior symbolically significant to the patient and, therefore, unreal. This can be minimized in several ways. These roles can be separated by using different offices for each, or by seeing the patient administratively in the presence of the secretary. The therapist should avoid casual contacts with the patient, and thus, minimize the confusion of roles. For example, if the patient calls on the phone, this may be left with the secretary. The therapist may even get into serious therapeutic impasses by such simple errors as giving the patient a ride home, or accepting a gift or an invitation to lunch. Sometimes he seriously errs by developing an implicit therapeutic relationship with another member of the family. He may do this by simply talking to the family about the patient. Generally, it is better not to handle any administrative details with the family. If the therapist must talk with the family, he should obtain the prior consent of the patient, and better yet speak to the family with the patient present. In summary, the therapeutic objective must be first. All other objectives must be secondary to the therapist lest he prove to the patient that the patient's wellness is not his primary objective.

Techniques in the Beginning Phase of Therapy

The techniques above dealt with the problems of administration in psychotherapy. The authors present below some of the techniques which they have found useful in psychotherapy itself. These are presented sequentially, beginning with the techniques and procedures most pertinent in the beginning phase of therapy. Some techniques pertinent and useful in one stage of the process are not relevant to the other stages. One mark of a professional therapist is the artistry of his timing in the use of techniques. At one point it may be of crucial significance that the therapist deny himself any satisfaction of his interest in the realities of the patient. At a later stage of therapy with the same patient, the therapist's failure to respond to the patient's offer of his outer world realities might be detrimental. The relationship of techniques to specific stages of therapy is crucial. The abuse of techniques in therapy stems most fundamentally from using them devoid of personal feeling and real affect, but secondarily stems from their use at an inappropriate time or with the wrong patient.

In the beginning phase of therapy, the objectives of the process as discussed throughout this book are essentially two: (1) the *objectives* achievement of adequate "isolation" of the relationship so that *of therapy* fantasy satisfaction is made possible, and (2) the rapid transition from the real to the symbolic—from the conscious to the unconscious. These two aims can be abetted through the use of specific techniques. Some of these techniques are commonplace, being utilized by many psychiatrists with or without awareness of their relationship to the patient's progress in therapy. Isolation of the relationship, for example, is furthered by the physical surroundings within which the therapy occurs. The therapist's consultation room becomes for him a place in which unconscious and acultural feelings are abreacted. The patient intuits the isolative feeling tones which pervade the therapist's office. The expediency of insisting that the patient come to the same place for therapy further heightens this isolation. For this reason, it is poor technique to allow constant change in the physical surroundings so that interviews take place in a number of different places.

Since isolation involves a deletion of the patient's realities from the therapeutic relationship, the therapist should not see the patient at a place or in a situation in which the patient's realities are dominant; for example, to do therapy in the patient's own home makes isolation extremely difficult. This technique of physical isolation to promote fantasy reflects somewhat the same principle which underlies the general rule that a therapist should not accept patients whose real lives approximate his own, for example, a close friend or relative.

One of the most difficult transitions the patient has to make in the beginning of therapy involves the termination of his relationship with his social therapist. Techniques which facilitate this

termination better isolate the professional therapeutic relationship. Some of these have been discussed in the previous section
dealing with administrative problems.

Perhaps the most useful technique for developing isolation is a
conscious deletion of the therapist's own realities from the therapeutic relationship. Thus, the therapist does not discuss the realities of his own living with a patient. He may also further the isolation by refusing to admit the immediate realities of his office
situation into the therapeutic relationship. Refusal to answer the
telephone during the interview and unwillingness to accept any
other interruption until the interview is terminated are illustrative
of techniques through which the therapist successfully isolates the
patient by deleting his own realities in the office situation. Refusal
to discuss the therapeutic relationship with the family, the referring doctor, or the employer constitutes another effective technique for isolation. A denial of the importance of the patient's past
life, and an insistence on the all-importance of the current feelings
of the patient in the relationship provides another means of isolation. This approach has an important bearing on how rapidly the
patient makes the transition into a symbolic fantasy relationship.

Techniques which have proven useful in facilitating the transition from a conscious, social relationship to an unconscious symbolic relationship between the patient and therapist can be
divided into four main groups. First are those techniques which
provide for the mutual acceptance of a reality frame of reference
as a point of departure into therapy. The patient will seldom enter
into a fantastic relationship unless he has assurance of reality foot-
holds to which he can return with ease whenever fantasy becomes
too threatening. In the beginning, the therapist easily tolerates the
patient's shifts from fantasy to reality. The patient's temporary
refuge in reality seems more acceptable at this point than during
the latter stages of therapy. The therapist waits for symbolic involvement at this stage without being too aggressively insistent on
the patient's fantasy participation. Thus, he may listen to a history
and recitation of the patient's past life or previous therapy without
insisting that the patient involve himself in an affective way with
the therapist. He must remain sensitive to the symbolic "castings"

of the patient nonetheless. The patient needs a reality basis for the therapeutic relationship. The imposition of very strict limitations around the therapeutic relationship becomes an important part of this reality framework. Thus, the therapist may limit the time he spends with the patient to 45 minutes or an hour and adhere to this limitation. To break this in the beginning phase of therapy may threaten the security which the patient needs and to stay beyond the allotted time may seriously threaten the patient's security. These limitations can be further implemented by the therapist's clear assurance that he will not see the patient except at scheduled interview times and in the usual place. Another technique which achieves the same aim involves the therapist's willingness for, and even insistence on, the patient making his own reality decisions. This may be crucial in the beginning phase of therapy. Thus, the therapist refuses to decide for the patient whether or not he should take a leave of absence from his job because of his emotional difficulties. The therapist may even insist that the patient make his own decision about the administration of the therapeutic process itself. Decisions about time, the number of interviews per week, whether the patient ought to return for subsequent interviews, even the decision to terminate an interview, are all specific bits of reality which, if constructively left to the patient, will build a substantial understructure to support the patient while he embarks into the unlimited world of his own fantasy. The therapist's direct, verbal, and honest acceptance of the patient's wellness, in addition to the sickness which brought him to the therapist, provides the patient with more security in the initial relationship. The patient deserves some assurance that the therapist sees his maturities so that the presentation of his immaturities becomes less threatening. Further, the therapist must constantly insist on maintaining his own personal reality satisfactions, so that at no point does he sacrifice any deep reality gratification because of pressure by the patient. Thus, if the patient should insist on seeing the therapist at a time inconvenient to the therapist, and the patient is able to come at another time, the therapist should not sacrifice his own convenience to satisfy the patient. The patient must come to know that this other person has sufficient integrity and cognizance of his own separateness and realness to refuse to sacrifice these for the fantasy relationship with the patient. Such assurance in the patient further facilitates his symbolic involvement. When the symbolic involvement of the patient seems premature and totally projective in nature, the therapist should deny the appropriateness of such projections. Thus, initially, the patient may project onto the therapist a magical capacity to alleviate some of his real needs, but one which is not pertinent to the therapeutic task of satisfying his symbolic needs.

A converse of this involves the therapist's presenting his own limitations and his immaturities to the patient. Expressed in an early stage of therapy, these constitute another segment of reality which supports the patient in his plunge into fantasy. The transition into the symbolic area may be facilitated by the techniques outlined above, which aim at providing a reality frame of reference from which the patient can embark into his fantasy.

Techniques aimed at directly developing fantasy are also useful in the beginning stages of therapy. Some which the authors have found useful include a participant response to everyday psychopathology, which the patient introduces either in the interview or in the management of his therapy. Thus, a slip of the tongue or any significant gesturing and posturing during the interview, when responded to by the therapist for their symbolic meaning, ease the patient's acceptance of his underlying need and establish some affective involvement. Simple interpretation is not usually the most adequate for this.

In addition, there are more positive techniques for the early development of a fantasy relationship. The isolation itself predisposes toward fantasy by its exclusion of the real. The fragments of fantasy life, e.g., loaded words or phrases, tone of voice, etc., which the patient presents in the beginning of therapy may be expanded, and the underlying symbolism of the therapeutic relationship implicit in the patient's coming to a psychiatrist thus transposed into a more explicit symbolic relationship. For years, both orthodox psychoanalysis and, to a large extent, all relationship therapists have utilized a technique of reflecting the patient's content back to him. The re-interpretation of all the patient's talk and behavior in terms of his relationship to his therapist increases the gain in this procedure. Everything the patient says emerges in the framework of this therapeutic relationship and has thereby some pertinence to the patient's symbolic pattern of relating to the therapist. By re-interpreting his discussion of his family life or his feeling about himself as though they were equally true about his relationship to the therapist, one pushes the patient farther and farther into cathecting the therapist himself. This amounts to the use of transference interpretations much as in orthodox therapy, and as such, needs little discussion. Its chief value as a technique, however, rests not only in the resulting insights which occur because of the re-interpretation. It also provides the patient with a sense of the many determinants of behavior and of the variability in the levels on which he relates to the therapist, as well as some concept of the fluidity of time and of expressions of the past in terms of the present. In general, it gives him some sense of the dimensions of symbolism, with an awareness of the timelessness of the unconscious and its poor regard for reality limitations.

Relationship interpretation in the beginning of therapy provides the patient with some feeling of the possibility of resolving his earlier transference relationships. Once his feelings for the original parents can be transferred to the therapist, the patient can work through and resolve feelings which hitherto had been historical and, therefore, unavailable for resolution. Relationship interpretations are but one of the many techniques based on the conviction that the patient's relationship to the therapist is essentially an unconscious one. This implies a readiness on the part of the therapist not only to hear what the patient says or means consciously, but also to be attentive to and respond verbally or behavioristically to what the patient says or means unconsciously. A therapist should be attentive to slips of the tongue, inappropriate behavior, inappropriate gestures, peculiar posturing, affectively loaded words, the manner in which the patient intrudes reality factors into the relationship at inappropriate times, and the whole gamut of what is ordinarily thought of as symbolic slips of the patient in therapy. The responsibility of the therapist at this point includes, primarily, attentiveness, instead of interpretations and translations of the symbolic language for the patient. The therapist needs only the conviction that everything the patient says after the early stages has symbolic portent for their relationship. His response at one point may be a rewording of what the patient has said, e.g., a re-interpretation of the patient's being late for an interview. More often, in the beginning phase of therapy, the therapist's responses consist only of his implicit understanding of the symbolic meaning of what the patient has said or done and an implicit response which most often stays within the confines of the patient's presenting symbolism. Most often in the beginning phase of therapy, the therapist functions best by responding with silence to the patient's symbolic presentations. This allows the patient's symbolic presentation to stimulate the therapist's own fantasy relationship to the patient. This implicit understanding of the patient and the patient's problem must be established before he begins responding on a more explicit behavioral or verbal level. Pure content interpretation of fantasy presentation often leads the therapist to preclude a deep relationship with the patient and, in essence, denies the symbolic fantasy relationship rather than expanding it. One can almost say that the earliest explicit interpretations should be interpretations by the therapist of his own symbolic fantasy, his own slips of the tongue, and his own psychopathology in the interview.

Another important element in the entrance into fantasy centers in the patient's concept of time. Any technique which succeeds in equating in the patient all time, whether past or future, with the present time, seems to have validity. Obviously, such a technique expands the unconscious component of the therapy.

To ask the patient to free associate as a procedural technique in the early phases of therapy is disappointing. The easiest and most complete transition into *felt free association* (similar to *felt insight* as against intellectual insight) for the patient develops through the therapist's willingness to utilize his own affective free associations and auto-fantasy as the basis for relating to his patient. The authors have found that in each instance where they could expand their own unconscious responses to a patient, the patient was more able and ready to respond with affect and with material which was more unconscious than that which could have been elicited by the artificial imposition of the rule of free association. Expansion of the fantasy component is also facilitated by sensitive selective deafness on the part of the therapist. By failure to respond to material which is real and is therefore not pertinent to the therapeutic problem, he effectively limits the patient's energies to the fantasy area. This technique of selective deafness, together with the traditional use of the "third ear," may be further reinforced with a firm denial of any interest in content or verbiage for its own sake. Technically, the fantasy relationship in therapy emerges more adequately and more rapidly by a firm and almost intractable concern with the affective elements during the initial phase of therapy. If the patient becomes convinced that the therapist is fundamentally concerned with his affective responses in the beginning phases of therapy, content and verbal material subsequently presented become meaningful and therapeutically valid. The principle that acceptance of content and verbiage in the beginning phases of therapy provides a bridge to a later affective involvement has not been validated in the authors' experiences. On the contrary, the affective elements become increasingly less available if the verbal and content defenses are tolerated in the beginning. In this phase of therapy, then, one of the most adequate techniques for developing fantasy involves silence on the part of the therapist. Since silence has manifold implications in therapy, it will be discussed at a later point in this chapter when those techniques which apply in all phases of therapy are presented.

In summary then, techniques for expanding the fantasy component of therapy are readily available to the therapist. Many of the orthodox, psychoanalytical techniques, and techniques used in child psychiatry have as their aim just such symbolic realization. The young therapist, in his initial interviews with patients, would do well to remain silent and to respond to as few of the realities of the patient as possible. Simultaneously, this will tend to expand his own fantasy reactions to the patient. Underlying this approach is the assumption that the patient's relationship to the therapist is basically symbolic. Everything the patient does or says has meaning in terms of his relationship to the therapist. Such meaning can be best understood and responded to only if the therapist has access to his own primary process which provides the most adequate basis for unconscious to unconscious communication.

Techniques which accelerate the transition into symbolic areas have counterparts in those methods used to block the patient's retreat from symbolization. When the therapist denies content and historical discussion, he says to the patient, "I will relate to you only on a symbolic level." As the patient's anxiety increases he will try to find other means to avoid a threatening symbolic relationship. This abrupt increase in anxiety reflects itself in greater confusion in the patient's real life adjustment during the period of transition. This activates his whole defensive armamentarium, associated with a retreat from fantasy. It then becomes a technical problem as to just how the therapist can block this retreat. The authors believe that this must be done firmly and surely, since any sense of the therapist's ambivalence about this by the patient increases his anxiety about their symbolic relationship. He comes to doubt the therapist's capacity to relate to him on a symbolic level. In certain instances, the anxiety provoked by the abrupt transition into an intense symbolic relationship may be so overwhelming that the therapist feels compelled to compromise the relationship in order to temporarily buffer the anxiety. Ordinarily this is not necessary, and patients tolerate anxiety with surprising homeostatic economy. The error usually lies in the direction of over-support and early compromise because of the uncertainty of the therapist. The techniques which prevent the patient's retreat from the relationship also serve to keep the therapist in the symbolic relationship. Acceptance by the therapist of his own affective involvement and participation at that level in the symbolic relationship strongly reinforce the patient's need for a deep, affective, unconscious relationship. Denial of content, the therapist's permitting his own fantasy to develop, deliberate use of his own slips of the tongue, behavioristic responses to the patient and, in general, his acceptance on an overt level of his own symbolic involvement, all serve to bring this about.

As the patient becomes more involved in the therapeutic process, he may utilize patterns of communication and symbolic referents which have served him in the past in the establishment of deeply affective relationships. For example, a businessman for whom fishing trips have been deep affective experiences may well begin to discuss his relationship to the therapist by things having to do with a fishing trip. If the therapist is willing to relate affectively to this analogic sort of symbolism, the relationship can develop apace. Within the superficial discussion of a fantasy fishing trip, the symbolic relationship may be established. Through this, a very deep relationship may develop, with the implicit understanding in each of the two participants of the two-level nature of their discussion.

These adult-oriented fantasy frameworks are less significant as methods of communication than are the symbolic forms which the culture provides. The language of religion exemplifies this very well. It is possible to communicate with the patient on a deeply symbolic level if the therapist feels free to use religious referents, and feels certain of the fundamental nature of the underlying affect and unconcerned with secondary cultural overtones. The therapist's own childhood experience in this area may persist as a distortion, and blind him to the commonalities of religious experience. If the therapist has worked this through, he can utilize the language of religion, both as a symbolic language relating to the therapy itself, and as an acceptable form for interpreting their relationship. More cogent still than the language of religion is the language that has to do with the structure and function of the body itself. Body image symbolism has been used frequently where physical symptoms are a presenting problem in the psychiatric patient. Initial discussions of symptoms can be converted into body image language which ordinarily has deep significance in the development of a symbolic relationship in therapy. Premature rejection of such presenting content as not pertinent to the problem at hand may delay the process. It must be emphasized again that the body language as a means of communication necessitates not only an understanding of the patient's multi-level use of it, but also, the therapist's awareness of the importance of his own body image in his responses to the patient. For example, rather than interpret a patient's complaint that he has "pains in the heart," acceptance of the underlying affect which he has attempted to communicate in this indirect manner has greater merit. Response to the patient who complains of a headache as if the patient were aggressing may move the process further along than interpreting the symptom as being aggressive. By the same token, presentation of the therapist's own physical sensations without interpretation has similar symbol value. Thus, it may be important for the patient to realize that you are indignant at his thinking so little of himself that he talks in a "tiny voice," but it is equally important for him to know that he had induced in you a stiffness of the neck or that he makes you tighten up the muscles of your legs. As the therapist in his body response says something about the relationship, he validates the patient's right to communicate with the therapist in an equally free-associative manner.

The peculiar appropriateness of using childhood, religious, and body image language in facilitating the patient's acceptance of symbolism arises out of the intimate manner in which these forms of communication approximate conscious to unconscious. The observation that these areas erupt early in the psychotic patient attests to this close relationship. Such a person, whether his psychosis be functional, organic, or a product of fatigue or drugs, presents his affect to others in the language of the child, in "religious" fantasies, and in the language of somatic sensations. It appears as if the basic psychological conflicts find an immediate expression in these forms when conventional forms of communication fail. In this sense then, the use of religious or body language has a psychological core, although the specific content may be culturally determined. It is valid to use these symbols, not because of their relevance in the patient's history or their cultural value, but simply because they comprise the most effective nontechnical language for communicating with the patient's unconscious. Both religious and agnostic patients understand the therapist when he says, "You do not believe you are made in the image of God." The primitiveness and universality of these three areas make them peculiarly fruitful in the process of symbolic communication and symbolic realization in psychotherapy.

Techniques in the Symbolic Phase of Psychotherapy

The techniques discussed previously were techniques which functioned to begin the process of psychotherapy. As was pointed out, initially one aims at achieving an isolation which favors a symbolic relationship and techniques which force, develop, and expand the fantasy relationship. These techniques have their greatest pertinence in Stages I and II (anamnesis and casting stages). Once the fantasy develops and goes beyond the casting stage into a deep, dynamic symbolic relationship with the therapist, i.e., beginning with the third stage (the Competitive Stage), the patient begins to relate to the therapist on an older sibling level. Techniques at this point assume less importance. Here the process of therapy has an emergent dynamic of its own. It involves, essentially, the inherent dynamics of the patient-vectors and the therapist-vectors in each person and in their interrelationships. Techniques in these areas are pertinent only when the process slows down or reaches some impasse. Ordinarily, if the beginning phase of therapy is adequate, the competitive, the regressive, and the core stages emerge and are completed with little or no difficulty. Technical implementation of this emergence is seldom necessary, and, when attempted, is ineffectual. The authors are convinced that once the patient enters the symbolic process of therapy, the process tends to grow to core stage unless serious patient-vectors in the therapist interfere with the emergent process. The distortions of the process through Stages III, IV, and V are essentially no different from any other impasse and resolve in much the same manner as other impasses.

The authors have found certain techniques useful in furthering their own adequacy when symbolically involved with the patient. During the competitive and regressive stages, where the patient projects onto the therapist, and relates to him with ever-changing and ever-deepening transferences, techniques should enable the therapist to be more deeply aware and more responsive to the patient's projections. Such techniques as free association, auto-fantasy, constant attention to and awareness of his own unconscious symbolization of the patient, and willingness to accept his deeper fantasy about the patient as a valid perception of the patient's symbolic use of him, may help.

During the competitive and regressive stage, the patient often develops new resistances. Frequently, he finds it difficult to move beyond certain critical areas in his regression. He tends to fix at a certain point and to repeat infantile behavior compulsively interview after interview. In such instances, the authors have found that aggression through a positive attack on the patient's fixation constitutes an effective dynamic. Like silence, however, aggression in psychotherapy has many facets, and since it comprises one of the major affective dynamics of psychotherapy, it will also be discussed in the latter part of this chapter. The therapist, during the stages of regression, often faces a lack of deep and appropriate affect in himself. The patient may come in deeply involved, and the therapist, who has been in a reality situation just prior to the interview or affectively involved with another patient, may find it difficult to respond with feelings of appropriate depth. The use of affectively loaded words or behavior, even though feelings and affective involvement are minimal, constitutes a valuable technique. This induces an unconscious set and involves the conviction that, although the affect is not immediately available, the use of words and behavior appropriate to such deep involvement effectively pushes the therapist's involvement. After technically responding to the patient who is on a deep level, the technical response may be automatically reinforced with appropriately deep feeling. Thus, the patient may come into an interview in the regressive stage with a dependent need, reinforced by or based on very deep affective symbolic ties to the therapist. The therapist may recognize his own response to the patient as shallow and affectively inappropriate. Technically, however, he can respond by offering to love, feed, hold, or mother the patient. In the beginning, his response may not have the necessary feeling reinforcing it. He ordinarily finds, however, that this verbal or behavioral response is followed by the emergence of feelings of sufficient depth and sincerity to satisfy the needs of the patient.

During the regressive and certainly in the core stage, the relationship is almost purely affective in character. Techniques contaminate such a relationship. Behaviorally, at any rate, silence comprises the framework within which regression occurs and core satisfactions are achieved. The authors have found that regression may, at times, be facilitated by certain props or auxiliaries. Thus, the therapists have used bottle feeding, physical rocking of patients, and other aids which stimulate in both therapist and patient the requisite affect for infantile satisfaction of the patient. It reproduces in therapy aspects of the mother-child relationship. More recently, the authors have found that if aggression is utilized at this point of therapy it most appropriately takes the form of spanking. These, however, are auxiliary techniques which compensate for the therapist's inadequacy by inducing the deep affect which the patient seeks for the satisfaction of his infantile and dependent needs. Theoretically, the authors are convinced that these regressive and core satisfactions can be provided without any props or auxiliary techniques since the process of therapy is essentially an intra-psychic one. Technical implementation must only reflect certain immaturities in the intra-psychic functioning of the therapist.

In the core stage of therapy, the experience is primarily a non-verbal shared fantasy experience. Each participant has unconscious access to the feelings and involvements of the other. This stage of therapy occurs spontaneously even though its emergence may have been facilitated by any number of techniques. Sometimes, when the final transition into the core fantasy is difficult, techniques have some pertinence. At this point, the relationship becomes purely symbolic in character. Affect is readily available to both participants. At the intermediate point, just anteceding the core experience, there may be some need to reassert the reality frame of reference in order to provide the necessary security for the patient. In addition to such reality affirmations, a final denial of the importance of content, verbiage, or reality factors may help to facilitate the transition into the core phase. The therapist may technically force the patient into the core experience only on the basis of his own inner assurance that the necessary affective and relationship ingredients are present so that the core experience can be satisfying to the patient. This takes the form of his activating a deep fantasy with the patient. The forced joint fantasy may, in its inception, be verbal. It is presented by the therapist as an experience in the present tense in which he relates to the patient with feeling and affect appropriate to the nursing mother who responds to a hungry child. The fantasy need not seek refuge in metaphor or allegory. The fantasy forced at this point becomes direct and primitive. If the patient is ready for the core experience in therapy, and the therapist is capable and sufficiently involved, the forced fantasy proceeds easily from the verbal presentation of it to the nonverbal experience itself. The verbal inception, or precipitation into the feeding experience, may be further implemented by techniques involving physical contact, changes in body posture, and a very frank, face to face relationship.

Techniques of Ending

Just as with the beginning phases of therapy, the ending phase requires technical adequacy. Both contrast, as indicated previously, with the lesser importance of technique in the core phase. As the relationship becomes less symbolic, technical maneuvers or moves by the therapist become useful and, sometimes, extremely significant. The most fundamental characteristic of the ending phase of therapy involves the expansion of the reality component within the patient himself. This correlates with an increasing amount of reality in the relationship between the patient and the therapist. One of the problems in this area, as discussed previously, has to do with the reluctance on the part of the therapist to leave the deeply satisfying relationship with the patient in the core phase. He may have to resort to the more technical aspects of the therapeutic experience in order to aid his own emergence into the ending experience.

The therapist can aid and abet the ending process by greater freedom to talk about real things. The reality decisions about the therapeutic relationship, the things having to do with their real life with each other, such as the interviews and their spacing, help to break up the symbolic relationship. They enable the patient to become increasingly independent of the therapist and take up his own living process again. In this connection, the authors have become increasingly aware of certain cues which emerge in the ending phase of treatment and indicate the patient's readiness to decathect the therapist and take over the management of his own living process. These are: (1) The patient may suddenly begin to talk in a casual manner where previously the talk has been affectively loaded. This change in voice tone may escape the therapist, but it should be taken at face value. (2) The patient may deny symbolic statements or ignore slips of the tongue which previously he had utilized for his own growth. Thus, he evidences his increased reality sense. (3) The patient may discuss a referral he has made to this therapist or another therapist, or sometimes tell how the day before, to his own amazement, he functioned as therapist to a friend or social acquaintance. (4) The patient may forget an appointment or be late for an appointment, and whereas in the beginning phase of therapy this might be thought of as a fear of becoming symbolically involved, it now signifies health and evidences his lessening need of the therapist. (5) The patient or the therapist may make slips of the tongue which have positive connotations, and infer their new faith in the maturity of the patient. (6) A confusing aspect of this phase of therapy may arise when the patient discusses with the therapist a situation laden with content, but in which the affect is minimal. This limited affect with serious content is indicative of the patient's desire to handle the problem by himself. (7) The authors have found that a very sure indication of imminent ending is revealed by the decreased affect in the therapist himself. He finds that his own affect in the interview diminishes suddenly. He even feels bored. (8) The patient may express his increasing maturity by offering to help the therapist with some aspect of his own immaturity, or reveal some psychopathology which he sees in the therapist. (9) The patient may take up the problem of finances, indicating in one way or another that he wants to pay the therapist off, and inferring thereby that he wants to be through with him. (10) The patient may take up, at some length, his real life successes, either in terms of the disappearance of one of his initial symptoms, or in a more specific way, describe his capacity as an adult in his real life situation. (11) The patient may visit his original referring physician. (12) Patients frequently denote their readiness to end by a recapitulation of the therapeutic process. Thus, the patient offers to pay the physician in the scientific medium of exchange. In addition to this, he makes the fantasy experience real by verbalizing it and binding it symbolically. (13) Lastly, the patient may take up the therapist's pathology on a fairly specific level and endeavor to or express his regret that he cannot help him work through this need.

It should be noted that cues for ending serve not only as communication, but also as a means by which the patient works through his relationship to the symbolic figure of the therapist. He simultaneously tests the therapist's faith in him, the therapist's capacity to see the wellness in him, and the therapist's willingness to let him grow up even though it means that the therapist will be left without "his child."

Techniques Involved in the Testing Stage

Once the therapist has accepted incipient ending by recognizing some of the cues, the patient is apt to flip rapidly into a testing phase. Here he puts increasing pressure upon the therapist to discover for himself whether the therapist really believes the patient capable of handling his own life even though the therapist knows, as the patient does, that there will be other times of stress and other periods of temporary regression. The testing may include a very direct invasion of the therapist's real life situation, both within the interview and outside it. This necessitates the therapist's firm recognition of the limitations of his own function. He had accepted the symbolic role. Now he must reaffirm his renunciation of the real relationship to his patient as a real person. For example, the therapist must not accept special appointments at this phase, even though on the basis of an acute anxiety episode. These anxiety attacks arise from the recognition that the patient is now responsible for himself in a new sense. Anxiety in the therapist, like anxiety in the parent of an adolescent, loads the patient with a further responsibility for reassuring the therapist. Furthermore, it impedes the progress of the patient's separation from the therapist. The therapist should deny any efforts the patient makes for the establishment of a social relationship since, if he accepts a social relationship, the therapist shows that he believes himself to be a necessity to the patient's adequate living.

The patient's insight into the therapist may lead him to point out the therapist's problems and offer him help in the resolution of these. Acceptance of this offer by the therapist imposes a responsibility which the patient is ordinarily not able to carry through. It results in the patient's staying in the core phase of the therapeutic relationship and being unable to end. Technically, the therapist does well to state openly his own residual needs, but reaffirm his capacity to continue to grow without the help of the patient. It must be clearly understood that this is quite different from the patient's function as a therapist to the relationship at an earlier stage when they switch roles temporarily. This post core stage offer amounts to a test of the therapist's readiness to accept the patient's ending.

The final termination of psychotherapy presents less problems than the period in which the patient makes his first tentative efforts at ending followed by a period of testing the therapist. The actual withdrawal of the patient may come easily, depending on the willingness of the therapist to accept the patient's explicit ending. During the withdrawal stage, however, techniques can precipitate the patient's deeper involvement in outside relationships, and this integration with reality often facilitates the terminal ending. Increasing the patient's responsibility for more decisive action in the management of the therapy often effectively aids withdrawal. For example, withdrawal may be facilitated by the therapist's willingness to accept the reality talk of the patient and/or a willingness to bring into the relationship some of his own realities, either professional or personal. At times, the therapist may have to reinforce reality participation by his explicit refusal to take up anew any fantasy vectors in the patient. Finally, in a rare instance, where termination of the relationship has resisted all other technical approaches, the therapy may be administratively ended by the therapist with the flat statement to the patient that he will not see the patient after a specific number of further interviews have ensued. Since the administrative ending occurs thus only after the process of therapy has been completed and the patient has had a core experience, such ending never amounts to a rejection. In contrast, administrative ending of a patient who had not successfully reached core phase in therapy would be tantamount to rejection and cause serious repercussions in the patient's emotional economy, whereas administrative ending is a declaration of faith in the patient and a statement of the limitations of the therapist's capacity.

Some days or weeks after the scheduled interviews conclude, the patient may call the therapist for an additional appointment because of a so-called relapse. No rule of thumb can be applied to these situations. The post-ending experience of the patient should be protected from too extensive reality (social) contact with the therapist. This precaution looms large in this period of transition. It is imperative that the patient find adequate reality stimulation in his real life situation apart from the therapist in order to develop and expand his ego component. The post-ending appointment, however, often constitutes a further testing. In such instances, refusal to see the patient may be the most valid procedure. Where the therapist is unsure of the motivation of the patient, subsequent interviews may be arranged. In these, the therapist can more definitely respond to either the wellness of the patient, or a need for deeper therapy. In the experience of the authors, post-ending appointments most often represent efforts at testing the therapist, with reference either to his perception and belief in the adequacy of the patient, or to the emotional validity of the ending process itself. At times, patients return for a post-ending interview in order to develop a relationship to the therapist now as a real person, and in so doing, decathect much of the fantasy experience of therapy. This decathecting makes their feelings and emotional energies available for use in real life relationships.

Techniques and Communication in Therapy

In speaking earlier of the dynamics of psychotherapy, constant reference was made to the importance of communication in the process of psychotherapy. In many ways, the process of psychotherapy can be equated with an emergent increase in the affective communication between the two participants in the therapeutic process. In much the same vein, techniques which develop fantasy and symbolic participation along with those which facilitate symbolic resolution and a reorientation toward reality, all function through increasing and clarifying the inter-subjective communication between the participants in psychotherapy. There are specific techniques related to communication in its most basic and pertinent form in psychotherapy, i.e., nonverbal communication, which the authors have found useful in the early stages of psychotherapy. One such technique involves the therapist's verbal response to non-verbal stimuli and cues from the patient. Simultaneously, his refusal to respond verbally to words spoken with little feeling by the patient develops the nonverbal communication bilaterally. Insistence on a face-to-face relationship in psychotherapy also facilitates such nonverbal communication. In contrast to the concern of many professional psychotherapists that patients cannot tolerate the stress and anxiety of a face-to-face relationship, the authors have found patients reassured by such a relationship. When the face-to-face encounter provokes excess anxiety in the patient, the patient's homeostatic dynamics economically buffer this interpersonal contact without untoward sequelae.

Technical Orientations Useful Throughout the Process

Techniques discussed so far have proven useful in psychotherapy during various stages of the process of psychotherapy. Such techniques are rather specific and their pertinence limited to recurrent problems arising at very definite stages in the process of psychotherapy. In contrast, certain major techniques apply throughout the whole process of psychotherapy. Their importance stems from a number of factors. First, these techniques have multiple functions. When used in one instance at a specific time in therapy, their function may be of an entirely different kind from that when used in a subsequent phase of psychotherapy. More significant, however, these techniques are used socially by people who do implicit psychotherapy in their everyday relationships with others. When one surveys the ordinary responses in society when an individual deals with a deep emotional reaction in another, one encounters these interpersonal "techniques." These include the importance of the present relationship and the manner in which it subsumes within it all of its past determinants; silence; aggression; physical contact; face-to-face relationships; and finally, they include the joint fantasy through which people normally communicate their unconscious feelings in an interpersonal relationship.

TRANSFERENCE AND EMPHASIS ON THE PRESENT RELATIONSHIP. All modern forms of psychotherapy are fundamentally based on the theory that transference problems can be expressed in the therapist-patient relationship. The first major technique presented here involves just this theory. The psychotherapist assumes that the patient will express in his relationship to the therapist all of the feelings and behavior appropriate to earlier infantile relationships. In this sense, the therapeutic relationship, a current and, therefore, a potentially modifiable relationship, contains the essential historical relationships which have determined the patient's personality. This provides a basis for structuring his future interpersonal relationships. Technically, the authors have accepted this tenet as being a fundamental principle in psychotherapy. Experience in brief depth therapy, however, has considerably modified the application of this transference principle. The authors have found it useful during therapy to assume that everything the patient says, his total behavior, has direct bearing on his relationship to the therapist during the interview. In brief depth therapy, the emphasis shifts from an objective analysis of the historical determinants in the patient's behavior to a contemporary participation and response to the patient's behavior during the interview. The therapist accepts, as a point of departure, the notion that all of the patient's therapeutic participation is essentially symbolic in character. He further accepts the fact that in brief psychotherapy the patient condenses all of his transference relationships into his emotional involvement with the therapist. At this point, the manner in which the therapist proceeds with the interviews differs considerably from the psychoanalyst who, of course, bases his therapy on much the same general principle. The psychoanalyst accepts his role as a time screen on which the patient projects his transference feelings and with whom the patient compulsively repeats his infantile patterns of behavior. The psychoanalyst, with this as a matrix, remains objectively detached from such transference projections and can, therefore, on the basis of his increasing understanding of the genetic determinants of the patient's behavior, interpretatively develop an understanding of how earlier infantile relationships determine the patient's current behavior with the analyst. The resulting insight and, to some extent, social correction ideally result in a deletion of these infantile determinants and a gradual resolution of the transference factors in the patient. The therapist interested in brief psychotherapy seldom utilizes interpretative techniques, nor does he overly concern himself with the patient's insight and understanding of the genetic determinants of his current behavior. He accepts the fact that his relationship to the patient is on the level of transference, and that, therefore, many of the patient's responses and feelings are inappropriate. He alters the nature of the patient's response, not by an intellectual or ego correction, but by way of his own emotional and personal participation in the relationship. In the context of this relationship, the patient becomes aware that his behavior and his feelings are inappropriate. Because of the therapist's partial involvement in the relationship, he can respond more appropriately, i.e., more maturely. Interpretations are always made in the present tense, set in the framework not of the patient's relationship to historical figures, but in the context of his current relationship to the therapist. For example, a patient who reveals a reluctance about, even fear of, his developing dependency on the therapist acts out, in a very direct way, a transference problem. Analytically, the treatment procedure would consist in bringing to bear on his present fear of dependency some awareness of unconscious fears relating to earlier dependency on his parents and the results of it in his own fantasy. In contrast, the brief therapist would approach the same transference problem with emphasis on the patient's current reluctance to become dependent upon him. This, in turn, aids the patient's perception of the inadequacies in the therapist which might make the present dependency simply a repetition of what had happened to him earlier. In summary then, the same general principles apply; the emphasis, however, shifts from the genetic determinants to the current determinants, from insight to corrective emotional factors involved in the present relationship with the therapist. Interpretations made by the brief therapist take on meaning in the context of the therapist's emotional response to the patient. The most important interpretations are made not verbally, but through the therapist's participation in the relationship, i.e., implicitly.

INSISTENCE ON A FACE-TO-FACE RELATIONSHIP. Such an emphasis on the current relationship, particularly its emotional dimension, calls for a re-evaluation of another technique utilized in orthodox analysis. Since analysis emphasizes the genetic determinants with the evocation of repressed memories and fantasies, the spatial relationship between the patient and the therapist must be such that the patient's memory and fantasy experience is maximal, and that the therapist intrude as little as possible into this experience. The usual couch promotes the patient's re-experience and his infantilism. The analyst's function remains essentially that of a screen so that his active participation can be as objective as possible. These aims are achieved in some measure by the patient's position on the couch, a position which stimulates reverie and infantilism. This permits the analyst some social distance (visual at any rate), leaving him free to participate only tangentially in the fantasy. In contrast, the brief therapist more actively participates in the current fantasies of the patient. He stresses what the patient is now, not what the patient has been historically. His orientation involves the conviction that he can alter what the patient is now through his present participation in the patient's deepest fantasy experiences. He does not remain "objective" but becomes subjectively involved with the patient.

The emphasis on the present, on the emotional, on the subjective, on the personal quality of the relationship between the patient and therapist, suggests some rearrangements in the interview situation. Brief therapy can best be accomplished with the patient in a sitting position, free to move and assume any position, but always in a face-to-face relationship with the therapist. This technique forces the patient's active, visual, even physical, participation. One of the most difficult problems in brief, intensive therapy is to help the patient dare to look directly at the therapist. As a corollary, one of the most difficult problems in training a therapist to do intensive, brief therapy is the development of a capacity to look directly at a patient.

THE USE OF SILENCE AS A TECHNICAL AID. Paradoxically silence assumes importance in therapy because of its significance in communication. In some respects its function in therapy runs counter to patterns of social communication. Probably the easiest utilization of silence is in the anamnestic stage in therapy. It creates a sort of vacuum and pushes the patient into taking the initiative in the relationship. Farther along in therapy, and specifically in the competitive stage, silence may serve as a very effective means for countering the patient's effort to break up his symbolization of the therapist. A non-verbal response by the therapist to the patient serves the purpose of helping the patient to hear his own superficial verbalization most clearly. It, thus, serves as a powerful means of precipitating the patient into a deeper level of transference. Silence also stimulates in the patient a fantasy response to his own verbalization, or augments the free-floating fantasy which forms such an important preliminary to the regressive stage. Silence can serve as a method for developing the patient's regression at a more rapid pace, increasing anxiety and helping the patient to carry a greater part of the initiative in an effort to resolve the disequilibrium involved in their affective exchange. Finally, therapy is usually non-verbal in the core phase. This silence effectively potentiates the affective communication which, by this time, is extremely accurate and exact.

Evaluating the function of silence on a more personal level, one finds that it serves as a means by which the therapist develops his own fantasy participation in the relationship. The authors have suspected that success in the use of silence in therapy leads to the therapist's willingness to sleep in the interview. It should not be necessary to clarify the fact that the therapist isn't being bored. Sleep does not signify either a positive or a negative relationship but has certain specific dynamics. Sleep, on the part of the therapist, may serve as a retreat from the relationship and an escape from his own anxiety. It may be a retreat from aggressive impulses or a yielding to sexual fantasies. A mature therapist will rapidly get past this phase and arrive at a point where going to sleep has a specific function and serves the therapeutic relationship. Then sleep becomes a means by which he expresses nonverbally the deepest positive feelings or negative feelings toward the patient. Further there are some patients with whom the symbolic relationship develops very slowly and, at times, the therapist can augment his own affect by allowing himself to go to sleep and thereby precipitating a dream in which he deepens the relationship through his own fantasy about this patient. This intra-psychic relating may serve to resolve his inability to relate to the patient on an interpersonal level. The authors often report these dreams to the patient without interpretation, knowing that communication may be better without any effort to interpret the dream to the patient or to himself. Lastly, it may well be that when the therapist sleeps he says to the patient, "Now I must deny all my reality to resolve my conflicting affects about you and I must be myself more completely before I can be more adequate to your needs." Obviously the therapist must grow beyond his own embarrassment at this socially unaccepted pattern in human relationships before he can develop it as a technique to serve the patient.

THE USE OF AGGRESSION AS A TECHNIQUE IN PSYCHOTHERAPY. One of the most controversial problems in contemporary psychotherapy is the function of aggression on the part of the therapist. American concepts about aggression in the therapeutic process are influenced by those cultural taboos which make aggression in its various forms such a difficult problem in our culture. It becomes even more of a problem when the aggression arises in a medical situation against the patient who has been historically categorized as a helpless individual, and whose very sickness is often thought to be the result of ill-considered hostility on the part of the parents. Hence, when psychotherapy involves the emotional participation of the therapist it runs up against this categorical exclusion of aggression as an appropriate feeling in therapy. The authors, in their growth as therapists, became convinced that many of their failures in psychotherapy could be attributed to an inability to adequately handle aggression in the therapeutic relationship. This included the aggression of the patient and the aggression felt against the patient. The medical ethic of protecting the patient against any assault, plus the guilt of repressed hostility against many patients, made a realistic approach to the problem even more difficult. Nonetheless, in examining interview records, aggression on the part of the therapist stands out as one of the most pervasive feeling tones in the therapeutic relationship. Because of its implicit and repressed quality, it often functions negatively and provides the basis for many therapeutic impasses.

Aggression, of course, can be expressed in a multitude of ways. It may be expressed by posture, by gestures of which the therapist is unaware, by facial expression, by words, and particularly by the tone, timbre and cadence associated with speech. It may be expressed administratively by the manner in which the therapist deals with the realities of his relationship to the patient. It may be expressed symbolically in the joint fantasy relationship with the patient. It may also be expressed in a displaced form. In all of these instances, a good portion of the affect itself remains repressed. Its repression, however, does not mitigate in the least the patient's perception of the therapist's hostility. His inability to bring to his relationship with the patient this feeling he has is an experiential negation of the very aim which he professes to have for the patient. In consequence, on the basis of these observations, the authors, during the past few years, have set out to express their hostility quite directly. This may be in silence, verbally, in body posture, or symbolically, but in each instance the therapist, contrary to his previous attitude, augments and develops his aggressive feelings and does not hesitate to express them in whatever way seems most suitable to the patient. Such free expression of hostility has resulted in fewer impasses and has provided a sound basis for dealing with the ever-present problem of ambivalence in patients. The patient learns emotionally, because of the therapist's active participation in this relationship with him, that aggression is possible without the loss of the underlying positive feeling which unites the patient and therapist.

Aggression by the therapist may be used to augment anxiety. It is used frequently to fragment the defenses of the patient and to break through the pseudo-adultness of the patient to find his infantile need. It appears many times as the earliest available expression of positive feeling since the first emotional awareness of the patient on the part of the therapist is often embodied in his hostile feelings against the patient for that inability to be and feel what the therapist fundamentally believes that patient can be and can feel at that given moment. Actual physical aggression has been used by the authors with deteriorated schizophrenic patients; and where, in some instances, years of therapeutic endeavor have failed to reach the psychotic patient, active and intense physical assault was effective in opening up an emotional relationship between the therapist and patient on the basis of which therapy could proceed.

Of the major techniques, however, aggression is most likely to be abused. When aggression is used solely as a technique, it often not only fails, but also may actually be detrimental to the therapeutic process itself. To be effective it must be felt in the therapist. To be adequate to the patient's needs, it must be personally appropriate to that patient and not displaced from another area. When these things are true, aggression provides a most functional means for establishing an emotional relationship with an *isolate* patient, for increasing the patient's anxiety in therapy, for providing the patient with the bipolar, love-hate experience so necessary in his emotional growth, and finally for expanding the beginning seeds of maturity in the growing patient.

THE USE OF PHYSICAL CONTACT AS A TECHNIQUE. The expression of affect in the therapeutic relationship by physical contact is less contrary to the culture when the affective response in the therapist is positive; however, there are still many therapists who have reservations about expressing their affect for the patient by any physical contact. The authors believe that physical contact is a technical aid in the therapeutic process. It is liable to the problems noted above, and it is as certainly true of positive affect and warmth as it is of aggression that unless the therapist has appropriate feeling in himself it can be dangerous. The authors have found that holding the patient during a crying episode, or offering to rock the patient during a period of deep regression into infantile living brings to the therapeutic relationship certain proprioceptive and sensory modalities which make a significant contribution to the therapeutic process itself. The therapist may also find help by utilizing the nursing bottle with nipple. Here the therapist assumes on a behavior level the active maternal role in the patient's regression to a crucial infantile experience.

THE JOINT FANTASY EXPERIENCE AS A TECHNICAL AID IN BRIEF PSYCHOTHERAPY. The authors have talked a good bit about the therapist's fantasy. Therapists have always assumed the presence of fantasy in the patient. One of the technical aids to developing a therapeutic relationship is the utilization of a joint fantasy. This fantasy may be a verbal one and may be initiated by the patient. In ordinary psychotherapy, the patient is allowed to go on with this fantasy. Many times the patient's fantasy is a silent one. If the therapist is able to participate in the fantasy on a verbal level, however, the patient can be helped to go further with his own fantasy living and thereby to develop a more profound affective relationship with the therapist. This fantasy between the two of them may also be pushed into the behavioral level, particularly with psychotics, and gain, thereby, still further affect in both the therapist and the patient. Such a joint fantasy serves not only to deepen the involvement of the patient, but possibly more significant, it serves to deepen the participation of the therapist. If the patient seems unable to inaugurate his own fantasy as a way of increasing regression and the depth of his affective participation in the therapeutic relationship, it may be possible for the therapist to inaugurate a joint fantasy or to force a fantasy. Once the patient accepts this, the fantasy becomes a bilateral process. Frequently, as the fantasy develops, the patient himself takes the initiative, moves the fantasy into the present tense, and utilizes it for his own purposes and for the expression of his own affect. This type of verbal fantasy with adult patients differs little from the long utilized play therapy in the child guidance clinic or in child analysis. The forced fantasy may also be extended into the behavioral field and may utilize whatever accoutrements the therapist feels are valid for him.

One of the hurdles in utilizing this technique arises from the inability of the therapist to tolerate the patient's initial rejection of the fantasy or the play therapy. For example, one of the authors has utilized clay and rubber knives on the desk between himself and the patient. The patient first regards this facetiously, but as the interview goes on, he begins to utilize it, first aimlessly, and then he integrates it with the interview and with the verbal communication. It may even be that some patients who have trouble developing a deep transference on a verbal or a purely affective level may be helped to a more significant therapeutic process by thus utilizing proprioceptive pathways and visual constructs which take on significance and become part of the relationship itself.

Pitfalls of Psychotherapy

The techniques utilized by the authors to facilitate the therapeutic process at various stages have been presented. Their presentation has been primarily from a positive point of view, in that these are operations which can be used to effect progress in dealing with patients. Out of the experience of the authors and the shared experiences of colleagues who are doing similar work, certain generalizations have emerged which are essentially negative in their significance. These represent those operations which are detrimental to progress in therapy and which, apparently, should not be utilized. They are presented here with very little discussion since the rationale for the dangers inherent in their use is meaningful only on the basis of the total philosophy presented in earlier chapters. They are presented here as rules which, if adhered to, may make the therapist function more adequately.

Sometimes we are asked to point out to a young therapist, in simple language, those things which he should never do if he is to be most adequate as a psychotherapist. Therapy is such a subtle process that rules are often of more hindrance than help, yet the authors present these generalizations which seem useful to the young therapist as the common pitfalls in the relationship to patients.

First, never diagnose the psychotherapeutic patient except insofar as the diagnosis of the patient emanates from the patient's personal relationship with the therapist, and is an integral part of the therapeutic process. In the early phases of therapy, many young therapists become involved in delineating the pathology of the patient and, even more naively, prematurely formulate the genesis of the patient's presenting pathology. The aim of the young therapist in the beginning phase of therapy should be to explicate the patient's needs, never his pathology. Since diagnosis in psychiatry is oriented essentially around psychopathology, diagnosis, as such, is often detrimental in that it becomes a way of rejecting the need of the patient. Patients will not return for therapy unless they feel that the therapist has some real, human concept of their needs and not simply an objective estimate of their deficiencies.

Second, the authors tell the young therapist not to accept acute anxiety as an emergency when the patient is in therapy. This is one of the most difficult lessons for the neophyte therapist to learn. In his effort to aid the growth of the patient, he often uses palliative measures in the face of acute anxiety in the patient. Were such anxiety rechanneled into the therapeutic interview, it might well assure a successful outcome to the treatment process. No treatment of any depth is possible without accompanying anxiety.

Third, the young therapist is told never to deliberately slow the process of therapy, either from diagnostic preconceptions or for technical reasons. The exception to this lies in the first phase of therapy where the patient has not yet entered into a symbolic relationship with the therapist. Deliberate slowing of the process even during this period, where there is not sufficient depth in the relationship to handle explosive affect, demands mature technical judgment. When the patient has entered the symbolic segment of therapy, however, the process seeks its own rate and technical intervention on the part of the therapist is usually out of his own pathology and dynamically dangerous.

Fourth, the young therapist is told something which he learns in his own therapeutic experience but which, because of the pressures put upon him by patients, he may forget. He is told he must never compromise his "self" or his social and professional life, i.e., integrity as a person, in his treatment of patients. This refers to the need for a self discipline, which sometimes seems cruel. He must maintain his separateness as a person. On this basis, he refuses to see the patient at times that would seriously interfere with the satisfaction he obtains in his own living. He would refuse to postpone a vacation out of concern for a patient's anxiety at his leaving. He would refuse to jeopardize his own physical safety when the patient acts out psychotic feelings without the assurances that the therapist feels are necessary to guarantee his own physical and emotional integrity. This is a difficult orientation for the young therapist, who in his enthusiasm often sacrifices himself for the patient, only to find that he has invariably sacrificed the patient concurrently.

Fifth, the young therapist is told never to verbalize without affect. Words which are not reinforced with personal feeling are not pertinent in psychotherapy, and function, primarily, to decathect the relationship of its therapeutic impact. This is particularly true of verbalizing the core of psychotherapy prematurely, i.e., without affect. The patient should for example never be told that he irritates the therapist if the therapist is not irritated. The stereotyped verbalization of an affect which is not felt in the therapist at the time constitutes one of the most serious detriments to effective psychotherapy. As a corollary of this, the therapist should never repeat verbalizations of affect he felt moments before and which were significant in his own experience with the patient, simply because the patient requests that he repeat it. That is, the therapist should never quote himself in therapy, since by so doing, he successfully externalizes himself and objectifies feeling which is pertinent only when subjectively integrated in the relationship to the patient. All this is subsumed under the general principle that, at no time, should a therapist verbalize when affect is not present. Nor should he hide his flatness from the patient.

Sixth, the young therapist is told never to interpret content which is presented by the patient with deep feeling, but to relate, as a person, with feeling to each symbol presented by the patient. He may successfully analyze the genetic and content elements in the symbol by interpreting it without participating but only by affectively participating in this process of symbolization can he develop the patient's integration. Developing his insight is not enough.

Seventh, the young therapist is told that he should never deny the least fragment of ending in the patient, and that, whenever he intuits subjectively or assays objectively, cues which indicate ending in the patient, he should verbalize his observations. The earlier the ending, the more effective is psychotherapy. Similarly, it seems important that the young therapist should set up as one of the criteria for his own growth that he will never transfer a patient to another therapist. There is no better way of his forcing his own development as a therapist than to arbitrarily determine to battle through the impasse situations since they arise out of the pathology in his own functioning.

Technical Aids in the Resolution of the Impasse

The authors have taken up the resolution of the impasse in the chapter on counter-transference. It is sufficient to mention here a few of the technical aids to this very personal problem. On a technical level, the therapist may be able to utilize almost any of the major therapeutic techniques outlined above. Particularly valuable is the use of silence and the use of aggression. Preliminary to this, the therapist must assume the patient's readiness to end. He may admit his inability to give further help and even offer the patient the right to terminate the therapeutic interviews since they seem to produce less and less movement. In this way, he infers that the prime objective of treatment is the patient's need. The patient is thus freed to terminate on a constructive level. It has been the experience of the authors that this type of ending, or this manner of resolving the impasse, is not rejecting the patient, since the patient has taken the initiative, and the therapist, thereby, admits the patient's strength.

Technical Aids in the Post Ending Relationship

The completion of the therapeutic relationship in its isolate framework ordinarily results in the patient returning to his environment. The therapist and patient may meet during the next weeks or months in a social setting. The tensions between them may then become quite severe, each one being anxious about the relationship to the other, and fearing lest he damage what has been real between them. The therapist's sense of responsibility may be a major factor in making him augment this tension to such a point that he avoids such social functions. If the therapist knows that there are resources in the community to which the patient can turn for those therapeutic needs which remain after the isolate relationship has been terminated, he should feel free to spontaneously participate on a social level, and deny any symbolic role, thus letting the chips fall where they may. In thus asserting his right to be a real person, he simultaneously gives expression to his faith in the patient's capacity to be a real person.

Glossary

Adaptation—The homeostatic response to immediate stress which increases the capacity of an organism to tolerate stress generally.

Adequacy—The utilization of maturity in interpersonal relationships—or—the ability to use the cultural patterns for personal satisfaction.

Adjustment—The homeostatic response to immediate stress without increase in the general capacity for adaptation.

Anxiety, negative—That anxiety which arises out of the breakdown of the defensive mechanisms of the individual in interpersonal relationships.

Anxiety, positive—The anxiety for growth which is mobilized by a therapeutic interpersonal relationship.

Biological potential—Any capacity, physical or psychological, not currently available for use by the individual.

Catalyzed adaptation—The more integrative response to stress which is made possible by the patient-therapist relationship.

Catalyzed therapy—Various methods for resolving therapeutic impasses. The term usually refers to a second therapist reactivating the relationship between a patient and therapist.

Child-self—The mature adult's memory residues of the intra-psychic representations of himself as a child, free of infantile affects.

Collaborative therapy—A term used to indicate the fact that therapy with some related person was inaugurated to complement the therapy of the patient. It usually refers to therapy of the nearest relative or the person whose psychopathology supports the patient's neurotic homeostasis.

Core stage—The stage of therapy in which maximal isolation and symbolic synchronization occurs, so that deepest patient-vectors are being responded to with deepest therapist-vectors and usually in joint fantasy, which may or may not be verbal.

Countertransference—Immature feelings aroused in the therapist by the patient which impair the process of psychotherapy.

Disequilibrium dynamics—The alternations in the expression of patient-vectors and therapist-vectors in the two participants.

Ending—The process of decathecting the therapist.

Fantasy—Non-reality-bound intra-psychic experiences.

231

Group therapy—The therapeutic process which takes place when a group of patients meet with a professional therapist.

Growth—The natural orderly emergence of potential forms and capacities of the total individual organism through maturation, differentiation, and integration.

Homeostasis—The maintenance of constant steady state. The mobilization and utilization of energy to maintain integration in a stress situation.

Impasse—A stalemate in the therapeutic process—sometimes called a transference-countertransference jam: both patient and therapist are maintaining the status quo interpersonally with a breakdown in emotional communication.

Interview segment—That part of therapy which occurs between the initial and ending interviews with the professional therapist.

Intra-psychic society—The key persons in the individual's growth who have been introjected, forming an intra-psychic framework for interpersonal behavior.

Introjection—The psychical assimilation (incorporation) of another individual to assure a constant togetherness and to avoid the anxiety of separation. The resultant intra-psychic representation is termed an introject.

Isolation—The deliberate dissociation of the therapeutic experience from the real life situations of each of the participants, providing the relationship with the quality of fantasy.

Maturity—The achievement of a growth level commensurate with age norms; intrapersonal availability of biological energy for interpersonal activity.

Movement (therapeutic)—Progress through successive stages of the process of psychotherapy with an underlying compulsion toward completion (growth).

Multiple therapy—The treatment of a single patient by two or more therapists who make up the therapeutic unit. The patient is seen only by this group.

Non-verbal communication—All those channels of communication which are not subsumed under the verbal content of the relationship—includes proprioceptive and other special receptors.

Patient-vectors—Immature transference needs expressed in an interpersonal relationship which offers some possibility of their satisfaction and resolution.

Pre-transference—Feelings extant in the patient when he perceives the therapist as a primordial parent. They imply a relationship in which the patient has lost his ego boundaries and perceives the therapist as part of himself.

Primordial parent (*parent image*)—The prototype of the parent—the source of all life. A stage prior to differentiation of mother and father.

Process of psychotherapy—An emotional exchange (process) in an interpersonal relationship which accelerates the growth of one or both participants.

Regression—A retreat to patterns of behavior which were appropriate at some earlier level of development.

Repetition compulsion—The tendency to repeat infantile patterns of behavior with the aim of obtaining the satisfactions necessary for further growth.

Re-repression—The post-therapeutic repression of fantasies made conscious in the therapeutic relationship, or the return to the unconscious of its normal functions in order to reassert the integration of the whole person.

Shared fantasy (*joint*)—Non-reality-bound experience in which both therapist and patient participate, the affects of each arising spontaneously in response to the productions of the other.

Sliver therapy—The resolution of a minor patient vector in a mature individual.

Social psychosis—Regression with personality disintegration which grossly disrupts adjustment to reality.

Social therapist—An individual in the culture who, because of his therapist-vectors, facilitates the transition of patients into and out of professional psychotherapy.

Therapeutic psychosis—Temporary regression occurring in therapy, with the emergence of primary process (the primitive ways of dealing with drives) which provides the basis for massive resynthesis of personality.

Therapeutic testing—The activity of a patient toward the end of therapy aimed at clarifying the therapist's personal feelings about the patient's adequacy.

Therapist-vector—Mature affect expressed in an interpersonal relationship in response to the immature needs of the other participant.

Transference—Feelings aroused by the therapist in the patient which result in his identification of the therapist with members of the patient's own intra-psychic society.

Bibliography

Foundation

Bridgeman, P. W.: *"Nature of Physical Theory,"* Princeton, N.J., Princeton Univ. Press, 1936.

——: *"Logic of Modern Physics,"* New York, Macmillan, 1927.

Brody, Samuel: *"Bioenergetics and Growth,"* New York, Reinhold, 1945.

Cohen, Morris Raphael: *"An Introduction to Logic and Scientific Method,"* New York, Harcourt, Brace & Co., c1934.

Einstein, Albert, and Leopold Infeld: *"The Evolution of Physics,"* New York, Simon & Schuster, 1938.

Freud, Sigmund: *"Collected Papers,"* New York, Int. Psychoanalytic Press, 1924–45, 4 v.

——: *"The Problem of Anxiety,"* New York, Norton, 1936.

——: *"Beyond the Pleasure Principle,"* London, Int. Psychoanalytic Press, 1922.

Ginsburg, Ethel, ed.: *"Public Health Is People,"* New York, Commonwealth Fund, 1950.

Goldstein, Kurt: *"The Organism, a Wholistic Approach to Biology Derived from Pathological Data in Order,"* New York, American Book Co., 1939.

Healy, William: *"Personality in Formation and Action,"* New York, Norton, 1938.

Hume, David: *"Treatise of Human Nature,"* New York, Dutton, 1911.

Kardiner, Abram: *"Psychological Frontiers of Society,"* New York, Columbia Univ. Press, 1945.

Lewin, Kurt: *"A Dynamic Theory of Personality,"* New York, McGraw-Hill Book Co., 1935.

——, and Grace Herder: *"Principles of Topological Psychology,"* New York and London, McGraw-Hill Book Co., 1936.

Lynd, R. S.: *"Knowledge for What?"* Princeton, N.J., Princeton Univ. Press, 1939.

Murphy, Gardner: *"Personality; A Biosocial Approach to Origins and Structures,"* New York, Harper, 1947.

Parsons, Talcott: *"The Structure of Social Action,"* New York and London, McGraw-Hill Book Co., 1937.

——, and E. A. Shils, eds.: *"Toward a General Theory of Action,"* Cambridge, Harvard Univ. Press, 1952 (c1951).

Peirce, Charles Santiago Sanders, and Morris Raphael Cohen: *"Chance, Love and Logic,"* New York, Harcourt, Brace & Co., Inc., 1923.

Piaget, Jean: *"The Moral Judgement of the Child,"* New York, Harcourt, Brace & Co., 1936.

Russell, Bertrand: *"The Analysis of Mind,"* New York, Macmillan, 1921.

Sapir, Edward: *"Selected Writings in Language, Culture and Personality,"* ed. by David G. Mandelbaum, Berkeley, University of California Press; Cambridge, England, 1949.

Sherrington, C. S.: *"The Integrative Action of the Nervous System,"* new ed., New Haven, Yale Univ. Press, 1948.

Sullivan, H. S.: *"Conceptions of Modern Psychiatry,"* Washington, D.C., William Alanson White Psychiatric Foundation, 1947.

Whitehead, Alfred North: *"Adventures of Ideas,"* New York, Macmillan, 1933.

——: *"Science and the Modern World,"* New York, Macmillan, 1925.

——, and Bertrand Russell: *"Principia Mathematica,"* Cambridge, England, University Press, 1927–1935.

Process

Alexander, Franz: *"Fundamentals of Psycho-Analysis,"* New York, Norton, 1948.

Allen, F. H.: *"Psychotherapy with Children,"* New York, Norton, 1942.

Brown, William: *"Psychology and Psychotherapy,"* Baltimore, Wood, 1934.

Bychowski, Gustav: *"Psychotherapy of Psychosis,"* New York, Grune and Stratton, 1952.

——: *"Specialized Technique in Psychotherapy,"* New York, Rhinehart & Co., 1952.

Cannon, W. B.: *"The Wisdom of the Body,"* New York, Norton, 1932.

Chicago Institute for Psychoanalysis: *"Proceedings of the Third Psychotherapy Council,"* Chicago, The Institute, 1946.

Eissler, K. R.: Remarks on the psycho-analysis of schizophrenia, *Internat. J. Psycho-Analysis,* Vol. XXXII, Part III, pp. 139–156.

Fenichel, Otto: *"The Psychoanalytic Theory of Neurosis,"* New York, Norton, 1945.

Fromm-Reichmann, Frieda: *"Principles of Intensive Psychotherapy,"* Chicago, Univ. of Chicago Press, 1950.

Glover, Edward, and Marjorie Brierley: *"An Investigation of the Technique of Psychoanalysis,"* Baltimore, Williams & Wilkins, 1940.

Glueck, Bernard, ed.: *"Current Therapies of Personality Disorders,"* New York, Grune & Stratton, 1946.

Groddeck, Georg: *"The Book of the It,"* New York, Funk & Wagnalls Co., 1950.

——: *"The Unknown Self,"* London, C. W. Daniel & Co., 1937.

——: *"Exploring the Unconscious,"* London, C. W. Daniel & Co., 1933.

Hoch, P. H., ed.: *"Failures in Psychiatric Treatment,"* New York, Grune & Stratton, 1948.

Rank, Otto: *"Will Therapy and Truth and Reality,"* New York, A. A. Knopf, 1947.

Robinson, G. C.: *"The Patient as a Person,"* New York, Commonwealth Fund, 1939.

Ruesch, Jurgen, and others: *"Chronic Disease and Psychological Invalidism,"* New York, American Society for Research in Psychosomatic Problems, 1946.

Schilder, Paul: *"The Image and Appearance of the Human Body,"* New York, International Universities Press, 1950.

——: *"Psychotherapy,"* New York, Norton, 1938.

Sears, Robert: *"Survey of Objective Studies of Psycho-Analytic Concepts,"* New York, Social Science Research Council, 1943.

Sechehaye, M. A.: *"Symbolic Realization,"* International Universities Press, 1951.

Witmer, H. S., ed.: *"Teaching Psychotherapeutic Medicine,"* N.Y. Commonwealth Fund, 1947.

Techniques

Alexander, Franz, and others: *"Psychoanalytic Therapy; Principles and Application,"* New York, Ronald, 1946.

Binger, Carl: *"The Doctor's Job,"* New York, Norton, 1945.

Fenichel, Otto: *"Problems of Psychoanalytic Technique,"* New York, Psychoanalytic Quarterly, 1941.

Ferenczi, Sandor: *"Further Contributions to the Theory and Technique of Psychoanalysis,"* London, Hogarth, 1926.

——: *"Contributions to Psycho-Analysis,"* Boston, R. C. Badger, 1916.

Glover, Edward, and Marjorie Brierley: *"An Investigation of the Technique of Psychoanalysis,"* Baltimore, Williams & Wilkins, 1940.

Kubie, L. S.: *"Practical and Theoretical Aspects of Psycho-Analysis,"* New York, International Universities Press, 1951.

Levine, Maurice: *"Psychotherapy in Medical Practice,"* New York, Macmillan, 1942.

Rogers, Carl Ransom: *"Counseling and Psychotherapy,"* Boston, Houghton Mifflin, 1942.

——, and others: *"Client-Centered Therapy,"* Boston, Houghton Mifflin, 1951.

Sears, R. R.: *"Survey of Objective Studies of Psycho-Analytic Concepts,"* New York, Social Science Research Council, 1943.